Skillbuilding
Building Speed and Accuracy on the Keyboard

3rd Edition

Carole Hoffman Eide
Consultant, Business and Office Education
Renton, Washington

Andrea Holmes Rieck
Instructor, Business and Office Education
Renton Technical College
Renton, Washington

V. Wayne Klemin, Ed.D.
Professor, Information Technology and Administrative Management
Central Washington University
Ellensburg, Washington

Boston   Burr Ridge, IL   Dubuque, IA   Madison, WI   New York   San Francisco   St. Louis
Bangkok   Bogotá   Caracas   Kuala Lumpur   Lisbon   London   Madrid   Mexico City
Milan   Montreal   New Delhi   Santiago   Seoul   Singapore   Sydney   Taipei   Toronto

ISBN 978-0-07-829801-1
MHID 0-07-829801-6

11 12 QPD/QPD 09 08 07

The McGraw-Hill Companies

CONTENTS

PREFACE

Objectives of the Skillbuilding Program

Skillbuilding: Building Speed and Accuracy on the Keyboard provides you with a thoroughly tested program to improve your proficiency in using a personal computer, word processor, typewriter, or any other machine with a similar keyboard. It contains materials specifically designed to:

- Measure your keyboarding speed and accuracy at the outset of the Skillbuilding program by typing the Course Entry Timing.

- Determine your specific keyboarding problems by analyzing the results of the diagnostic tests that appear at the beginning of sections 2 and 12 of the program.

- Select appropriate practice lessons based on diagnostic tests, your personal choice of lessons, or teacher-prescribed lessons.

- Establish your particular skill-improvement goal for each practice lesson by typing the lesson pretest.

- Provide you with specially designed skillbuilding exercises in a prescribed manner.

- Determine whether or not you have achieved your practice goal for each lesson by typing the lesson posttest.

- Measure your overall skill-development progress at regular intervals during the Skillbuilding course by typing special Progress Check Timings and at the end of the course by typing the Course Exit Timing.

Skillbuilding reflects the philosophy and research findings of Dr. Fred E. Winger, former professor of office administration and business education at Oregon State University. His research found that the appropriate type of practice material, when practiced systematically and in the correct way, produces statistically significant gains in speed and in accuracy.

OVERVIEW OF THE PROGRAM SECTIONS

This text contains a variety of special practice materials organized in the following sections:

1. **Course Entry and Exit.** This section provides a 3- or 5-minute timing for use in measuring your speed and accuracy at the beginning of the course and again at the end of the course.

2. **Alphabet Practice, Lessons 1–26.** Two diagnostic timings determine which letters you mistype most often. Separate skillbuilding lessons for each letter of the alphabet are provided.

3. **Individual Finger Practice, Lessons 27–31.** Each of the five lessons presents exercises that emphasize the use of specific fingers.

4. **Word-Level Keystroking Practice, Lessons 32–36.** When you learn to type, you begin by stroking individual letters. As you become more fluent, you type entire words rather than separating them into individual keystrokes. You will practice word-level responses in this five-lesson section.

5. **Frequently Used Words Practice, Lessons 37–41.** Research indicates that certain English words are used more often than others. These five lessons provide practice on some of the most frequently used words.

6. **Horizontal/Vertical Reaches Practice, Lessons 42–51.** Ten lessons are devoted to improving your stroking on reaches that require your fingers to move sideways on the rows of the keyboard (horizontal reaches) or to move from one row of keys to another (vertical reaches).

7. **Word Family Practice, Lessons 52–56.** The five lessons in this section provide practice on some of the most commonly used word beginnings and endings found in the English language.

8. **Concentration Practice, Lessons 57–66.** Concentration Practice is divided into two sets of five lessons each. Accuracy is the primary focus. The first set concentrates on the most commonly transposed letters. The second set focuses on such problems as transposition on adjacent-key reaches, opposite-finger reaches, and vertical-key reaches. *To achieve the maximum benefit from these additional concentration lessons, do one or more other skillbuilding sections **before** you do the second set of concentration lessons.*

9. **Frequently Misspelled Words Practice, Lessons 67–71.** Commonly misspelled words are the focus of these five lessons.

10. **Alternate-Hand Words Practice, Lessons 72–76.** Each of the five lessons builds speed through practice on words that require the alternate use of the right and left hands.

11. **Double-Letter Words Practice, Lessons 77–81.** The five lessons cover all the letters frequently doubled in English words, and they help you overcome the common problem of misstroking the second letter in double-letter combinations.

12. **Right-Hand and Left-Hand Words Practice, Lessons 82–91.** A surprising number of English words are typed entirely with the fingers of one hand, and most people who type over 30 words per minute have a stroking speed imbalance between their hands. The Diagnostic Timings and the ten lessons in this section are designed to detect and reduce or eliminate the stroking imbalance between your hands.

13. **Punctuation Practice, Lessons 92–96.** Intensive practice on all the punctuation keys is provided in these five lessons.

14. **Number Practice, Lessons 97–106.** In addition to ten skillbuilding lessons, this section includes three entry and exit timings—numbers in phrases, in sentences, and in a paragraph. These timings are used to measure your skill in typing numbers before and after completing the lessons. There are two versions of Lesson 102: page 123 is for standard keyboards and page 124 is for ergonomic keyboards.

15. **Symbol Practice, Lessons 107–111.** These five lessons provide practice on the most commonly used symbols.

16. **Keypad Practice, Lessons 112–116.** The five lessons in this section will help you build your skill in using the keypad on computers and calculators. In addition, the correlated software provides an introduction to the keypad and additional practice exercises.

17. **Progress Check Timings, Progress Checks 1–35.** The lesson materials are heavily weighted with special features to assist you in developing your speed and accuracy and they are inappropriate for assessing your overall keyboarding skill. The Progress Check Timings, however, provide you with realistic copy of normal difficulty for measuring speed and accuracy on 3- or 5-minute timings. You will use the Progress Check Timings at regular intervals during your skillbuilding class. A chart on which you can record your scores is provided on page xv and xvi.

18. **Pacing Practice, Pacing Paragraphs 20 wpm through 100 wpm.** In addition to the Placement Timing, this section provides 1-minute timings for building speed and accuracy from 20 through 100 words per minute in increments of one or two words per minute. The markers in each timing indicate where you should be at the end of each quarter of a minute.

SPECIAL ACKNOWLEDGMENT

The authors wish to give special recognition to linguist Dr. Donald W. Cummings, Professor of English, Central Washington University, and author of *American English Spelling* (The Johns Hopkins University Press, 1988), for his professional assistance and research in identifying common letter patterns in the English language.

Carole Hoffman Eide
Andrea Holmes Rieck
V. Wayne Klemin, Ed.D.

90-HOUR/18-WEEK SKILLBUILDING COURSE

If you are enrolled in a 90-hour/18-week skillbuilding course, you will follow the course plan outline below. Use Level 1 if your speed is below 40 words per minute; use Level 2 if your speed is above 40 words per minute. As you complete each assignment, check off the box next to the assignment. Note: (?) denotes a computer-assigned lesson. Optional activities (*) include Pacing Practice, Keypad Practice, and Open-Screen Practice.

Week	Level 1 — Day 1	Level 1 — Day 2	Level 1 — Day 3	Level 1 — Day 4	Level 1 — Day 5	Level 2 — Day 1	Level 2 — Day 2	Level 2 — Day 3	Level 2 — Day 4	Level 2 — Day 5
	Level 1—for keyboarding speed below 40 words per minute					**Level 2—for keyboarding speed above 40 words per minute**				
1	☐ Entry Timing ☐ Alpha. Diag. ☐ Number Entry	☐ Alphabet ? ☐ Number 97 ☐ Pacing Place	☐ Alphabet ? ☐ Number 98 ☐ Pacing	☐ Alphabet ? ☐ Number 99 ☐ Pacing	☐ Alphabet ? ☐ Pro Chk 1 ☐ Pacing	☐ Entry Timing ☐ Alpha. Diag. ☐ Number Entry	☐ Alphabet ? ☐ Number 97 ☐ Pacing Place	☐ Alphabet ? ☐ Number 98 ☐ Pacing	☐ Alphabet ? ☐ Number 99 ☐ Pacing	☐ Alphabet ? ☐ Pro Chk 1 ☐ Pacing
2	☐ Alphabet ? ☐ Number 100 ☐ *Option Act	☐ Alphabet ? ☐ Number 101 ☐ Pacing	☐ Alphabet ? ☐ Pro Chk 2 ☐ *Option Act	☐ Alphabet ? ☐ Number 102 ☐ Pacing	☐ Alphabet ? ☐ Pro Chk 3 ☐ *Option Act	☐ Alphabet ? ☐ Number 100 ☐ *Option Act	☐ Alphabet ? ☐ Number 101 ☐ Pacing	☐ Alphabet ? ☐ Pro Chk 2 ☐ *Option Act	☐ Alphabet ? ☐ Number 102 ☐ Pacing	☐ Alphabet ? ☐ Pro Chk 3 ☐ *Option Act
3	☐ Ind Fing 27 ☐ Number 103 ☐ *Option Act	☐ Ind Fing 28 ☐ Number 104 ☐ Pacing	☐ Ind Fing 29 ☐ Pro Chk 4 ☐ *Option Act	☐ Ind Fing 30 ☐ Number 105 ☐ Pacing	☐ Ind Fing 31 ☐ Pro Chk 5 ☐ *Option Act	☐ Ind Fing 27 ☐ Number 103 ☐ *Option Act	☐ Ind Fing 28 ☐ Number 104 ☐ Pacing	☐ Ind Fing 29 ☐ Pro Chk 4 ☐ *Option Act	☐ Ind Fing 30 ☐ Number 105 ☐ Pacing	☐ Ind Fing 31 ☐ Pro Chk 5 ☐ *Option Act
4	☐ Word Lev 32 ☐ Number 106 ☐ Number Exit	☐ Word Lev 33 ☐ Punct 92 ☐ Pacing	☐ Word Lev 34 ☐ Pro Chk 6 ☐ *Option Act	☐ Word Lev 35 ☐ Punct 93 ☐ Pacing	☐ Word Lev 36 ☐ Pro Chk 7 ☐ *Option Act	☐ Word Lev 32 ☐ Number 106 ☐ Number Exit	☐ Word Lev 33 ☐ Punct 92 ☐ Pacing	☐ Word Lev 34 ☐ Pro Chk 6 ☐ *Option Act	☐ Word Lev 35 ☐ Punct 93 ☐ Pacing	☐ Word Lev 36 ☐ Pro Chk 7 ☐ *Option Act
5	☐ Freq Use 37 ☐ Punct 94 ☐ *Option Act	☐ Freq Use 38 ☐ Punct 95 ☐ Pacing	☐ Freq Use 39 ☐ Pro Chk 8 ☐ *Option Act	☐ Freq Use 40 ☐ Punct 96 ☐ Pacing	☐ Freq Use 41 ☐ Pro Chk 9 ☐ *Option Act	☐ Freq Use 37 ☐ Punct 94 ☐ *Option Act	☐ Freq Use 38 ☐ Punct 95 ☐ Pacing	☐ Freq Use 39 ☐ Pro Chk 8 ☐ *Option Act	☐ Freq Use 40 ☐ Punct 96 ☐ Pacing	☐ Freq Use 41 ☐ Pro Chk 9 ☐ *Option Act
6	☐ Horz/Ver 42 ☐ Symbol 107 ☐ *Option Act	☐ Horz/Ver 43 ☐ Symbol 108 ☐ Pacing	☐ Horz/Ver 44 ☐ Pro Chk 10 ☐ *Option Act	☐ Horz/Ver 45 ☐ Symbol 109 ☐ Pacing	☐ Horz/Ver 46 ☐ Pro Chk 11 ☐ *Option Act	☐ Horz/Ver 42 ☐ Symbol 107 ☐ *Option Act	☐ Horz/Ver 43 ☐ Symbol 108 ☐ Pacing	☐ Horz/Ver 44 ☐ Pro Chk 10 ☐ *Option Act	☐ Horz/Ver 45 ☐ Symbol 109 ☐ Pacing	☐ Horz/Ver 46 ☐ Pro Chk 11 ☐ *Option Act
7	☐ Horz/Ver 47 ☐ Symbol 110 ☐ *Option Act	☐ Horz/Ver 48 ☐ Symbol 111 ☐ Pacing	☐ Horz/Ver 49 ☐ Pro Chk 12 ☐ *Option Act	☐ Horz/Ver 50 ☐ Number Entry ☐ Number 97	☐ Horz/Ver 51 ☐ Pro Chk 13 ☐ *Option Act	☐ Horz/Ver 47 ☐ Symbol 110 ☐ *Option Act	☐ Horz/Ver 48 ☐ Symbol 111 ☐ Pacing	☐ Horz/Ver 49 ☐ Pro Chk 12 ☐ *Option Act	☐ Horz/Ver 50 ☐ Number Entry ☐ Number 97	☐ Horz/Ver 51 ☐ Pro Chk 13 ☐ *Option Act
8	☐ Word Fam 52 ☐ Number 98 ☐ *Option Act	☐ Word Fam 53 ☐ Number 99 ☐ Pacing	☐ Word Fam 54 ☐ Pro Chk 14 ☐ *Option Act	☐ Word Fam 55 ☐ Number 100 ☐ Pacing	☐ Word Fam 56 ☐ Pro Chk 15 ☐ *Option Act	☐ RH/LH ? ☐ Number 98 ☐ *Option Act	☐ RH/LH ? ☐ Number 99 ☐ Pacing	☐ RH/LH ? ☐ Pro Chk 14 ☐ *Option Act	☐ RH/LH ? ☐ Number 100 ☐ Pacing	☐ RH/LH ? ☐ Pro Chk 15 ☐ RH/LH Diag.
9	☐ Concen 57 ☐ Number 101 ☐ *Option Act	☐ Concen 58 ☐ Number 102 ☐ Pacing	☐ Concen 59 ☐ Pro Chk 16 ☐ *Option Act	☐ Concen 60 ☐ Number 103 ☐ Pacing	☐ Concen 61 ☐ Pro Chk 17 ☐ *Option Act	☐ RH/LH ? ☐ Number 101 ☐ *Option Act	☐ RH/LH ? ☐ Number 102 ☐ Pacing	☐ RH/LH ? ☐ Pro Chk 16 ☐ *Option Act	☐ RH/LH ? ☐ Number 103 ☐ Pacing	☐ RH/LH ? ☐ Pro Chk 17 ☐ RH/LH Diag.

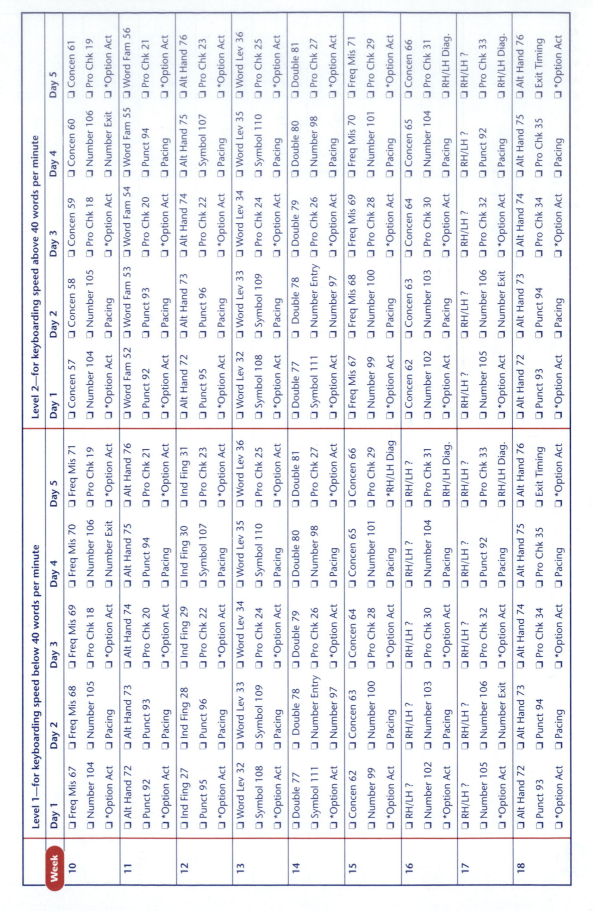

Week		Level 1—for keyboarding speed below 40 words per minute					Level 2—for keyboarding speed above 40 words per minute				
		Day 1	Day 2	Day 3	Day 4	Day 5	Day 1	Day 2	Day 3	Day 4	Day 5
10		Freq Mis 67	Freq Mis 68	Freq Mis 69	Freq Mis 70	Freq Mis 71	Concen 57	Concen 58	Concen 59	Concen 60	Concen 61
		Number 104	Number 105	Pro Chk 18	Number 106	Pro Chk 19	Number 104	Number 105	Pro Chk 18	Number 106	Pro Chk 19
		*Option Act	Pacing	*Option Act	Number Exit	*Option Act	*Option Act	Pacing	*Option Act	Number Exit	*Option Act
11		Alt Hand 72	Alt Hand 73	Alt Hand 74	Alt Hand 75	Alt Hand 76	Word Fam 52	Word Fam 53	Word Fam 54	Word Fam 55	Word Fam 56
		Punct 92	Punct 93	Pro Chk 20	Punct 94	Pro Chk 21	Punct 92	Punct 93	Pro Chk 20	Punct 94	Pro Chk 21
		*Option Act	Pacing	*Option Act	Pacing	*Option Act	*Option Act	Pacing	*Option Act	Pacing	*Option Act
12		Ind Fing 27	Ind Fing 28	Ind Fing 29	Ind Fing 30	Ind Fing 31	Alt Hand 72	Alt Hand 73	Alt Hand 74	Alt Hand 75	Alt Hand 76
		Punct 95	Punct 96	Pro Chk 22	Symbol 107	Pro Chk 23	Punct 95	Punct 96	Pro Chk 22	Symbol 107	Pro Chk 23
		*Option Act	Pacing	*Option Act	Pacing	*Option Act	*Option Act	Pacing	*Option Act	Pacing	*Option Act
13		Word Lev 32	Word Lev 33	Word Lev 34	Word Lev 35	Word Lev 36	Word Lev 32	Word Lev 33	Word Lev 34	Word Lev 35	Word Lev 36
		Symbol 108	Symbol 109	Pro Chk 24	Symbol 110	Pro Chk 25	Symbol 108	Symbol 109	Pro Chk 24	Symbol 110	Pro Chk 25
		*Option Act	Pacing	*Option Act	Pacing	*Option Act	*Option Act	Pacing	*Option Act	Pacing	*Option Act
14		Double 77	Double 78	Double 79	Double 80	Double 81	Double 77	Double 78	Double 79	Double 80	Double 81
		Symbol 111	Number Entry	Pro Chk 26	Number 98	Pro Chk 27	Symbol 111	Number Entry	Pro Chk 26	Number 98	Pro Chk 27
		*Option Act	Number 97	*Option Act	Pacing	*Option Act	*Option Act	Number 97	*Option Act	Pacing	*Option Act
15		Concen 62	Concen 63	Concen 64	Concen 65	Concen 66	Freq Mis 67	Freq Mis 68	Freq Mis 69	Freq Mis 70	Freq Mis 71
		Number 99	Number 100	Pro Chk 28	Number 101	Pro Chk 29	Number 99	Number 100	Pro Chk 28	Number 101	Pro Chk 29
		*Option Act	Pacing	*Option Act	Pacing	*RH/LH Diag	*Option Act	Pacing	*Option Act	Pacing	*Option Act
16		RH/LH ?	RH/LH ?	RH/LH ?	RH/LH ?	RH/LH ?	Concen 62	Concen 63	Concen 64	Concen 65	Concen 66
		Number 102	Number 103	Pro Chk 30	Number 104	Pro Chk 31	Number 102	Number 103	Pro Chk 30	Number 104	Pro Chk 31
		*Option Act	Pacing	*Option Act	Pacing	RH/LH Diag.	*Option Act	Pacing	*Option Act	Pacing	RH/LH Diag.
17		RH/LH ?	RH/LH ?	RH/LH ?	RH/LH ?	RH/LH ?	RH/LH ?	RH/LH ?	RH/LH ?	RH/LH ?	RH/LH ?
		Number 105	Number 106	Pro Chk 32	Punct 92	Pro Chk 33	Number 105	Number 106	Pro Chk 32	Punct 92	Pro Chk 33
		*Option Act	Number Exit	*Option Act	Pacing	RH/LH Diag.	*Option Act	Number Exit	*Option Act	Pacing	RH/LH Diag.
18		Alt Hand 72	Alt Hand 73	Alt Hand 74	Alt Hand 75	Alt Hand 76	Alt Hand 72	Alt Hand 73	Alt Hand 74	Alt Hand 75	Alt Hand 76
		Punct 93	Punct 94	Pro Chk 34	Pro Chk 35	Exit Timing	Punct 93	Punct 94	Pro Chk 34	Pro Chk 35	Exit Timing
		*Option Act	Pacing	*Option Act	Pacing	*Option Act	*Option Act	Pacing	*Option Act	Pacing	*Option Act

60-HOUR/12-WEEK SKILLBUILDING COURSE

If you are enrolled in a **60-hour/12-week** skillbuilding course, you will follow the course plan outlined below. Use Level 1 if your speed is below 40 words per minute; use Level 2 if your speed is above 40 words per minute. As you complete each assignment, check off the box next to the assignment. Note: (?) denotes a computer-assigned lesson. Optional activities (*) include Pacing Practice, Keypad Practice, and Open-Screen Practice.

Level 1—for keyboarding speed below 40 words per minute

Week	Day 1	Day 2	Day 3	Day 4	Day 5
1	☐ Entry Timing ☐ Alpha. Diag. ☐ Number Entry	☐ Alphabet ? ☐ Number 97 ☐ Pacing Place	☐ Alphabet ? ☐ Number 98 ☐ Pacing	☐ Alphabet ? ☐ Number 99 ☐ Pacing	☐ Alphabet ? ☐ Pro Chk 1 ☐ Pacing
2	☐ Alphabet ? ☐ Number 100 ☐ *Option Act	☐ Alphabet ? ☐ Number 101 ☐ Pacing	☐ Alphabet ? ☐ Pro Chk 2 ☐ *Option Act	☐ Alphabet ? ☐ Number 102 ☐ Pacing	☐ Alphabet ? ☐ Pro Chk 3 ☐ *Option Act
3	☐ Ind Fing 27 ☐ Number 103 ☐ *Option Act	☐ Ind Fing 28 ☐ Number 104 ☐ Pacing	☐ Ind Fing 29 ☐ Pro Chk 4 ☐ *Option Act	☐ Ind Fing 30 ☐ Number 105 ☐ Pacing	☐ Ind Fing 31 ☐ Pro Chk 5 ☐ *Option Act
4	☐ Word Lev 32 ☐ Number 106 ☐ Number Exit	☐ Word Lev 33 ☐ Punct 92 ☐ Pacing	☐ Word Lev 34 ☐ Pro Chk 6 ☐ *Option Act	☐ Word Lev 35 ☐ Punct 93 ☐ Pacing	☐ Word Lev 36 ☐ Pro Chk 7 ☐ *Option Act
5	☐ Concen 57 ☐ Punct 94 ☐ *Option Act	☐ Concen 58 ☐ Punct 95 ☐ Pacing	☐ Concen 59 ☐ Pro Chk 8 ☐ *Option Act	☐ Concen 60 ☐ Punct 96 ☐ Pacing	☐ Concen 61 ☐ Pro Chk 9 ☐ *Option Act
6	☐ Freq Use 37 ☐ Symbol 107 ☐ *Option Act	☐ Freq Use 38 ☐ Symbol 108 ☐ Pacing	☐ Freq Use 39 ☐ Pro Chk 10 ☐ *Option Act	☐ Freq Use 40 ☐ Symbol 109 ☐ Pacing	☐ Freq Use 41 ☐ Pro Chk 11 ☐ *Option Act

Level 2—for keyboarding speed above 40 words per minute

Week	Day 1	Day 2	Day 3	Day 4	Day 5
1	☐ Entry Timing ☐ Alpha. Diag. ☐ Number Entry	☐ Alphabet ? ☐ Number 97 ☐ Pacing Place	☐ Alphabet ? ☐ Number 98 ☐ Pacing	☐ Alphabet ? ☐ Number 99 ☐ Pacing	☐ Alphabet ? ☐ Pro Chk 1 ☐ Pacing
2	☐ Alphabet ? ☐ Number 100 ☐ *Option Act	☐ Alphabet ? ☐ Number 101 ☐ Pacing	☐ Alphabet ? ☐ Pro Chk 2 ☐ *Option Act	☐ Alphabet ? ☐ Number 102 ☐ Pacing	☐ Alphabet ? ☐ Pro Chk 3 ☐ *Option Act
3	☐ Ind Fing 27 ☐ Number 103 ☐ *Option Act	☐ Ind Fing 28 ☐ Number 104 ☐ Pacing	☐ Ind Fing 29 ☐ Pro Chk 4 ☐ *Option Act	☐ Ind Fing 30 ☐ Number 105 ☐ Pacing	☐ Ind Fing 31 ☐ Pro Chk 5 ☐ *Option Act
4	☐ Word Lev 32 ☐ Number 106 ☐ Number Exit	☐ Word Lev 33 ☐ Punct 92 ☐ Pacing	☐ Word Lev 34 ☐ Pro Chk 6 ☐ *Option Act	☐ Word Lev 35 ☐ Punct 93 ☐ Pacing	☐ Word Lev 36 ☐ Pro Chk 7 ☐ *Option Act
5	☐ Concen 57 ☐ Punct 94 ☐ *Option Act	☐ Concen 58 ☐ Punct 95 ☐ Pacing	☐ Concen 59 ☐ Pro Chk 8 ☐ *Option Act	☐ Concen 60 ☐ Punct 96 ☐ Pacing	☐ Concen 61 ☐ Pro Chk 9 ☐ *Option Act
6	☐ Freq Use 37 ☐ Symbol 107 ☐ *Option Act	☐ Freq Use 38 ☐ Symbol 108 ☐ Pacing	☐ Freq Use 39 ☐ Pro Chk 10 ☐ *Option Act	☐ Freq Use 40 ☐ Symbol 109 ☐ Pacing	☐ Freq Use 41 ☐ Pro Chk 11 ☐ *Option Act

Level 1—for keyboarding speed below 40 words per minute

Week	Day 1	Day 2	Day 3	Day 4	Day 5
7	☐ Alt Hand 72 ☐ Symbol 110 ☐ *Option Act	☐ Alt Hand 73 ☐ Symbol 111 ☐ Pacing	☐ Alt Hand 74 ☐ Pro Chk 12 ☐ *Option Act	☐ Alt Hand 75 ☐ Number Entry ☐ Number 97	☐ Alt Hand 76 ☐ Pro Chk 13 ☐ *Option Act
8	☐ Horz/Ver 42 ☐ Number 98 ☐ *Option Act	☐ Horz/Ver 43 ☐ Number 99 ☐ Pacing	☐ Horz/Ver 44 ☐ Pro Chk 14 ☐ *Option Act	☐ Horz/Ver 45 ☐ Number 100 ☐ Pacing	☐ Horz/Ver 46 ☐ Pro Chk 15 ☐ *Option Act
9	☐ Horz/Ver 47 ☐ Number 101 ☐ *Option Act	☐ Horz/Ver 48 ☐ Number 102 ☐ Pacing	☐ Horz/Ver 49 ☐ Pro Chk 16 ☐ *Option Act	☐ Horz/Ver 50 ☐ Number 103 ☐ Pacing	☐ Horz/Ver 51 ☐ Pro Chk 17 ☐ *Option Act
10	☐ Freq Mis 67 ☐ Number 104 ☐ *Option Act	☐ Freq Mis 68 ☐ Number 105 ☐ Pacing	☐ Freq Mis 69 ☐ Pro Chk 18 ☐ *Option Act	☐ Freq Mis 70 ☐ Number 106 ☐ Number Exit	☐ Freq Mis 71 ☐ Pro Chk 19 ☐ *Option Act
11	☐ Word Fam 52 ☐ Punct 92 ☐ *Option Act	☐ Word Fam 53 ☐ Punct 93 ☐ Pacing	☐ Word Fam 54 ☐ Pro Chk 20 ☐ *Option Act	☐ Word Fam 55 ☐ Punct 94 ☐ Pacing	☐ Word 56 ☐ Pro Chk 21 ☐ *Option Act
12	☐ Alt Hand 72 ☐ Punct 95 ☐ *Option Act	☐ Alt Hand 73 ☐ Punct 96 ☐ Pacing	☐ Alt Hand 74 ☐ Pro Chk 22 ☐ *Option Act	☐ Alt Hand 75 ☐ Pro Chk 23 ☐ Pacing	☐ Alt Hand 76 ☐ Exit Timing ☐ *Option Act

Level 2—for keyboarding speed above 40 words per minute

Week	Day 1	Day 2	Day 3	Day 4	Day 5
7	☐ Alt Hand 72 ☐ Symbol 110 ☐ *Option Act	☐ Alt Hand 73 ☐ Symbol 111 ☐ Pacing	☐ Alt Hand 74 ☐ Pro Chk 12 ☐ *Option Act	☐ Alt Hand 75 ☐ Number Entry ☐ Number 97	☐ Alt Hand 76 ☐ Pro Chk 13 ☐ *Option Act
8	☐ Horz/Ver 42 ☐ Number 98 ☐ *Option Act	☐ Horz/Ver 43 ☐ Number 99 ☐ Pacing	☐ Horz/Ver 44 ☐ Pro Chk 14 ☐ *Option Act	☐ Horz/Ver 45 ☐ Number 100 ☐ Pacing	☐ Horz/Ver 46 ☐ Pro Chk 15 ☐ *Option Act
9	☐ Horz/Ver 47 ☐ Number 101 ☐ *Option Act	☐ Horz/Ver 48 ☐ Number 102 ☐ Pacing	☐ Horz/Ver 49 ☐ Pro Chk 16 ☐ *Option Act	☐ Horz/Ver 50 ☐ Number 103 ☐ Pacing	☐ Horz/Ver 51 ☐ Pro Chk 17 ☐ RH/LH Diag.
10	☐ RH/LH ? ☐ Number 104 ☐ *Option Act	☐ RH/LH ? ☐ Number 105 ☐ Pacing	☐ RH/LH ? ☐ Pro Chk 18 ☐ *Option Act	☐ RH/LH ? ☐ Number 106 ☐ Number Exit	☐ RH/LH ? ☐ Pro Chk 19 ☐ RH/LH Diag.
11	☐ RH/LH ? ☐ Punct 92 ☐ *Option Act	☐ RH/LH ? ☐ Punct 93 ☐ Pacing	☐ RH/LH ? ☐ Pro Chk 20 ☐ *Option Act	☐ RH/LH ? ☐ Punct 94 ☐ Pacing	☐ RH/LH ? ☐ Pro Chk 21 ☐ RH/LH Diag.
12	☐ Double 77 ☐ Punct 95 ☐ *Option Act	☐ Double 78 ☐ Punct 96 ☐ Pacing	☐ Double 79 ☐ Pro Chk 22 ☐ *Option Act	☐ Double 80 ☐ Pro Chk 23 ☐ Pacing	☐ Double 81 ☐ Exit Timing ☐ *Option Act

45-HOUR/9-WEEK SKILLBUILDING COURSE

If you are enrolled in a **45-hour/9-week** skillbuilding course, you will follow the course plan outline below. Use Level 1 if your speed is below 40 words per minute; use Level 2 if your speed is above 40 words per minute. As you complete each assignment, check off the box next to the assignment. Note: (?) denotes a computer-assigned lesson. Optional activities (*) include Pacing Practice, Keypad Practice, and Open-Screen Practice.

Level 1—for keyboarding speed below 40 words per minute

Week	Day 1	Day 2	Day 3	Day 4	Day 5
1	☐ Entry Timing ☐ Alpha. Diag. ☐ Number Entry	☐ Alphabet ? ☐ Number 97 ☐ Pacing Place	☐ Alphabet ? ☐ Number 98 ☐ Pacing	☐ Alphabet ? ☐ Number 99 ☐ Pacing	☐ Alphabet ? ☐ Pro Chk 1 ☐ Pacing
2	☐ Alphabet ? ☐ Number 100 ☐ *Option Act	☐ Alphabet ? ☐ Number 101 ☐ Pacing	☐ Alphabet ? ☐ Pro Chk 2 ☐ *Option Act	☐ Alphabet ? ☐ Number 102 ☐ Pacing	☐ Alphabet ? ☐ Pro Chk 3 ☐ *Option Act
3	☐ Ind Fing 27 ☐ Number 103 ☐ *Option Act	☐ Ind Fing 28 ☐ Number 104 ☐ Pacing	☐ Ind Fing 29 ☐ Pro Chk 4 ☐ *Option Act	☐ Ind Fing 30 ☐ Number 105 ☐ Pacing	☐ Ind Fing 31 ☐ Pro Chk 5 ☐ *Option Act
4	☐ Word Lev 32 ☐ Number 106 ☐ Number Exit	☐ Word Lev 33 ☐ Punct 92 ☐ Pacing	☐ Word Lev 34 ☐ Pro Chk 6 ☐ *Option Act	☐ Word Lev 35 ☐ Punct 93 ☐ Pacing	☐ Word Lev 36 ☐ Pro Chk 7 ☐ *Option Act
5	☐ Concen 57 ☐ Punct 94 ☐ *Option Act	☐ Concen 58 ☐ Punct 95 ☐ Pacing	☐ Concen 59 ☐ Pro Chk 8 ☐ *Option Act	☐ Concen 60 ☐ Punct 96 ☐ Pacing	☐ Concen 61 ☐ Pro Chk 9 ☐ *Option Act
6	☐ Freq Use 37 ☐ Symbol 107 ☐ *Option Act	☐ Freq Use 38 ☐ Symbol 108 ☐ Pacing	☐ Freq Use 39 ☐ Pro Chk 10 ☐ *Option Act	☐ Freq Use 40 ☐ Symbol 109 ☐ Pacing	☐ Freq Use 41 ☐ Pro Chk 11 ☐ *Option Act
7	☐ Horz/Ver 42 ☐ Symbol 110 ☐ *Option Act	☐ Horz/Ver 43 ☐ Symbol 111 ☐ Pacing	☐ Horz/Ver 44 ☐ Pro Chk 12 ☐ *Option Act	☐ Horz/Ver 45 ☐ Punct 92 ☐ Pacing	☐ Horz/Ver 46 ☐ Pro Chk 13 ☐ *Option Act
8	☐ Horz/Ver 47 ☐ Punct 93 ☐ *Option Act	☐ Horz/Ver 48 ☐ Punct 94 ☐ Pacing	☐ Horz/Ver 49 ☐ Pro Chk 14 ☐ *Option Act	☐ Horz/Ver 50 ☐ Punct 95 ☐ Pacing	☐ Horz/Ver 51 ☐ Pro Chk 15 ☐ *Option Act
9	☐ Alt Hand 72 ☐ Punct 96 ☐ *Option Act	☐ Alt Hand 73 ☐ Pro Chk 16 ☐ Pacing	☐ Alt Hand 74 ☐ Pro Chk 17 ☐ *Option Act	☐ Alt Hand 75 ☐ Pro Chk 18 ☐ Pacing	☐ Alt Hand 76 ☐ Exit Timing ☐ *Option Act

Level 2—for keyboarding speed above 40 words per minute

Week	Day 1	Day 2	Day 3	Day 4	Day 5
1	☐ Entry Timing ☐ Alpha. Diag. ☐ Number Entry	☐ Alphabet ? ☐ Number 97 ☐ Pacing Place	☐ Alphabet ? ☐ Number 98 ☐ Pacing	☐ Alphabet ? ☐ Number 99 ☐ Pacing	☐ Alphabet ? ☐ Pro Chk 1 ☐ Pacing
2	☐ Alphabet ? ☐ Number 100 ☐ *Option Act	☐ Alphabet ? ☐ Number 101 ☐ Pacing	☐ Alphabet ? ☐ Pro Chk 2 ☐ *Option Act	☐ Alphabet ? ☐ Number 102 ☐ Pacing	☐ Alphabet ? ☐ Pro Chk 3 ☐ *Option Act
3	☐ Ind Fing 27 ☐ Number 103 ☐ *Option Act	☐ Ind Fing 28 ☐ Number 104 ☐ Pacing	☐ Ind Fing 29 ☐ Pro Chk 4 ☐ *Option Act	☐ Ind Fing 30 ☐ Number 105 ☐ Pacing	☐ Ind Fing 31 ☐ Pro Chk 5 ☐ *Option Act
4	☐ Concen 57 ☐ Number 106 ☐ Number Exit	☐ Concen 58 ☐ Punct 92 ☐ Pacing	☐ Concen 59 ☐ Pro Chk 6 ☐ *Option Act	☐ Concen 60 ☐ Punct 93 ☐ Pacing	☐ Concen 61 ☐ Pro Chk 7 ☐ *Option Act
5	☐ Horz/Ver 42 ☐ Punct 94 ☐ *Option Act	☐ Horz/Ver 43 ☐ Punct 95 ☐ Pacing	☐ Horz/Ver 44 ☐ Pro Chk 8 ☐ *Option Act	☐ Horz/Ver 45 ☐ Punct 96 ☐ Pacing	☐ Horz/Ver 46 ☐ Pro Chk 9 ☐ *Option Act
6	☐ Horz/Ver 47 ☐ Symbol 107 ☐ *Option Act	☐ Horz/Ver 48 ☐ Symbol 108 ☐ Pacing	☐ Horz/Ver 49 ☐ Pro Chk 10 ☐ *Option Act	☐ Horz/Ver 50 ☐ Symbol 109 ☐ Pacing	☐ Horz/Ver 51 ☐ Pro Chk 11 ☐ *Option Act
7	☐ RH/LH ? ☐ Symbol 110 ☐ *Option Act	☐ RH/LH ? ☐ Symbol 111 ☐ Pacing	☐ RH/LH ? ☐ Pro Chk 12 ☐ *Option Act	☐ RH/LH ? ☐ Punct 92 ☐ Pacing	☐ RH/LH ? ☐ Pro Chk 13 ☐ RH/LH Diag.
8	☐ RH/LH ? ☐ Punct 93 ☐ *Option Act	☐ RH/LH ? ☐ Punct 94 ☐ Pacing	☐ RH/LH ? ☐ Pro Chk 14 ☐ *Option Act	☐ RH/LH ? ☐ Punct 95 ☐ Pacing	☐ RH/LH ? ☐ Pro Chk 15 ☐ RH/LH Diag.
9	☐ Alt Hand 72 ☐ Punct 96 ☐ *Option Act	☐ Alt Hand 73 ☐ Pro Chk 16 ☐ Pacing	☐ Alt Hand 74 ☐ Pro Chk 17 ☐ *Option Act	☐ Alt Hand 75 ☐ Pro Chk 18 ☐ Pacing	☐ Alt Hand 76 ☐ Exit Timing ☐ *Option Act

30-HOUR/6-WEEK SKILLBUILDING COURSE

If you are enrolled in a 30-hour/6-week skillbuilding course, you will follow the course plan outline below. Use Level 1 if your speed is below 40 words per minute; use Level 2 if your speed is above 40 words per minute. As you complete each assignment, check off the box next to the assignment. Note: (?) denotes a computer-assigned lesson. Optional activities (*) include Pacing Practice, Keypad Practice, and Open-Screen Practice.

Level 1—for keyboarding speed below 40 words per minute

Week	Day 1	Day 2	Day 3	Day 4	Day 5
1	☐ Entry Timing ☐ Alpha. Diag. ☐ Number Entry	☐ Alphabet ? ☐ Number 97 ☐ Pacing Place	☐ Alphabet ? ☐ Number 98 ☐ Pacing	☐ Alphabet ? ☐ Number 99 ☐ Pacing	☐ Alphabet ? ☐ Pro Chk 1 ☐ Pacing
2	☐ Alphabet ? ☐ Number 100 ☐ *Option Act	☐ Alphabet ? ☐ Number 101 ☐ Pacing	☐ Alphabet ? ☐ Pro Chk 2 ☐ *Option Act	☐ Alphabet ? ☐ Number 102 ☐ Pacing	☐ Alphabet ? ☐ Pro Chk 3 ☐ *Option Act
3	☐ Ind Fing 27 ☐ Number 103 ☐ *Option Act	☐ Ind Fing 28 ☐ Number 104 ☐ Pacing	☐ Ind Fing 29 ☐ Pro Chk 4 ☐ *Option Act	☐ Ind Fing 30 ☐ Number 105 ☐ Pacing	☐ Ind Fing 31 ☐ Pro Chk 5 ☐ *Option Act
4	☐ Word Lev 32 ☐ Number 106 ☐ Number Exit	☐ Word Lev 33 ☐ Punct 92 ☐ Pacing	☐ Word Lev 34 ☐ Pro Chk 6 ☐ *Option Act	☐ Word Lev 35 ☐ Punct 93 ☐ Pacing	☐ Word Lev 36 ☐ Pro Chk 7 ☐ *Option Act
5	☐ Freq Use 37 ☐ Punct 94 ☐ *Option Act	☐ Freq Use 38 ☐ Punct 95 ☐ Pacing	☐ Freq Use 39 ☐ Pro Chk 8 ☐ *Option Act	☐ Freq Use 40 ☐ Punct 96 ☐ Pacing	☐ Freq Use 41 ☐ Pro Chk 9 ☐ *Option Act
6	☐ Alt Hand 72 ☐ Word Fam 52 ☐ *Option Act	☐ Alt Hand 73 ☐ Word Fam 53 ☐ Pacing	☐ Alt Hand 74 ☐ Pro Chk 10 ☐ *Option Act	☐ Alt Hand 75 ☐ Word Fam 54 ☐ Pacing	☐ Alt Hand 76 ☐ Exit Timing ☐ *Option Act

Level 2—for keyboarding speed above 40 words per minute

Week	Day 1	Day 2	Day 3	Day 4	Day 5
1	☐ Entry Timing ☐ Alpha. Diag. ☐ Number Entry	☐ Alphabet ? ☐ Number 97 ☐ Pacing Place	☐ Alphabet ? ☐ Number 98 ☐ Pacing	☐ Alphabet ? ☐ Number 99 ☐ Pacing	☐ Alphabet ? ☐ Pro Chk 1 ☐ Pacing
2	☐ Alphabet ? ☐ Number 100 ☐ *Option Act	☐ Alphabet ? ☐ Number 101 ☐ Pacing	☐ Alphabet ? ☐ Pro Chk 2 ☐ *Option Act	☐ Alphabet ? ☐ Number 102 ☐ Pacing	☐ Alphabet ? ☐ Pro Chk 3 ☐ *Option Act
3	☐ Ind Fing 27 ☐ Number 103 ☐ *Option Act	☐ Ind Fing 28 ☐ Number 104 ☐ Pacing	☐ Ind Fing 29 ☐ Pro Chk 4 ☐ *Option Act	☐ Ind Fing 30 ☐ Number 105 ☐ Pacing	☐ Ind Fing 31 ☐ Pro Chk 5 ☐ RH/LH Diag.
4	☐ RH/LH ? ☐ Number 106 ☐ Number Exit	☐ RH/LH ? ☐ Punct 92 ☐ Pacing	☐ RH/LH ? ☐ Pro Chk 6 ☐ *Option Act	☐ RH/LH ? ☐ Punct 93 ☐ Pacing	☐ RH/LH ? ☐ Pro Chk 7 ☐ RH/LH Diag.
5	☐ RH/LH ? ☐ Punct 94 ☐ *Option Act	☐ RH/LH ? ☐ Punct 95 ☐ Pacing	☐ RH/LH ? ☐ Pro Chk 8 ☐ *Option Act	☐ RH/LH ? ☐ Punct 96 ☐ Pacing	☐ RH/LH ? ☐ Pro Chk 9 ☐ RH/LH Diag.
6	☐ Alt Hand 72 ☐ Horz/Ver 42 ☐ *Option Act	☐ Alt Hand 73 ☐ Horz/Ver 43 ☐ Pacing	☐ Alt Hand 74 ☐ Pro Chk 10 ☐ *Option Act	☐ Alt Hand 75 ☐ Horz/Ver 44 ☐ Pacing	☐ Alt Hand 76 ☐ Exit Timing ☐ *Option Act

Progress

Name _____ Class _____ Period _____

Record the words per minute and errors of your more accurate timing. First, mark the speed with a dot at the junction of the speed (WPM) scale and the Progress Check number. Then, write the number of errors and the date in the appropriate boxes at the bottom of the graph.

WPM	ENTRY	1	2	3	4	5	6	7	8	9	10	11	12	13	14	15	16	17	18	WPM
100																				100
98																				98
96																				96
94																				94
92																				92
90																				90
88																				88
86																				86
84																				84
82																				82
80																				80
78																				78
76																				76
74																				74
72																				72
70																				70
68																				68
66																				66
64																				64
62																				62
60																				60
58																				58
56																				56
54																				54
52																				52
50																				50
48																				48
46																				46
44																				44
42																				42
40																				40
38																				38
36																				36
34																				34
32																				32
30																				30
28																				28
26																				26
24																				24
22																				22
20																				20
18																				18
16																				16
14																				14
12																				12
10																				10
ERRORS																				ERRORS
DATE																				DATE

Progress

Record the words per minute and errors of your more accurate timing. First, mark the speed with a dot at the junction of the speed (WPM) scale and the Progress Check number. Then, write the number of errors and the date in the appropriate boxes at the bottom of the graph.

WPM	ENTRY	1	2	3	4	5	6	7	8	9	10	11	12	13	14	15	16	17	18	WPM
100																				100
98																				98
96																				96
94																				94
92																				92
90																				90
88																				88
86																				86
84																				84
82																				82
80																				80
78																				78
76																				76
74																				74
72																				72
70																				70
68																				68
66																				66
64																				64
62																				62
60																				60
58																				58
56																				56
54																				54
52																				52
50																				50
48																				48
46																				46
44																				44
42																				42
40																				40
38																				38
36																				36
34																				34
32																				32
30																				30
28																				28
26																				26
24																				24
22																				22
20																				20
18																				18
16																				16
14																				14
12																				12
10																				10
ERRORS																				ERRORS
DATE																				DATE

Course Entry and Exit

Entry Timing or Exit Timing

COURSE ENTRY TIMING

CONTENT

This section provides material for use in measuring your speed and accuracy on a 3- or 5-minute timing at the beginning of the course.

OBJECTIVE

To determine keyboarding speed and accuracy at the beginning of this course.

COURSE EXIT TIMING

OBJECTIVE

To measure keyboarding speed and accuracy at the end of this course.

After completing the Course Exit Timing, compare your scores on this timing with those you achieved on the Course Entry Timing, and note your skill gains!

TECHNIQUE TIP

Position the keyboard even with the front of the desk.

Practice the following paragraph. *Time—2 minutes.*

Most people think that the paper punch is a simple office tool. Projects may be destroyed if the paper punch is not used properly. One error is punching the wrong edge of the paper.

`00.00` **TIMING**

Business today needs to be in touch with its patrons. Cell 13
phones, pagers, personal data assistants, and pocket computers 26
provide businesses with the power to do so in a quick, precise, 39
and timely way. 42

A pager lets its owner know that someone is trying to call. 55
It stores the telephone number of the calling person until the 68
owner can return the call. Some pagers just store voice calls. 81
Pagers make it easy for the owner to move away from the phone 93
and still be informed of any calls. 100

Cell phones provide telephone services around the world. 112
The pocket phones travel anywhere the user wants to go and can 125
be used to call or receive calls. Simple cell phones have a few 138
service features, but more complex phones can send and receive 151
data, voice messages, and videos. They will store phone numbers, 164
save phone messages, display written messages, and show movies. 177
Cell phone towers dot the landscape across the country and send 190
the cell phone traffic. 195

The personal data assistant will help its user to set up 207
meetings, to take typed or handwritten notes, to store phone 219
numbers, and to remind its user of meetings. These very tiny 231
devices can hook up to other computers, printers, and modems. 243

A pocket computer is a small computer the size of your 255
hand. It can do many of the common tasks of a large computer, 267
but it has less memory, uses a little keyboard, and has a small 280
display. It too can hook up to other computers as well as to 292
printers and modems. 296

New devices to send, receive, process, and store data are 309
made almost daily, making the old devices obsolete. What does 321
the future hold? Time will tell, but most likely, the devices 333
will make using data fast, easy, and cheap. 342

| 1 | 2 | 3 | 4 | 5 | 6 | 7 | 8 | 9 | 10 | 11 | 12 | 13 |

99 wpm through 100 wpm

99 WORDS

There always has been a great deal of sound advice written for the person seeking employment. Much of this writing stresses[1] the importance of making a great first impression, and research does support the fact that the first minutes are very[2] crucial to one's chances of being selected for the new job. This means the interviewee should do some careful wardrobe planning[3] before that important interview. The apparel chosen must be neat, clean, and very appropriate for this major occasion.[4]

| 1 | 2 | 3 | 4 | 5 | 6 | 7 | 8 | 9 | 10 | 11 | 12 | 13 |

100 WORDS

There always has been a great deal of sound advice written for the person seeking employment. Much of this writing stresses[1] the importance of making a good first impression, and research does support the fact that the first minutes are indeed critical[2] to one's chances of being selected for the job. This means the interviewee should do some careful wardrobe planning[3] before the important interview. The apparel chosen must be neat, clean, and appropriate for this very important occasion.[4]

| 1 | 2 | 3 | 4 | 5 | 6 | 7 | 8 | 9 | 10 | 11 | 12 | 13 |

Alphabet Practice

Lessons 1–26

ALPHABET DIAGNOSTIC TIMING

CONTENT

The 3-minute timing in this lesson consists of 15 lines, each of which contains all the letters of the alphabet.

OBJECTIVE

To determine which letters are mistyped most often and to help you select practice lessons.

TECHNIQUE TIP

Keep wrists straight and curve fingers naturally over the home position.

PACING PRACTICE

95 wpm through 97 wpm

95 WORDS
There always has been a great deal of sound advice written for a person seeking employment. Much of this writing stresses the importance of making a good first impression, and research does support the fact that the first minutes are indeed critical to one's chances of being selected. This means the interviewee should do some careful wardrobe planning before each interview. The outfit that is selected should be appropriate, neat, and clean for this important event.

| 1 | 2 | 3 | 4 | 5 | 6 | 7 | 8 | 9 | 10 | 11 | 12 | 13 |

97 WORDS
There always has been a great deal of sound advice written for the person seeking employment. Much of this writing stresses the importance of making a good first impression, and research supports the fact that the first minutes are indeed critical to one's chances of being selected for the position. This means the interviewee should do some careful wardrobe planning before the interview. The selected outfit must be neat, clean, and most appropriate for the important event.

| 1 | 2 | 3 | 4 | 5 | 6 | 7 | 8 | 9 | 10 | 11 | 12 | 13 |

ALPHABET PRACTICE—DIAGNOSTIC TIMING

Press ENTER at the end of each line. Type the following, and make sure you do not skip any lines. *Time—2 minutes.*

1 Zak Wagner explained verbs quite carefully to John at home.

2 Lazy Herb picked very few quince to fill my six glass jars.   12

3 Pamy realized Jinx had not acquired five big working vests.   24

4 Jumpy nurses gave quick smallpox shots to Buzz and Winfred.   36

5 Max Jason may quickly play golf having won the ritzy derby.   48

| 1 | 2 | 3 | 4 | 5 | 6 | 7 | 8 | 9 | 10 | 11 | 12 | 60

`03.00` **TIMING**

Take two 3-minute timings on the following lines.

6 Jerry Rieck got his video prize for many quality workboxes.

7 Carollyn viewed amazing exhibits of pretty jonquil baskets.   12

8 Josh develops job questions for excellent weekly magazines.   24

9 Anxious buzzards quickly flew over eight jumpy jackrabbits.   36

10 A lynx quickly fled the zoo by jumping over the west gates.   48

11 Jayne squeezed five large boxes of limes to make new punch.   60

12 Brave horses quickly jump six water hazards and four gates.   72

13 Jodie very quickly went to get six zinc bears for the camp.   84

14 Dozens of women quietly joined six victims in the big park.   96

15 Five onyx and jade plaques grew dusty by my prized kitchen.   108

16 Aza will very quickly export huge jonquil blooms to Freddy.   120

17 Bejay gave Flip extra video cameras with quick zoom lenses.   132

18 Martha and Jeff quickly won luxury vacations as big prizes.   144

19 Quincy exports zebras and jackals for famous English wives.   156

20 Six antique owners quickly approved sizable jugs of shrimp.   168

  180

| 1 | 2 | 3 | 4 | 5 | 6 | 7 | 8 | 9 | 10 | 11 | 12 |

90 wpm through 94 wpm

90 WORDS

The work ethic and attitude of a new employee will do much to determine the employee's success at work. Employers are more than willing to spend time to assist new trainees in learning the most appropriate procedures of the office when they exhibit enthusiasm for a job and a strong desire to learn. It is a very interesting, but sad, fact that more people lose jobs because of poor attitudes than for their weak skills or a lack of training.

| 1 | 2 | 3 | 4 | 5 | 6 | 7 | 8 | 9 | 10 | 11 | 12 | 13 |

92 WORDS

The work ethic and attitude of a new employee will do much to determine the employee's success at work. Employers are more than willing to spend time to assist new trainees in learning the most appropriate procedures for the office when they exhibit enthusiasm for the job and a sincere desire to learn. It is an extremely interesting, but sad, fact that more people lose jobs because of their poor attitudes than for weak skills or poor job training.

| 1 | 2 | 3 | 4 | 5 | 6 | 7 | 8 | 9 | 10 | 11 | 12 | 13 |

94 WORDS

The work ethic and attitude of a new employee will do much to determine the employee's success at work. Employers are more than willing to spend the extra effort to assist new trainees in learning correct procedures for the office when they exhibit enthusiasm for the job and a sincere desire to learn. It is an extremely interesting, but sad, fact that more people lose their jobs because of poor attitude and work ethic than for weak or inadequate job training.

| 1 | 2 | 3 | 4 | 5 | 6 | 7 | 8 | 9 | 10 | 11 | 12 | 13 |

ALPHABET PRACTICE LESSONS

CONTENT
Separate skillbuilding lessons for each letter of the alphabet are provided. Use those Alphabet Practice lessons that correspond to the mistyped/difficult letters.

OBJECTIVE
To improve accuracy on the letters of the alphabet mistyped most often (as indicated by the diagnostic timings or personal selection) and increase speed in typing alphabetic copy.

PACING PRACTICE

85 wpm through 89 wpm

85 WORDS

Telecommunications is a term that simply means the transfer of data over a distance. The business that sends its data by telephone wire wants to increase its profits and to decrease its expenses at the same time. In order to achieve these goals, the correct use of all hardware and software is of major importance. The business also should give thoughtful consideration to the speed at which it can send its information.

| 1 | 2 | 3 | 4 | 5 | 6 | 7 | 8 | 9 | 10 | 11 | 12 | 13 |

87 WORDS

Telecommunications is a term that simply means the transfer of data over a distance. The business that sends its data by a telephone wire wants to increase its profits and to decrease its expenses at the same time. In order to achieve these goals, the correct use of all hardware is of the utmost importance to the firm. The business also should give thoughtful consideration to the speed at which it can transmit data by wire.

| 1 | 2 | 3 | 4 | 5 | 6 | 7 | 8 | 9 | 10 | 11 | 12 | 13 |

89 WORDS

Telecommunications is simply a term used to mean the speedy transfer of data over a distance. The business that sends data via telephone wire wishes to increase its profits and decrease its expenses at the same time. In order to achieve these goals, the correct use of hardware and software is of utmost importance to managers. A company must give very careful consideration to the rapidity with which it may send its critical data by wire.

| 1 | 2 | 3 | 4 | 5 | 6 | 7 | 8 | 9 | 10 | 11 | 12 | 13 |

WARMUP

Practice the following lines. *Time—2 minutes.*

Fluency	1	socks clans snaps docks envy jams isle name fog irk cow bob	12
Accuracy	2	yews cozy onyx even buoy aqua king join bump dirt file hunt	24
Numbers	3	air 1 air 2 air 3 air 4 air 5 air 6 air 7 air 8 air 9 air 0	36
Symbols	4	ss @ ss @ ss @ jj & jj & jj & ;; = ;; = ;; = ;; + ;; + ;; +	48

PRETEST

Take one 1-minute timing.

	5	Adam asked his aide to analyze the data for the Alaska	12
	6	and Canada caravan. Our caravan of boats will take the long	24
	7	canal with a load of azaleas and alfalfa to Asia via Japan.	36

| 1 | 2 | 3 | 4 | 5 | 6 | 7 | 8 | 9 | 10 | 11 | 12 |

PRACTICE

Type lines for speed or accuracy. *Time—3 or 5 minutes.*

Key Review: A	8	aaa asa aaa ada aaa afa aqa aza aAa AaA AaA Ala Ana Ava aaa	12
	9	aqua Asia canal kayak banana cabana cabbage garbage Pancake	24
	10	gala papa carat salad Canada llamas panacea caravan Albania	36
	11	aura data fatal Japan casaba azalea anagram Baggage cantata	48
	12	alpaca alfalfa lasagna Alabama bandanna aardvarks Americana	60
	13	Alaska mascara malaria Barbara panorama barracuda appraisal	72

⏱ 00.30 30-SECOND OKS

SPEED: 2 errors allowed

ACCURACY: 0 errors allowed

Take a 30-second OK timing on each line. Repeat.

	14	Jodie very quickly examined and sewed the five big zippers.	12
	15	Roxy picked five jonquils while Buz stayed with my grandpa.	12
	16	Just fifty hands were picked to excavate my blazing quarry.	12

| 1 | 2 | 3 | 4 | 5 | 6 | 7 | 8 | 9 | 10 | 11 | 12 |

TECHNIQUE CHECK

Proper position at machine.

Control hand bounce.

Eyes on copy.

Type for 30 seconds on each line.

	17	ace act add age ago aid ail aim air ale all Art Ada Abe Amy	12
	18	afar away alas aria Adam Alta naval radar nasal salad Sarah	12
	19	area aroma arena apart appall appear appeal airfare airmail	12

⏱ 01.00 1-MINUTE OKS

SPEED: 3 errors allowed

ACCURACY: 1 error allowed

Take one 1-minute OK timing on each line.

	20	Sarah wore an aqua bandanna in a kayak in an Alabama canal.	12
	21	Adam gave Barbara lasagna while Anabel ate banana pancakes.	12

| 1 | 2 | 3 | 4 | 5 | 6 | 7 | 8 | 9 | 10 | 11 | 12 |

POSTTEST

Repeat the Pretest.

80 wpm through 84 wpm

80 WORDS

Most management personnel spend a good deal of time placing phone calls that do not reach their intended parties. Statistics on calls that are successfully completed the first time they are dialed show that a low percentage of calls reach the intended party on the first attempt. Thus, voice messaging can eliminate this waste of time. The messages are stored until a person can answer the call.

| 1 | 2 | 3 | 4 | 5 | 6 | 7 | 8 | 9 | 10 | 11 | 12 | 13 |

82 WORDS

Some key office personnel spend a good deal of time making phone calls that do not reach the intended people. Statistics on calls that are successfully completed the first time they are dialed show that a low percentage of our phone calls reach the intended party on the first try. Voice messaging can eliminate the waste of time. Electronic computers can store messages until someone can take the call.

| 1 | 2 | 3 | 4 | 5 | 6 | 7 | 8 | 9 | 10 | 11 | 12 | 13 |

84 WORDS

Some key office personnel spend a good deal of time making phone calls that never reach the right parties. Statistics on calls that are successfully completed the first time they are dialed show that a low percentage of these phone calls reach the intended party on the first try. Voice messaging can very easily eliminate the waste of time. Electronic computers will store messages until someone is able to answer.

| 1 | 2 | 3 | 4 | 5 | 6 | 7 | 8 | 9 | 10 | 11 | 12 | 13 |

WARMUP

Practice the following lines. *Time—2 minutes.*

Fluency	1	neighbor visitor visuals panels bushel rigid fight dial she	12
Accuracy	2	lamb fret clog jump quit hour evil next axis kill doze away	24
Numbers	3	may 1 may 2 may 3 may 4 may 5 may 6 may 7 may 8 may 9 may 0	36
Symbols	4	dd # dd # dd # jj ^ jj ^ jj ^ ;; [;; [;; [;;] ;;] ;;]	48

PRETEST

Take one 1-minute timing.

5	Bobby and Barb quibbled over bonbons served by busboys	12
6	in the lobby while Gabby nibbled on a kabob. My bubbly baby	24
7	dribbled on his bib while Robby babbled at the big baboons.	36

| 1 | 2 | 3 | 4 | 5 | 6 | 7 | 8 | 9 | 10 | 11 | 12 |

PRACTICE

Type lines for speed or accuracy. *Time—3 or 5 minutes.*

Key Review: B

8	fbf bbb fbf bbb fbf bbb bob bib fBf BfB bBb BbB Bub Bob bbb	12
9	bibs baby kabob Bobby babble Hubbub busboys baboons blabbed	24
10	Barb blob bribe Gabby suburb cobweb clobber blubber dribble	36
11	bulb ebbs lobby nubby bubbly hobnob Nibbles rubbery Robbins	48
12	bibbed bobbled Quibble slobber babbling Bubbletop gibberish	60
13	Rabbit stubbed stubble Scrubby bubblier bubbliest blubberer	72

00.30 30-SECOND OKS

Take a 30-second OK timing on each line. Repeat.

SPEED: 2 errors allowed
ACCURACY: 0 errors allowed

14	Victor zipped through quickly but just finished with exams.	12
15	Jake expects Ward to acquire seven prize goldfish by March.	12
16	He examined a few subjects and very quickly recognized pox.	12

| 1 | 2 | 3 | 4 | 5 | 6 | 7 | 8 | 9 | 10 | 11 | 12 |

TECHNIQUE CHECK

Type for 30 seconds on each line.

Wrists low, not touching.
Proper finger position and curve.
Efficient use of right shift key.

17	bad bag ban bar bat bee bag bet cab cob jab jib job Lab Mob	12
18	bomb hubby blurb hobby bauble barber bamboo bobbins Bonbons	12
19	bBb Cabby Robby Abbey Bedbug Bobble Bubbles Bombard Bobbies	12

01.00 1-MINUTE OKS

Take one 1-minute OK timing on each line.

SPEED: 3 errors allowed
ACCURACY: 1 error allowed

20	Bob bribed the busboys to bring rabbit kabobs to the lobby.	12
21	His baboon nibbled bamboo while Bub quibbled in the suburb.	12

| 1 | 2 | 3 | 4 | 5 | 6 | 7 | 8 | 9 | 10 | 11 | 12 |

POSTTEST

Repeat the Pretest.

75 wpm through 79 wpm

75 WORDS

Today there is a great deal of interest in the offices of the future. The modern office uses a wide range of equipment for various kinds of jobs. The jobs utilize modern phone systems, microfilm or microfiche for the storage and recall of records, and computers for the processing of both words and numbers. The move is toward upgrading in all kinds of office equipment.

| 1 | 2 | 3 | 4 | 5 | 6 | 7 | 8 | 9 | 10 | 11 | 12 | 13 |

77 WORDS

Today there is a great deal of interest in the offices of the future. The modern office uses a wide range of equipment for many different kinds of jobs. The tasks utilize modern phone systems, microfilm or microfiche for the storage and recall of records, and computers for the processing of both numbers and words. The trend is toward improvement in all kinds of office machines.

| 1 | 2 | 3 | 4 | 5 | 6 | 7 | 8 | 9 | 10 | 11 | 12 | 13 |

79 WORDS

Today there is a great deal of interest in the offices of the future. The modern office uses a wide range of equipment for many different kinds of jobs. The tasks utilize modern phone systems, microfilm or microfiche for the storage and recall of records, and computers for the processing of both numbers and words. The trend is toward even more improvement in all kinds of office equipment.

| 1 | 2 | 3 | 4 | 5 | 6 | 7 | 8 | 9 | 10 | 11 | 12 | 13 |

WARMUP Practice the following lines. *Time—2 minutes.*

Fluency	1	tutorial bushels problem dismal eighth shape giant work but	12
Accuracy	2	junk asks dove quiz cold flex moat bank give hour pure wavy	24
Numbers	3	set 1 set 2 set 3 set 4 set 5 set 6 set 7 set 8 set 9 set 0	36
Symbols	4	ff $ ff $ ff $ 11 (11 (11 (;;) ;;) ;;) ;; / ;; / ;; /	48

PRETEST Take one 1-minute timing.

5   An eccentric doc called Cicely and Chuck to cancel the   12
6 vaccines at the council clinic for their cat and raccoon so   24
7 that comical circus clowns could get a colicky cub checked.   36

| 1 | 2 | 3 | 4 | 5 | 6 | 7 | 8 | 9 | 10 | 11 | 12 |

PRACTICE Type lines for speed or accuracy. *Time—3 or 5 minutes.*

Key Review: C
8   dcd ccc dcd ccc dcd ccc car cot dCd CdC dCd CdC cam Cec ccc   12
9   coco cabs cache cocky cancer Critic Hiccups succeed succumb   24
10   cafe cats check Cecil citric cancel piccolo Picnics chances   36
11   chic cage cacti Yucca circus coccyx raccoon Vaccine colicky   48
12   Cicely choices comical copycat accuracy eccentric Occupancy   60
13   clinic crewcut Council corncob cuticles Accessory backspace   72

00.30 30-SECOND OKS Take a 30-second OK timing on each line. Repeat.

SPEED: 2 errors allowed
ACCURACY: 0 errors allowed

14   Mike Wiley acquired visiting exhibits for the Japanese zoo.   12
15   Zak was given a free smallpox vaccine by the jealous squad.   12
16   Jo zipped her brown jacket and fixed her gloves on my quay.   12

| 1 | 2 | 3 | 4 | 5 | 6 | 7 | 8 | 9 | 10 | 11 | 12 |

TECHNIQUE CHECK Type for 30 seconds on each line.

Back erect, lean forward.
Smooth stroking, even pace.
Space bar—thumb close.

17   cad cab can cap car cob cop cot cub doc arc tic Ace act ice   12
18   cocoa cycle chick Chuck cinch click clock could couch crock   12
19   c c c ccc c c c ccc cat cod cur cup cut calm came card Carl   12

01.00 1-MINUTE OKS Take one 1-minute OK timing on each line.

SPEED: 3 errors allowed
ACCURACY: 1 error allowed

20   A cocky critic succumbs to hiccups and can cancel a circus.   12
21   The clinic can cut crewcuts or cuticles for Cecil and Carl.   12

| 1 | 2 | 3 | 4 | 5 | 6 | 7 | 8 | 9 | 10 | 11 | 12 |

POSTTEST Repeat the Pretest.

70 wpm through 74 wpm

70 WORDS

The need for good language skills has become very vital to all office workers. In addition to both grammar and word usage,[1] language arts include listening and speaking skills.[2] Although there has been a good deal of progress made in the ease of using modern machines,[3] the employee is always responsible for properly spelling and punctuating work.[4]

| 1 | 2 | 3 | 4 | 5 | 6 | 7 | 8 | 9 | 10 | 11 | 12 | 13 |

72 WORDS

The need for good language skills has become very vital to all office workers. In addition to both grammar and word usage,[1] language arts include listening and speaking skills.[2] Although there has been a good deal of progress made in the ease of using modern office machines,[3] the workers are still responsible for correctly spelling and punctuating documents.[4]

| 1 | 2 | 3 | 4 | 5 | 6 | 7 | 8 | 9 | 10 | 11 | 12 | 13 |

74 WORDS

The need for strong language skills has become increasingly vital to the busy office worker. In addition to good grammar and[1] word usage, the language arts include listening and speaking[2] skills. Although there has been a great deal of progress made in the ease of using modern office equipment,[3] the employee is still responsible for correct spelling and punctuation.[4]

| 1 | 2 | 3 | 4 | 5 | 6 | 7 | 8 | 9 | 10 | 11 | 12 | 13 |

WARMUP

Practice the following lines. *Time—2 minutes.*

Fluency	1	rifle bugle corks soaps corn clay fowl busy dug lay toe men	12
Accuracy	2	coax join very shag fizz bout riot paid soap kilt meow quit	24
Numbers	3	got 1 got 2 got 3 got 4 got 5 got 6 got 7 got 8 got 9 got 0	36
Symbols	4	ff % ff % ff % kk * kk * kk * ;; \ ;; \ ;; \ ;; | ;; | ;; |	48

PRETEST

Take one 1-minute timing.

5	Dazed Donald kidded Edward as Dede dawdled in her dyed	12
6	beaded wedding dress. Her addled daddy decided to ask David	24
7	to play his dandy fiddle during the dreaded wedding dinner.	36

| 1 | 2 | 3 | 4 | 5 | 6 | 7 | 8 | 9 | 10 | 11 | 12 |

PRACTICE

Type lines for speed or accuracy. *Time—3 or 5 minutes.*

Key Review: D

8	ddd dsd ddd dfd ddd dad ded dcd dDd DdD DdD Dud Don Dad ddd	12
9	deed dads dandy ended Donald padded deduced cuddled Peddled	24
10	dude dyed faded David deeded Kidded caddied wedding riddled	36
11	dead Odds added dress doodad Edward muddied fiddled huddled	48
12	wedded Decided decoded deluded embedded Shuddered gladdened	60
13	Nodded divided dreaded defends Reddened addressed disdained	72

00.30 30-SECOND OKS

Take a 30-second OK timing on each line. Repeat.

SPEED: 2 errors allowed

ACCURACY: 0 errors allowed

14	Pa lugs my extra fuzzy jacket to squelch bitter river wind.	12
15	Gaby Koch will adjust my quota level for Cadiz expeditions.	12
16	Jacques gave Micky a balloon while we fixed pizza for Todd.	12

| 1 | 2 | 3 | 4 | 5 | 6 | 7 | 8 | 9 | 10 | 11 | 12 |

TECHNIQUE CHECK

Type for 30 seconds on each line.

Eyes on copy.

Feet on floor.

Control hand bounce.

17	dazed diced dined addled adored edited banded beaded candid	12
18	adds Dede dread daddy chided eluded dawdled doodled dredged	12
19	did dad dud Dan day den dew die dig dip dog dot due add odd	12

01.00 1-MINUTE OKS

Take one 1-minute OK timing on each line.

SPEED: 3 errors allowed

ACCURACY: 1 error allowed

20	Donald kidded Edward as they decided to defend their deeds.	12
21	Daddy was dazed as Dede wedded Don in a dyed wedding dress.	12

| 1 | 2 | 3 | 4 | 5 | 6 | 7 | 8 | 9 | 10 | 11 | 12 |

POSTTEST

Repeat the Pretest.

64 wpm through 69 wpm

64 WORDS

Today more than ever before, it is critical for each of us to have a course in economics. Astute shopping is one important phase of our sound economic awareness. Two other main areas are the role that the government plays in all of our lives and what inflation is doing to our purchasing power at home and abroad.

| 1 | 2 | 3 | 4 | 5 | 6 | 7 | 8 | 9 | 10 | 11 | 12 | 13 |

65 WORDS

Students are very wise if they leave school with some basic ability in bookkeeping and business math. Whether they continue in school or enter the workforce, these basic skills will help each of them manage their business and personal finances more easily. Learning to use a computer and calculator is important also.

| 1 | 2 | 3 | 4 | 5 | 6 | 7 | 8 | 9 | 10 | 11 | 12 | 13 |

67 WORDS

Students are very wise if they leave school with some basic ability in bookkeeping and business math. Whether they continue in school or enter the workforce, they will use the basic skills to help them manage their business and personal finances much more easily. Knowing how to use the computer or calculator is needed and helpful.

| 1 | 2 | 3 | 4 | 5 | 6 | 7 | 8 | 9 | 10 | 11 | 12 | 13 |

69 WORDS

Students are very wise if they leave school with some basic skills in accounting and business math. Whether they choose to continue in college or enter the workforce, basic skills will help all of them cope more easily with any business and personal finances. Learning how to use the computer and a calculator is needed and useful for them.

| 1 | 2 | 3 | 4 | 5 | 6 | 7 | 8 | 9 | 10 | 11 | 12 | 13 |

WARMUP   Practice the following lines. *Time—2 minutes.*

Fluency	1	mementos auditor socials formal island handy civic city got	12
Accuracy	2	quiz axle jaws easy brew camp dent flop high kits vain lock	24
Numbers	3	pay 1 pay 2 pay 3 pay 4 pay 5 pay 6 pay 7 pay 8 pay 9 pay 0	36
Symbols	4	kk < kk < kk < ll > ll > ll > ;; { ;; { ;; { ;; } ;; } ;; }	48

PRETEST   Take one 1-minute timing.

5	Eugene believed he was one of eleven engineers elected	12
6	to emcee for the employees of Evergreen in Seattle. He said	24
7	Ellen and Helen were also elected to emcee for every event.	36

| 1 | 2 | 3 | 4 | 5 | 6 | 7 | 8 | 9 | 10 | 11 | 12 |

PRACTICE   Type lines for speed or accuracy. *Time—3 or 5 minutes.*

Key Review: E

8	ded eee ded eee ded eee eel eye dEd EdE eEe EeE Ede Eve eee	12
9	ease eyes elect eject Helena esteem elected escapee Element	24
10	edge else Tepee geese secret Peewee essence secedes secrete	36
11	even Erie emcee event Decree eleven recedes expense evacuee	48
12	settee deplete Believe referee reseeded refreezes Evergreen	60
13	Eugene refugee retiree relieve Redeemed engineers employees	72

00.30 30-SECOND OKS   Take a 30-second OK timing on each line. Repeat.

SPEED: 2 errors allowed

ACCURACY: 0 errors allowed

14	Kit and Bob have acquired my five expensive jigsaw puzzles.	12
15	Big Alex quickly drank five whole cups of zesty plum juice.	12
16	Dwight Ek explores amazing folklore movies in jolly Quebec.	12

| 1 | 2 | 3 | 4 | 5 | 6 | 7 | 8 | 9 | 10 | 11 | 12 |

TECHNIQUE CHECK   Type for 30 seconds on each line.

Wrists low, not touching.

Efficient use of shift keys.

Sharp, quick keystroking.

17	eye eel bee fee Lee see tee wee ebb err ear eat ego elk elm	12
18	eEe Emerge Eyelet Severe Needle Revere Deeper Teethe Delete	12
19	every exert eager easel eaten edged egret Ellen Helen expel	12

01.00 1-MINUTE OKS   Take one 1-minute OK timing on each line.

SPEED: 3 errors allowed

ACCURACY: 1 error allowed

20	Lee created eleven expensive tepees for esteemed engineers.	12
21	Ellen believed the referee emceed the secret event in Erie.	12

| 1 | 2 | 3 | 4 | 5 | 6 | 7 | 8 | 9 | 10 | 11 | 12 |

POSTTEST   Repeat the Pretest.

57 wpm through 62 wpm

57 WORDS

A few workers still use shorthand on the job. This skill is used to take minutes of meetings as well as memos, letters, and reports. Some may even use their shorthand skill to write phone messages. Everyone who knows shorthand finds it to be a helpful tool for home or office.

| 1 | 2 | 3 | 4 | 5 | 6 | 7 | 8 | 9 | 10 | 11 | 12 | 13 |

59 WORDS

A few workers still use shorthand on the job. This skill is used to take minutes of meetings as well as memos, letters, and reports. Some may even use shorthand to take telephone messages. Office workers who know shorthand find it a convenient and handy tool for their home and office work.

| 1 | 2 | 3 | 4 | 5 | 6 | 7 | 8 | 9 | 10 | 11 | 12 | 13 |

60 WORDS

More than ever before, it is true that each of us needs a good course in economics. Smart shopping is but one important phase of sound economic awareness. Two other major areas are the role of government in our lives and what inflation is doing to our purchasing power both at home and overseas.

| 1 | 2 | 3 | 4 | 5 | 6 | 7 | 8 | 9 | 10 | 11 | 12 | 13 |

62 WORDS

More than ever before, it is true that each of us needs a good course in economics. Prudent shopping is but one important phase of sound economic awareness. Two other areas are the role the government plays in our lives and what inflation seems to be doing to our purchasing power both at home and abroad.

| 1 | 2 | 3 | 4 | 5 | 6 | 7 | 8 | 9 | 10 | 11 | 12 | 13 |

WARMUP   Practice the following lines. *Time—2 minutes.*

Fluency	1	neuritis element emblems eighty chapel amend signs maps the	12
Accuracy	2	joys dark jump balk cave zest file hung grew copy quit taxi	24
Numbers	3	bid 1 bid 2 bid 3 bid 4 bid 5 bid 6 bid 7 bid 8 bid 9 bid 0	36
Symbols	4	ss @ ss @ ss @ jj & jj & jj & ;; = ;; = ;; = ;; + ;; + ;; +	48

PRETEST   Take one 1-minute timing.

	5	The gruff officers made few efforts to diffuse traffic	12
	6	while the offended chauffeur scoffed. Faith was fearful for	24
	7	she had offered to ferry the foodstuff to the office staff.	36

| 1 | 2 | 3 | 4 | 5 | 6 | 7 | 8 | 9 | 10 | 11 | 12 |

PRACTICE   Type lines for speed or accuracy. *Time—3 or 5 minutes.*

Key Review: F	8	fff fdf fsf faf frf ftf fvf fbf fgf fFf FfF FfF Fad Fay fff	12
	9	buff doff daffy Taffy affect effort Offbeat firefly falsify	24
	10	cuff fief Muffy fifth offers Fluffy liftoff officer fortify	36
	11	fife huff Jiffy fluff Afford fitful fearful offside flyleaf	48
	12	affirm baffled Gruffly sniffle riffraff Flagstaff affection	60
	13	Office chiffon buffalo traffic daffodil foodstuff Chauffeur	72

`00.30` 30-SECOND OKS   Take a 30-second OK timing on each line. Repeat.

SPEED: 2 errors allowed

ACCURACY: 0 errors allowed

	14	Happy Muf quickly seized live jaguars at the new Bronx Zoo.	12
	15	His deft joking brought quizzical expressions to my viewer.	12
	16	Jack Quigley poorly reviewed many fine exhibits at the zoo.	12

| 1 | 2 | 3 | 4 | 5 | 6 | 7 | 8 | 9 | 10 | 11 | 12 |

TECHNIQUE CHECK   Type for 30 seconds on each line.

Back erect, lean forward.

Proper position at machine.

Proper finger position and curve.

	17	fad fan far fat Fay fee few fib fig fit fix fly fog fox fun	12
	18	chaff Cliff gruff scoff sniff skiff staff stuff offer affix	12
	19	muff tiff fifty Puffy fluffs offend diffuse efforts effects	12

`01.00` 1-MINUTE OKS   Take one 1-minute OK timing on each line.

SPEED: 3 errors allowed

ACCURACY: 1 error allowed

	20	A chauffeur offered Taffy a daffodil from the office staff.	12
	21	Efforts to diffuse traffic by a fearful officer were daffy.	12

| 1 | 2 | 3 | 4 | 5 | 6 | 7 | 8 | 9 | 10 | 11 | 12 |

POSTTEST   Repeat the Pretest.

PACING PRACTICE

50 wpm through 55 wpm

50 WORDS

When one is writing a story, it is wise to think about good[1] writing skills. A story that has been written well gives your[2] reader the chance to become involved in the problem or plot. The[3] problem or plot must be developed carefully and precisely.[4]

| 1 | 2 | 3 | 4 | 5 | 6 | 7 | 8 | 9 | 10 | 11 | 12 | 13 |

52 WORDS

When you are writing any story, it is smart to think about[1] good writing skills. A story that has been written well gives a[2] reader the chance to become involved in the problem or plot. The[3] problem or plot always must be written carefully and precisely.[4]

| 1 | 2 | 3 | 4 | 5 | 6 | 7 | 8 | 9 | 10 | 11 | 12 | 13 |

54 WORDS

When you are going to create a story, it is wise to think[1] about good writing skills. A story that has been written well[2] gives the reader a chance to become involved in the problems and[3] plots. The problems and plots always must be developed with care[4] and precision.

| 1 | 2 | 3 | 4 | 5 | 6 | 7 | 8 | 9 | 10 | 11 | 12 | 13 |

55 WORDS

A few workers still use shorthand on the job. This skill is[1] used to take minutes of meetings as well as memos, letters, and[2] reports. Some may even use their shorthand to write telephone[3] messages. Office workers who take shorthand find it useful for[4] work as well as home.

| 1 | 2 | 3 | 4 | 5 | 6 | 7 | 8 | 9 | 10 | 11 | 12 | 13 |

WARMUP

Practice the following lines. *Time—2 minutes.*

Fluency	1	burns bland girls world land paid melt lame bud hay box tot	12
Accuracy	2	quay apex zinc bevy said fire gape hope jowl keep mine tire	24
Numbers	3	for 1 for 2 for 3 for 4 for 5 for 6 for 7 for 8 for 9 for 0	36
Symbols	4	dd # dd # dd # jj ^ jj ^ jj ^ ;; [;; [;; [;;] ;;] ;;]	48

PRETEST

Take one 1-minute timing.

5	Georgie and Greg were giggling and gasping about their	12
6	big biology and geology tests. Maggie was glaring since she	24
7	was getting groggy waiting for Greg in the muggy gymnasium.	36

| 1 | 2 | 3 | 4 | 5 | 6 | 7 | 8 | 9 | 10 | 11 | 12 |

PRACTICE

Type lines for speed or accuracy. *Time—3 or 5 minutes.*

Key Review: G

8	fgf ggg fgf ggg gGg gGg fgf ggg gGg GgG ggg Gal Gig Gay ggg	12
9	grin Gong gaged gates gaggle gagged gadgets Garages garbage	24
10	Greg agog glare gorge giggle goggle gargles Georgia geology	36
11	Eggs gags gauge gouge groggy bigger gasping granges Gregory	48
12	Beggar gauging getting glaring gargling Floggings gymnasium	60
13	eggnog Gouging gorging glowing gurgling debugging Zigzagged	72

`00.30` 30-SECOND OKS

Take a 30-second OK timing on each line. Repeat.

SPEED: 2 errors allowed

ACCURACY: 0 errors allowed

14	Jojo frequently publicized expensive hacksaws in magazines.	12
15	Joy Polyk acquired six amazing velvet hats with fine braid.	12
16	Margy fixed five dozen jonquil baskets with pretty candles.	12

| 1 | 2 | 3 | 4 | 5 | 6 | 7 | 8 | 9 | 10 | 11 | 12 |

TECHNIQUE CHECK

Type for 30 seconds on each line.

Smooth stroking, even pace.

Space bar—thumb close.

Feet on floor.

17	going gages egged baggy buggy foggy muggy soggy Peggy Gregg	12
18	g g g ggg g g g ggg gag gig egg gab gad gal gas gem get Gym	12
19	gate gape gaze gain gala Gale game Gary gift give golf gone	12

`01.00` 1-MINUTE OKS

Take one 1-minute OK timing on each line.

SPEED: 3 errors allowed

ACCURACY: 1 error allowed

20	Georgia giggled as she and Greg got eggnog for a golf gala.	12
21	Peggy was agog as Gary was getting gadgets from the garage.	12

| 1 | 2 | 3 | 4 | 5 | 6 | 7 | 8 | 9 | 10 | 11 | 12 |

POSTTEST

Repeat the Pretest.

42 wpm through 49 wpm

42 WORDS

The banking industry is a good example of how computers may[1] be used to streamline the flow of paperwork.[2] It is now possible to take care of your business needs without ever entering the[3] doors of the bank.[4]

| 1 | 2 | 3 | 4 | 5 | 6 | 7 | 8 | 9 | 10 | 11 | 12 | 13 |

44 WORDS

The banking industry is a fine example of how the computer[1] is being used to streamline the processing of paper.[2] It is now possible to meet most or all of your banking needs without ever[3] passing through the doors.[4]

| 1 | 2 | 3 | 4 | 5 | 6 | 7 | 8 | 9 | 10 | 11 | 12 | 13 |

45 WORDS

The history of the typewriter is really very brief.[1] In its early days it was built by people who developed sewing machines.[2] This could be one of the reasons why it looked like a sewing[3] machine with a very big foot pedal.[4]

| 1 | 2 | 3 | 4 | 5 | 6 | 7 | 8 | 9 | 10 | 11 | 12 | 13 |

47 WORDS

The history of the typewriter is really very brief.[1] In its early days it was built by people who developed sewing machines.[2] This could be one of the reasons why it looked so much like a[3] sewing machine with a huge metal foot pedal.[4]

| 1 | 2 | 3 | 4 | 5 | 6 | 7 | 8 | 9 | 10 | 11 | 12 | 13 |

49 WORDS

The history of the typewriter is really very brief.[1] In its early days it was built by people who developed sewing machines.[2] This could be one of the reasons why it looked much like the old[3] sewing machines with those large metal foot pedals.[4]

| 1 | 2 | 3 | 4 | 5 | 6 | 7 | 8 | 9 | 10 | 11 | 12 | 13 |

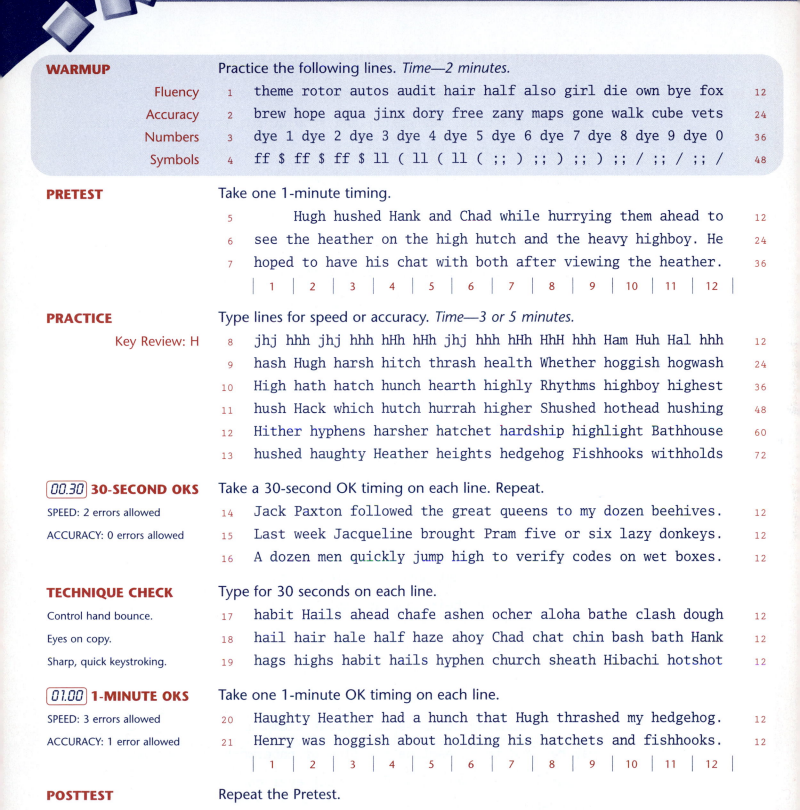

WARMUP

Practice the following lines. *Time—2 minutes.*

Fluency	1	theme rotor autos audit hair half also girl die own bye fox	12
Accuracy	2	brew hope aqua jinx dory free zany maps gone walk cube vets	24
Numbers	3	dye 1 dye 2 dye 3 dye 4 dye 5 dye 6 dye 7 dye 8 dye 9 dye 0	36
Symbols	4	ff $ ff $ ff $ ll (ll (ll (;;) ;;) ;;) ;; / ;; / ;; /	48

PRETEST

Take one 1-minute timing.

5   Hugh hushed Hank and Chad while hurrying them ahead to   12

6   see the heather on the high hutch and the heavy highboy. He   24

7   hoped to have his chat with both after viewing the heather.   36

| 1 | 2 | 3 | 4 | 5 | 6 | 7 | 8 | 9 | 10 | 11 | 12 |

PRACTICE

Type lines for speed or accuracy. *Time—3 or 5 minutes.*

Key Review: H

8   jhj hhh jhj hhh hHh hHh jhj hhh hHh HhH hhh Ham Huh Hal hhh   12

9   hash Hugh harsh hitch thrash health Whether hoggish hogwash   24

10   High hath hatch hunch hearth highly Rhythms highboy highest   36

11   hush Hack which hutch hurrah higher Shushed hothead hushing   48

12   Hither hyphens harsher hatchet hardship highlight Bathhouse   60

13   hushed haughty Heather heights hedgehog Fishhooks withholds   72

00.30 30-SECOND OKS

SPEED: 2 errors allowed

ACCURACY: 0 errors allowed

Take a 30-second OK timing on each line. Repeat.

14   Jack Paxton followed the great queens to my dozen beehives.   12

15   Last week Jacqueline brought Pram five or six lazy donkeys.   12

16   A dozen men quickly jump high to verify codes on wet boxes.   12

TECHNIQUE CHECK

Control hand bounce.

Eyes on copy.

Sharp, quick keystroking.

Type for 30 seconds on each line.

17   habit Hails ahead chafe ashen ocher aloha bathe clash dough   12

18   hail hair hale half haze ahoy Chad chat chin bash bath Hank   12

19   hags highs habit hails hyphen church sheath Hibachi hotshot   12

01.00 1-MINUTE OKS

SPEED: 3 errors allowed

ACCURACY: 1 error allowed

Take one 1-minute OK timing on each line.

20   Haughty Heather had a hunch that Hugh thrashed my hedgehog.   12

21   Henry was hoggish about holding his hatchets and fishhooks.   12

| 1 | 2 | 3 | 4 | 5 | 6 | 7 | 8 | 9 | 10 | 11 | 12 |

POSTTEST

Repeat the Pretest.

32 wpm through 40 wpm

32 WORDS

No one will argue the impact of a computer in our everyday life. If you bank, buy gifts, and stop at gas stations, you will see many computers being used.

| 1 | 2 | 3 | 4 | 5 | 6 | 7 | 8 | 9 | 10 | 11 | 12 | 13 |

34 WORDS

No one will argue the impact of a computer in our everyday life. If you bank, buy gifts, and stop at a gas station, you may see computers being used by many workers.

| 1 | 2 | 3 | 4 | 5 | 6 | 7 | 8 | 9 | 10 | 11 | 12 | 13 |

35 WORDS

Every firm must have its own rules to build a smooth flow of work and to use the company employees wisely. Such rules may well stress basic working conditions and salary.

| 1 | 2 | 3 | 4 | 5 | 6 | 7 | 8 | 9 | 10 | 11 | 12 | 13 |

37 WORDS

Every firm must have its own rules to build a smooth flow of work and to use the company employees wisely. Establishing such rules may well stress good working conditions and wages.

| 1 | 2 | 3 | 4 | 5 | 6 | 7 | 8 | 9 | 10 | 11 | 12 | 13 |

39 WORDS

Every firm must have its rules to build a smooth flow of work and to use their company employees wisely. Such established rules will probably stress the basic working conditions and the wages.

| 1 | 2 | 3 | 4 | 5 | 6 | 7 | 8 | 9 | 10 | 11 | 12 | 13 |

40 WORDS

The banking business is a great example of how computers may be used to streamline the flow of paperwork. It is possible to handle your banking needs without ever entering the doors of the bank.

| 1 | 2 | 3 | 4 | 5 | 6 | 7 | 8 | 9 | 10 | 11 | 12 | 13 |

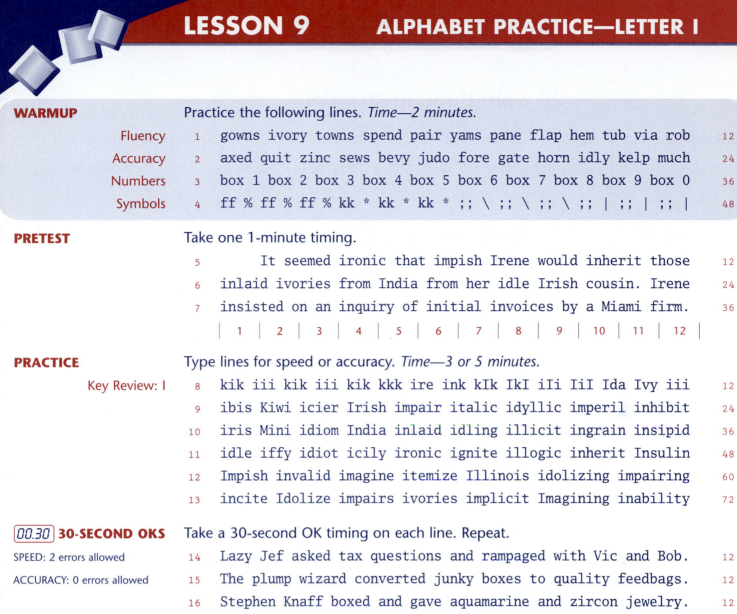

WARMUP

Practice the following lines. *Time—2 minutes.*

Fluency	1	gowns ivory towns spend pair yams pane flap hem tub via rob	12
Accuracy	2	axed quit zinc sews bevy judo fore gate horn idly kelp much	24
Numbers	3	box 1 box 2 box 3 box 4 box 5 box 6 box 7 box 8 box 9 box 0	36
Symbols	4	ff % ff % ff % kk * kk * kk * ;; \ ;; \ ;; \ ;; | ;; | ;; |	48

PRETEST

Take one 1-minute timing.

5   It seemed ironic that impish Irene would inherit those   12
6 inlaid ivories from India from her idle Irish cousin. Irene   24
7 insisted on an inquiry of initial invoices by a Miami firm.   36

| 1 | 2 | 3 | 4 | 5 | 6 | 7 | 8 | 9 | 10 | 11 | 12 |

PRACTICE

Type lines for speed or accuracy. *Time—3 or 5 minutes.*

Key Review: I   8   kik iii kik iii kik kkk ire ink kIk IkI iIi IiI Ida Ivy iii   12
9 ibis Kiwi icier Irish impair italic idyllic imperil inhibit   24
10 iris Mini idiom India inlaid idling illicit ingrain insipid   36
11 idle iffy idiot icily ironic ignite illogic inherit Insulin   48
12 Impish invalid imagine itemize Illinois idolizing impairing   60
13 incite Idolize impairs ivories implicit Imagining inability   72

⏱00.30 30-SECOND OKS

SPEED: 2 errors allowed

ACCURACY: 0 errors allowed

Take a 30-second OK timing on each line. Repeat.

14   Lazy Jef asked tax questions and rampaged with Vic and Bob.   12
15   The plump wizard converted junky boxes to quality feedbags.   12
16   Stephen Knaff boxed and gave aquamarine and zircon jewelry.   12

| 1 | 2 | 3 | 4 | 5 | 6 | 7 | 8 | 9 | 10 | 11 | 12 |

TECHNIQUE CHECK

Proper finger position and curve.

Wrists low, not touching.

Proper position at machine.

Type for 30 seconds on each line.

17   icy ilk ill imp ink inn ire Ivy aid bib did die fib hid jig   12
18   ills inch icing Miami indict infirm inspire invoice ironies   12
19   inking inning inside insist incline inflict initial inquire   12

⏱01.00 1-MINUTE OKS

SPEED: 3 errors allowed

ACCURACY: 1 error allowed

Take one 1-minute OK timing on each line.

20   Ivy was illogic about inheriting inlaid ivories from India.   12
21   Millie was inclined to itemize invoices of irises and kiwi.   12

| 1 | 2 | 3 | 4 | 5 | 6 | 7 | 8 | 9 | 10 | 11 | 12 |

POSTTEST

Repeat the Pretest.

20 wpm through 30 wpm

20 WORDS

It is wise to learn to type data while in school. This is a skill used at home and in business.

| 1 | 2 | 3 | 4 | 5 | 6 | 7 | 8 | 9 | 10 | 11 | 12 | 13 |

22 WORDS

It is very wise to learn to type data while in school. This is a good skill for personal use or business.

| 1 | 2 | 3 | 4 | 5 | 6 | 7 | 8 | 9 | 10 | 11 | 12 | 13 |

24 WORDS

It is very wise to learn to type data while in high school. This is a good skill for your personal use or business.

| 1 | 2 | 3 | 4 | 5 | 6 | 7 | 8 | 9 | 10 | 11 | 12 | 13 |

25 WORDS

The printer is hooked to your computer with a short cable. Your printer will print a user a hard copy when it is needed.

| 1 | 2 | 3 | 4 | 5 | 6 | 7 | 8 | 9 | 10 | 11 | 12 | 13 |

27 WORDS

A color printer is hooked to the new computer with a short cable. Your printer will print the users a hard copy when it is needed.

| 1 | 2 | 3 | 4 | 5 | 6 | 7 | 8 | 9 | 10 | 11 | 12 | 13 |

29 WORDS

A color printer is very often hooked to your new computer with a short cable. Your printer will give the user a hard copy when it is needed.

| 1 | 2 | 3 | 4 | 5 | 6 | 7 | 8 | 9 | 10 | 11 | 12 | 13 |

30 WORDS

No one will argue the impact of a computer in our everyday lives. If you bank, buy gifts, and stop at a gas station, you will see computers used.

| 1 | 2 | 3 | 4 | 5 | 6 | 7 | 8 | 9 | 10 | 11 | 12 | 13 |

WARMUP

Practice the following lines. *Time—2 minutes.*

Fluency	1	angle works firms dials both keys such fish box spa man fir	12
Accuracy	2	next flog home zest code jaws pica able yolk vast quit rail	24
Numbers	3	end 1 end 2 end 3 end 4 end 5 end 6 end 7 end 8 end 9 end 0	36
Symbols	4	kk < kk < kk < ll > ll > ll > ;; { ;; { ;; { ;; } ;; } ;; }	48

PRETEST

Take one 1-minute timing.

5	Jittery but jovial Joe was in jeopardy as he jaywalked	12
6	across Jefferson Jetty and was jolted by a jitney driven by	24
7	Jocelyn. Joe adjourned to the jazzy Jacuzzi for his injury.	36

| 1 | 2 | 3 | 4 | 5 | 6 | 7 | 8 | 9 | 10 | 11 | 12 |

PRACTICE

Type lines for speed or accuracy. *Time—3 or 5 minutes.*

Key Review: J	8	jjj jkj jlj j;j juj jyj jnj jmj jhj jJj JjJ JjJ Jon Jay jjj	12
	9	jade Josh jazzy major jujube adjust jujitsu jackpot Jacuzzi	24
	10	jail Fiji jetty enjoy jacket object January majesty injures	36
	11	join ajar Eject jewel Jackie pajama javelin adjourn jealous	48
	12	jitney janitor jittery Rejects jaywalks Jefferson flapjacks	60
	13	jovial journal Rejoice project jeopardy jellyfish Misjudged	72

`00.30` 30-SECOND OKS

Take a 30-second OK timing on each line. Repeat.

SPEED: 2 errors allowed

ACCURACY: 0 errors allowed

14	Jack objectively examined prize aquarium fish with Grandma.	12
15	Mike Bingham was saving old crazy jars for antique experts.	12
16	Mike Cowen qualified the expert jury while visiting Brazil.	12

| 1 | 2 | 3 | 4 | 5 | 6 | 7 | 8 | 9 | 10 | 11 | 12 |

TECHNIQUE CHECK

Type for 30 seconds on each line.

Efficient use of left shift key.

Back erect, lean forward.

Smooth stroking, even pace.

17	jJj Jaguar Jargon Jaunty Jeered Jersey Jockey Jokers Jovial	12
18	jab jag jam Jan jar jaw jay jet jig Jim job joy Joe jug jut	12
19	jaded jails jeans jeers Jacob jelly jiffy joins joker jolts	12

`01.00` 1-MINUTE OKS

Take one 1-minute OK timing on each line.

SPEED: 3 errors allowed

ACCURACY: 1 error allowed

| 20 | Jovial Joyce enjoys a major jellyfish project by the jetty. | 12 |
| 21 | The jittery janitor had a job in a jail in Fiji in January. | 12 |

| 1 | 2 | 3 | 4 | 5 | 6 | 7 | 8 | 9 | 10 | 11 | 12 |

POSTTEST

Repeat the Pretest.

PACING—PLACEMENT TIMING

WARMUP

Practice the following paragraph. *Time—2 minutes.*

Tracy Billie plans to use the vivid fabrics on the lapel of her new coat. Her mom is going to help her cut the fabric and pin the pattern. It will take many hours of sewing before Tracy will be able to wear it.

`01.00` **TIMING**

Take one 1-minute timing on the paragraph below.

12

In this section you will be developing your accuracy and speed by taking timings on paragraphs that are designed to be completed within a minute at a specified speed with no more than one error. These paced timings help increase your stroking rate by indicating where you should be at the end of each quarter of a minute, and they encourage you to type more accurately. Your speed and errors on this placement timing will suggest to you which of the pacing paragraphs to practice first.

24
37
50
63
76
88
98

| 1 | 2 | 3 | 4 | 5 | 6 | 7 | 8 | 9 | 10 | 11 | 12 | 13 |

WARMUP		Practice the following lines. *Time—2 minutes.*	
	Fluency	1 visit title worms corps risk turn then lake six key ham bug	12
	Accuracy	2 hoax omen rope haze jinx give bulk quiz cork yard fire west	24
	Numbers	3 row 1 row 2 row 3 row 4 row 5 row 6 row 7 row 8 row 9 row 0	36
	Symbols	4 ss @ ss @ ss @ jj & jj & jj & ;; = ;; = ;; = ;; + ;; + ;; +	48

PRETEST Take one 1-minute timing.

5   Keen Kenneth in the kidskin mukluks kicked Kirk in the   12

6   kneecap. Kirk kept his knee on kapok in my kayak and yakked   24

7   with my Kodiak kinfolk about their checkbook and keepsakes.   36

| 1 | 2 | 3 | 4 | 5 | 6 | 7 | 8 | 9 | 10 | 11 | 12 |

PRACTICE Type lines for speed or accuracy. *Time—3 or 5 minutes.*

Key Review: K

8   kkk klk kkk kjk kkk k;k kik k,k kKk KkK KkK Kay Kim Kip kkk   12

9   Kirk kink kicks khaki Kodiak yakked kinfolk Bangkok knights   24

10   king keen kapok kayak mukluk kicked Trekked Kenneth ketchup   36

11   kook King knack knock skunks Skulks keepers keyhole kittens   48

12   Kiosks knuckle kickoff skyjack Bookmark blackjack keepsakes   60

13   kickup Skylark kidskin skywalk Kickback checkbook cookbooks   72

`00.30` **30-SECOND OKS** Take a 30-second OK timing on each line. Repeat.

SPEED: 2 errors allowed

ACCURACY: 0 errors allowed

14   Holly Pike was fixing my unique adjectives and crazy verbs.   12

15   Lizzy brought from Iraq six cans wrapped in jute for Vicky.   12

16   Five junky taxicabs were bumping along the quite dim zones.   12

| 1 | 2 | 3 | 4 | 5 | 6 | 7 | 8 | 9 | 10 | 11 | 12 |

TECHNIQUE CHECK Type for 30 seconds on each line.

Space bar—thumb close.

17   k k k kkk k k k kkk kit kept keys kiln kilt kind KiKi Kirby   12

Sharp, quick keystroking.

18   kite knee pukka kinks kookie kicker kneecap Knowing blocker   12

Control hand bounce.

19   kabob Kathy kazoo keeps Kelly alike banks books check drink   12

`01.00` **1-MINUTE OKS** Take one 1-minute OK timing on each line.

SPEED: 3 errors allowed

20   A keen keeper kept a kettle of kale for kittens and skunks.   12

ACCURACY: 1 error allowed

21   Ken and Kirk trekked with a kayak to see kinfolk in Kodiak.   12

| 1 | 2 | 3 | 4 | 5 | 6 | 7 | 8 | 9 | 10 | 11 | 12 |

POSTTEST Repeat the Pretest.

Pacing Practice

Paragraphs 20 wpm–100 wpm

CONTENT

In addition to the placement timing, this section provides 1-minute timings for building speed and accuracy from 20 through 100 words per minute in increments of one or two words per minute. The markers within each timing indicate where you should be at the end of each quarter minute.

OBJECTIVE

To improve overall speed and accuracy.

LESSON 12   ALPHABET PRACTICE—LETTER L

WARMUP   Practice the following lines. *Time—2 minutes.*

Fluency	1	quantity ancient enamels turkey profit proxy vivid when bid	12
Accuracy	2	gain quip duck bevy five hoax joke loan west part sore zoom	24
Numbers	3	tow 1 tow 2 tow 3 tow 4 tow 5 tow 6 tow 7 tow 8 tow 9 tow 0	36
Symbols	4	dd # dd # dd # jj ^ jj ^ jj ^ ;; [;; [;; [;;] ;;] ;;]	48

PRETEST   Take one 1-minute timing.

5	Lively and likable Laura and Lucille longed to fulfill	12
6	a lifelong dream to help the local ballet. They were likely	24
7	to sell little glass lilies using locally printed leaflets.	36

| 1 | 2 | 3 | 4 | 5 | 6 | 7 | 8 | 9 | 10 | 11 | 12 |

PRACTICE   Type lines for speed or accuracy. *Time—3 or 5 minutes.*

Key Review: L

8	lll l;l lll lkl lll ljl lol l.l lLl LlL LlL Lon Lan Lin lll	12
9	loll Lull label lapel likely little legally Locally illegal	24
10	lilt Lily legal level lonely lovely loyally Lucille liberal	36
11	ball bell Glass loyal lilies lively Lullaby willful fulfill	48
12	lawful lanolin likable Helpful lollygag laterally Illogical	60
13	Laurel leaflet levelly Anthill lifelong cellblock parallels	72

00.30 **30-SECOND OKS**   Take a 30-second OK timing on each line. Repeat.

SPEED: 2 errors allowed

ACCURACY: 0 errors allowed

14	Big Vic Knox zealously performs jury duty with quiet class.	12
15	Jovial Debra Frantz swims quickly with grace and expertise.	12
16	Bud Jarvis may quit paying awful taxes on his snazzy ketch.	12

| 1 | 2 | 3 | 4 | 5 | 6 | 7 | 8 | 9 | 10 | 11 | 12 |

TECHNIQUE CHECK   Type for 30 seconds on each line.

Wrists low, not touching.

Arms quiet.

Space bar—thumb close.

17	fall hall lass half slag lads shall falls flash flags Allan	12
18	ally bills calls falls ballet billow callow cowbell eyeball	12
19	lad lap all law lay ill led leg let lid lip log lop low lye	12

01.00 **1-MINUTE OKS**   Take one 1-minute OK timing on each line.

SPEED: 3 errors allowed

ACCURACY: 1 error allowed

20	Laurel Fuller left leaflets on anthills in local landfills.	12
21	Lucille Miller is likely to sell the lovely little cowbell.	12

| 1 | 2 | 3 | 4 | 5 | 6 | 7 | 8 | 9 | 10 | 11 | 12 |

POSTTEST   Repeat the Pretest.

PROGRESS CHECK TIMINGS

WARMUP

Practice the following paragraph. *Time—2 minutes.*

Some writers feel that we are moving toward a paperless society. A society without paper is hard to imagine, but the use of the computer has moved the business world steps closer to this possibility.

`00.00` **TIMING**

(SI = 1.65)

Although your hard work has paid off and you have secured	13
the job, it is not time to rest. It is time to learn your job	25
and show that you were the right one to hire. You may be given	38
an orientation and special job training.	46
To orient you to your new job, many firms give you a tour	59
of the building, describe all the company benefits, and provide	72
safety guidelines. Some firms rotate you in various jobs before	85
assigning you to your final job. This practice acquaints you	97
with the whole firm and shows you how your job fits within it.	110
Other companies give you explicit classroom training about your	123
job, then permit you to work. Still others provide training on	136
the job; that is, you work under supervision.	145
Many firms today provide employees with the opportunity for	158
personal and professional growth. Company classes on a variety	171
of subjects may be offered, and some earn college credit. Other	184
firms give tuition credits for employees who complete classes at	197
nearby schools.	200
Some firms might encourage participation in professional	212
organizations and conferences. Employers see direct increases in	225
productivity when employees grow professionally. They also see	238
improved morale and heightened motivation when employees become	251
involved in professional activities. Professional growth and	263
increased productivity can add up to a raise, increased personal	276
satisfaction, and even a promotion.	283

| 1 | 2 | 3 | 4 | 5 | 6 | 7 | 8 | 9 | 10 | 11 | 12 | 13 |

WARMUP

Practice the following lines. *Time—2 minutes.*

Fluency	1	rocks usury wicks focus dish worn duty bowl big apt fix fit	12
Accuracy	2	quad axis zeal jury yoke calm drum frog vows best pony itch	24
Numbers	3	due 1 due 2 due 3 due 4 due 5 due 6 due 7 due 8 due 9 due 0	36
Symbols	4	ff $ ff $ ff $ ll (ll (ll (;;) ;;) ;;) ;; / ;; / ;; /	48

PRETEST

Take one 1-minute timing.

5   Mimi wanted Mama to comment from her hammock about the   12
6   midsummer melodrama of that mermaid from Miami. Mama smiled   24
7   remembering the gimmicks of the old drummer and the comics.   36

| 1 | 2 | 3 | 4 | 5 | 6 | 7 | 8 | 9 | 10 | 11 | 12 |

PRACTICE

Type lines for speed or accuracy. *Time—3 or 5 minutes.*

Key Review: M

8   jmj mmm jmj mmm jmj mmm met mum jMj MjM mMm MmM Mae Mom mmm   12
9   maim Mama madam modem mammal dimmed mammoth Maximum minimum   24
10   memo mime maxim Mommy hammer Simmer midterm hammock mummify   36
11   Mimi ammo mimic Miami summit clammy mermaid mailman milkman   48
12   chummy command comment Gimmick momentum microfilm Melodrama   60
13   museum macrame Rummage summary Mealtime midsummer memoranda   72

00.30 30-SECOND OKS

SPEED: 2 errors allowed
ACCURACY: 0 errors allowed

Take a 30-second OK timing on each line. Repeat.

14   Paddy and Jeb will give many quick extra tours of this zoo.   12
15   Pat Wolfe has judged very excellent bronze antique monkeys.   12
16   Jon Witz can quickly pedal his large bike five extra miles.   12

| 1 | 2 | 3 | 4 | 5 | 6 | 7 | 8 | 9 | 10 | 11 | 12 |

TECHNIQUE CHECK

Eyes on copy.
Proper position at machine.
Proper finger position and curve.

Type for 30 seconds on each line.

17   made meal mumps comma commit common drummer grammar swimmer   12
18   mom mum mad man map mat men met mew mix mob mud Max Mel Moe   12
19   mMm Mayhem Medium Miriam Memory Marmot Murmur Muumuu Member   12

01.00 1-MINUTE OKS

SPEED: 3 errors allowed
ACCURACY: 1 error allowed

Take one 1-minute OK timing on each line.

20   Members commented on the mermaid in my midsummer melodrama.   12
21   Mimi was a mime in Miami before making the mammoth hammock.   12

| 1 | 2 | 3 | 4 | 5 | 6 | 7 | 8 | 9 | 10 | 11 | 12 |

POSTTEST

Repeat the Pretest.

PROGRESS CHECK TIMINGS

WARMUP

Practice the following paragraph. *Time—2 minutes.*

A computer operator must possess keyboarding skills to type data quickly and accurately. Of equal importance is the ability to spell and punctuate correctly. A sound knowledge of grammar is also vital.

00.00 TIMING

(SI = 1.62)

The best way to build keyboarding speed and to improve	12
your accuracy is selecting the right practice pattern, using the	25
correct practice material, and maintaining a positive attitude.	38
This approach will ensure improved keyboarding skill.	49
Research findings suggest that the right type of practice	62
requires a pretest on the skills to be improved, followed by	74
practice using the appropriate material, and ending with the	86
posttest. The pretest determines what improvement in skill is	98
needed, either speed or accuracy. Based on the pretest results,	111
a goal for speed or accuracy is set, and the practice material	124
for that goal is assigned. The results of the posttest compared	137
to those of the pretest reveal the progress toward the goal.	149
If quick keying is the expected goal, use material that	161
requires the alternate use of the fingers of the right and left	174
hands, that uses very easy words, and that allows the typing of	187
words as whole words rather than single keystrokes. To improve	200
stroking accuracy, use material that forces concentration, that	213
uses doubled letters, and that includes word families.	224
The most important part of building typing skill is your	236
attitude. That attitude includes focus, resolve, and commitment.	249
Focus means reducing outside distractions and attending to quick	262
or accurate typing. Resolve means keeping a positive attitude	274
that you will succeed. Commitment means having a strong desire	287
and zeal to succeed. With just the right attitude, coupled with	300
the practice pattern and the right material, success will come.	313

| 1 | 2 | 3 | 4 | 5 | 6 | 7 | 8 | 9 | 10 | 11 | 12 | 13 |

LESSON 14   ALPHABET PRACTICE—LETTER N

WARMUP

Practice the following lines. *Time—2 minutes.*

Fluency	1	laugh cycle whale forms sock owls rich woe rub sit is do so	12
Accuracy	2	yoga meow zinc even buoy junk flop hoax dirt stem quad hurt	24
Numbers	3	map 1 map 2 map 3 map 4 map 5 map 6 map 7 map 8 map 9 map 0	36
Symbols	4	ff % ff % ff % kk * kk * kk * ;; \ ;; \ ;; \ ;; | ;; | ;; |	48

PRETEST

Take one 1-minute timing.

5   The announcers mentioned that Danny Jonson was driving   12

6 in the afternoon race. Danny knew an engineer who could fix   24

7 his engine. He won the race and went to dinner with Lynnea.   36

| 1 | 2 | 3 | 4 | 5 | 6 | 7 | 8 | 9 | 10 | 11 | 12 |

PRACTICE

Key Review: N

Type lines for speed or accuracy. *Time—3 or 5 minutes.*

8 jnj nnn jnj nnn jnj nnn njn nnn jNj NjN nNn NnN Nic Nan nnn   12

9 nuns neon ninth nanny Engine Jonson innings funnier nominal   24

10 noun noon known union anyone Hansen running mention Winning   36

11 nine inns nylon Nancy infant Cannot lantern uncanny pension   48

12 Dinner antenna condemn Lincoln engineer announcer nonentity   60

13 ninety tension Antonio nunnery nineteen afternoon Nonpaying   72

`00.30` 30-SECOND OKS

SPEED: 2 errors allowed

ACCURACY: 0 errors allowed

Take a 30-second OK timing on each line. Repeat.

14 Laurie Wold jumps quickly by the vicious lynx seizing fish.   12

15 Jack gave gifts to the lazy men who acquired six pegboards.   12

16 Marvin Bille waxes jet skis and quickly zips to freighters.   12

| 1 | 2 | 3 | 4 | 5 | 6 | 7 | 8 | 9 | 10 | 11 | 12 |

TECHNIQUE CHECK

Proper finger position and curve.

Arms quiet.

Space bar—thumb close.

Type for 30 seconds on each line.

17 net nay nor nut non nap new nod nil now not Nat Nix Dan Nan   12

18 onion annoy Denny unpin ninny bunny Danny nouns funny linen   12

19 n n n nnn n n n nnn ton bun sun ban ran none Lynn Finn Anne   12

`01.00` 1-MINUTE OKS

SPEED: 3 errors allowed

ACCURACY: 1 error allowed

Take one 1-minute OK timing on each line.

20 Nineteen engineers in Ansonia mentioned the running engine.   12

21 Nancy Johnson was known for running unions for ninety inns.   12

| 1 | 2 | 3 | 4 | 5 | 6 | 7 | 8 | 9 | 10 | 11 | 12 |

POSTTEST

Repeat the Pretest.

TIMING 33

PROGRESS CHECK TIMINGS

WARMUP

Practice the following paragraph. *Time—2 minutes.*

Revise your study time if you need to spend more time on one subject than on others. If you focus better at a certain time of the day, then study your most difficult subject then.

`00.00` **TIMING**

(SI = 1.62)

You need car insurance for several reasons. Most states by	13
law require you to purchase auto insurance. Usually financial	25
institutions that loan you money to buy a car emphasize that you	38
purchase car insurance. Plus, you need auto insurance for your	51
personal peace of mind and economic welfare. From what varieties	64
of insurance can you choose?	70
Your liability insurance covers you for bodily injury and	83
property damage of another person if you are legally responsible	96
for damages. This type of insurance is required by most states	109
and banks. You want this liability insurance to protect your	121
assets. If you are sued in court and damages are awarded to the	134
plaintiff, you will have to pay unless you have this insurance.	147
However, the insurance company will pay only up to the limits of	160
your policy. Any amount over the limit is excluded and is then	173
your responsibility.	177
Who pays for your car if you damage it? You do, unless you	190
have collision insurance. This type of auto insurance protects	203
your car if you have an accident.	210
Comprehensive coverage pays for theft losses and for damage	223
from flying objects, wind, water, and other acts of God. The	235
expense of towing your car to a repair shop may be covered under	248
your insurance package. Medical insurance covers medical bills	261
that are incurred by you or any passenger in your car, even if	274
you are at fault. Uninsured motorist coverage pays in the event	287
that you are hit by a driver who does not have insurance.	298

| 1 | 2 | 3 | 4 | 5 | 6 | 7 | 8 | 9 | 10 | 11 | 12 | 13 |

WARMUP   Practice the following lines. *Time—2 minutes.*

Fluency	1	ducks fuels prism endow soap town soak halt sod fur oak wit	12
Accuracy	2	hive same bunk zero text join club drew flag most quay pure	24
Numbers	3	did 1 did 2 did 3 did 4 did 5 did 6 did 7 did 8 did 9 did 0	36
Symbols	4	kk < kk < kk < ll > ll > ll > ;; { ;; { ;; { ;; } ;; } ;; }	48

PRETEST   Take one 1-minute timing.

5	Morton cooks onions at that old outdoor cookout at the	12
6	bottom of the hollow for the Johnston Hoedown. He also will	24
7	cook for some sophomores in Ohio where he is the zoologist.	36

| 1 | 2 | 3 | 4 | 5 | 6 | 7 | 8 | 9 | 10 | 11 | 12 |

PRACTICE   Type lines for speed or accuracy. *Time—3 or 5 minutes.*

Key Review: O

8	lol ooo lol ooo lol ooo oar oil lOl OlO oOo OoO Ody Ole ooo	12
9	oboe Oslo outdo torso oriole oblong outdoor Cookout logbook	24
10	Ohio odor outgo motto bottom hollow monsoon Forlorn lotions	36
11	Book loop Olson polio doctor voodoo boxwood outlook pontoon	48
12	Olcott boyhood Johnson comfort dogwoods sociology sophomore	60
13	Morton oxblood cocoons hoedown mongoose footstool Zoologist	72

`00.30` 30-SECOND OKS   Take a 30-second OK timing on each line. Repeat.

SPEED: 2 errors allowed

ACCURACY: 0 errors allowed

14	Mack vowed to quit playing his sax for five big jazz bands.	12
15	Judy Fox took very bright pictures with a unique zoom lens.	12
16	Vicky quietly exited while Suzie bought the farm in Joplin.	12

| 1 | 2 | 3 | 4 | 5 | 6 | 7 | 8 | 9 | 10 | 11 | 12 |

TECHNIQUE CHECK   Type for 30 seconds on each line.

Sharp, quick keystroking.

Control hand bounce.

Eyes on copy.

17	boom food cooks donor bonbon coupon forsook hotfoot pothook	12
18	books color combo cools bongo doors folio looks onion floor	12
19	old one ore own oaf oak oar off odd out owl ohm oil owe orb	12

`01.00` 1-MINUTE OKS   Take one 1-minute OK timing on each line.

SPEED: 3 errors allowed

ACCURACY: 1 error allowed

20	Morton Olcott and the polio doctor from Oslo comfort a boy.	12
21	The Ohio sophomore enjoyed the outdoor cookout and hoedown.	12

| 1 | 2 | 3 | 4 | 5 | 6 | 7 | 8 | 9 | 10 | 11 | 12 |

POSTTEST   Repeat the Pretest.

PROGRESS CHECK TIMINGS

WARMUP

Practice the following paragraph. *Time—2 minutes.*

An appropriate place to study is very important. Sitting upright at a desk or table keeps you alert and in the mood to study. Distracting items cause the mind to wander and should be hidden away.

`00.00` TIMING

(SI = 1.61)

A facsimile machine, often called a fax, converts printed	13
text and graphic images into either analog or digital signals.	26
The machine transfers those signals over a telephone or network	39
line to a receiving fax machine. This receiving machine then	51
converts the signals back into printed text or graphics.	62
Fax equipment enables the immediate sending of sketches,	74
photographs, line illustrations, signed documents, and annotated	87
documents. A fax can erase the largest, and most vital, hidden	100
business cost. This cost is that of time and money lost in just	113
waiting for vital information.	119
The right hardware and software are required to communicate	132
via fax. This includes a sending and a receiving fax device, one	145
at each end of the line; data transmission software; and special	158
hookup connections.	162
To send a fax document, you manually or automatically dial	175
the receiving station, feed the hard copy through the machine,	188
and wait for the transmission to be completed. Once the document	201
is sent, the fax machine prints a record of the transmitted fax.	214
Some newer fax machines keep an organized list of all documents	227
sent and received.	231
To receive a fax document, the power to your fax machine	243
must be turned on. Transmissions arrive stacked in a receiving	256
tray. Some fax machines sound a tone when a document arrives. It	269
is good practice to check the tray regularly for documents even	282
if your machine sounds a tone.	288

| 1 | 2 | 3 | 4 | 5 | 6 | 7 | 8 | 9 | 10 | 11 | 12 | 13 |

WARMUP

Practice the following lines. *Time—2 minutes.*

Fluency	1	gland slept roams bowls them oboe make torn dig pal cod due	12
Accuracy	2	days vote jerk exit bars wolf gone echo zeal huts mean quip	24
Numbers	3	big 1 big 2 big 3 big 4 big 5 big 6 big 7 big 8 big 9 big 0	36
Symbols	4	ss @ ss @ ss @ jj & jj & jj & ;; = ;; = ;; = ;; + ;; + ;; +	48

PRETEST

Take one 1-minute timing.

5   The peppy puppy was happy to be plopped beside the old   12

6   playpen. She promptly found an appetite for snappy pumps or   24

7   posh apparel. Paul did not approve. The puppy was punished.   36

| 1 | 2 | 3 | 4 | 5 | 6 | 7 | 8 | 9 | 10 | 11 | 12 |

PRACTICE

Type lines for speed or accuracy. *Time—3 or 5 minutes.*

Key Review: P

8   ;p; ppp ;p; ppp ;p; ppp pip pep ;P; P;P pPp PpP Pop Peg ppp   12

9   pipe pope Poppy pumps pepper Tiptop pappose propped puppies   24

10   prep pulp peppy pappy Pappas oppose plopped puppets Bagpipe   36

11   papa prop apply happy choppy prepay Poppins apparel Cripple   48

12   Hopper poppies Approve upsweep appetite sparkplug pineapple   60

13   prompt prepped playpen Phillip lollipop pawnshops Spaceship   72

00.30 30-SECOND OKS

SPEED: 2 errors allowed

ACCURACY: 0 errors allowed

Take a 30-second OK timing on each line. Repeat.

14   Crazy viewers jumping frequently excite bored hockey idols.   12

15   The judges quickly absolved the crazy man of swiping foxes.   12

16   Any excited fish may just zoom quickly by my viewing perch.   12

| 1 | 2 | 3 | 4 | 5 | 6 | 7 | 8 | 9 | 10 | 11 | 12 |

TECHNIQUE CHECK

Feet on floor.

Back erect, lean forward.

Smooth stroking, even pace.

Type for 30 seconds on each line.

17   pups nippy pupil paper popped pamper poppet playpen poppers   12

18   pep pop pin pit pod ply pal par pry pet pan pie pip pun pen   12

19   peep pops plops apple props prepays peppier pippins opposed   12

01.00 1-MINUTE OKS

SPEED: 3 errors allowed

ACCURACY: 1 error allowed

Take one 1-minute OK timing on each line.

20   Pappy and Hopper promptly approved the apparel for Phillip.   12

21   A happy and peppy pupil promptly approved of my old papers.   12

| 1 | 2 | 3 | 4 | 5 | 6 | 7 | 8 | 9 | 10 | 11 | 12 |

POSTTEST

Repeat the Pretest.

TIMING 31

PROGRESS CHECK TIMINGS

WARMUP

Practice the following paragraph. *Time—2 minutes.*

To improve the quality of your study time, consider some basic ideas. Set up a study pattern and conscientiously follow it. You might study for fifty minutes and then relax for ten minutes. This is an efficient use of time.

00.00 TIMING

(SI = 1.60)

In a modern business office, records management deals with   13
the entire cycle of manual and electronic handling of data. The   26
individual in charge must perform all of the standard functions   39
of controlling data as well as any of the other jobs required to   52
maintain the flow of records.   58

The people involved in managing records use many media to   71
complete their tasks. The tools may include a records inventory   84
and a retention schedule. The records inventory specifies the   96
records that are present, where these records are stored, and   108
how long they have been stored. A retention schedule can be made   121
from the records inventory.   127

Data taken from the inventory and past experience determine   140
the life cycle of each record. Retention includes the process of   153
deciding how long a record will be stored. A retention schedule   166
is made, which includes a list of each record with its retention   179
date. The retention schedule controls the movement of records in   192
the system and throughout the life cycle of the record.   203

The life cycle of a record includes its creation, use, and   216
final destruction. Thus the safe storage of records has become a   229
very costly and complex task. The records manager performs a   241
more indispensable role than ever before in minimizing the cost   254
of storing records and in storing records safely.   264

| 1 | 2 | 3 | 4 | 5 | 6 | 7 | 8 | 9 | 10 | 11 | 12 | 13 |

WARMUP

Practice the following lines. *Time—2 minutes.*

Fluency	1	cubic goals lapel turns rush flap wish icy aid sue of it us	12
Accuracy	2	jerk figs wart oozy oxen move quay cask jolt drip hogs brat	24
Numbers	3	cut 1 cut 2 cut 3 cut 4 cut 5 cut 6 cut 7 cut 8 cut 9 cut 0	36
Symbols	4	dd # dd # dd # jj ^ jj ^ jj ^ ;; [;; [;; [;;] ;;] ;;]	48

PRETEST

Take one 1-minute timing.

5	Quincy had qualms about those unique techniques of the	12
6	qualified squad in the quagmire after the quake. Quinn then	24
7	requested an inquiry of the squad and the unique equipment.	36

| 1 | 2 | 3 | 4 | 5 | 6 | 7 | 8 | 9 | 10 | 11 | 12 |

PRACTICE

Type lines for speed or accuracy. *Time—3 or 5 minutes.*

Key Review: Q

8	aqa qqq aqa qqq aqa qqq qua que aQa QaQ qQq QqQ Qui Quo qqq	12
9	quad quiz quack quake qualms Quayle qualify Conquer quality	24
10	quit quip pique quart Opaque quarry Quigley inquiry request	36
11	quay aqua Quann equal quench quests inquest Liquids sequels	48
12	Unique plaques quarter Quakers quagmire equipment turquoise	60
13	Quinto racquet Jonquil unequal quantify qualified technique	72

00.30 30-SECOND OKS

SPEED: 2 errors allowed

ACCURACY: 0 errors allowed

Take a 30-second OK timing on each line. Repeat.

14	Six jovial men on the flying trapeze quake when crowds boo.	12
15	Baking an extra dozen lovely quiches would just fill me up.	12
16	Pretty Delores quickly bought five extra wigwams in Juarez.	12

| 1 | 2 | 3 | 4 | 5 | 6 | 7 | 8 | 9 | 10 | 11 | 12 |

TECHNIQUE CHECK

Efficient use of right shift key.

Arms quiet.

Control hand bounce.

Type for 30 seconds on each line.

17	qQq Quail Quaint Quincy Equity Quartz Equate Quiche Quantum	12
18	quest quire queen query equip quilt squad squid quiet queue	12
19	quid quay quad quire quota quits squab liquid sequel plaque	12

01.00 1-MINUTE OKS

SPEED: 3 errors allowed

ACCURACY: 1 error allowed

Take one 1-minute OK timing on each line.

20	Quincy and Quigley may both qualify for the unique plaques.	12
21	Quann quit my quarry because of his qualms about equipment.	12

| 1 | 2 | 3 | 4 | 5 | 6 | 7 | 8 | 9 | 10 | 11 | 12 |

POSTTEST

Repeat the Pretest.

PROGRESS CHECK TIMINGS

WARMUP

Practice the following paragraph. *Time—2 minutes.*

The home shopping industry via computers makes it easy to shop without leaving home. Industry analysts expect this type of shopping to show enormous growth over the next few years.

`00.00` **TIMING**

(SI = 1.59)

The topology of a local area network is characterized by	12
its physical or geometric shape and its logical layout of data	25
flow. Physically, a local area network, as it typically may be	38
labeled, can take the shape of a star, ring, bus, or tree. The	51
signal flow may not emulate the physical layout of the network.	64
For instance, the complex token ring network has the physical	76
shape of a star while signals logically flow in a ring.	87
Star networks resemble a radial pattern with a controlling	100
requisite hub and multiple lines radiating from the center to	112
every device. If the central computer goes down, the network	124
becomes inoperative because all data flow must travel through	136
the central control device. This pattern is analogous to sharing	149
mainframe time or to a dedicated word processor employing shared	162
logic.	163
Ring networks take the contour of a circle with one device	176
linked to another in an unbroken chain fashion. Signals pass	188
from one device to another in a loop. Failure of a device in the	201
ring normally causes the entire network to stop functioning.	213
The most common network layout, the bus, forms a single	225
line from one end of the network to the other end, with many	237
connections attached all along the line, much like a public	249
transit bus route with stops along the way. The simple design	261
plus its ease of expansion justly contribute to the use of this	274
network design.	277

| 1 | 2 | 3 | 4 | 5 | 6 | 7 | 8 | 9 | 10 | 11 | 12 | 13 |

WARMUP Practice the following lines. *Time—2 minutes.*

Fluency	1	flays hairy shame soaks rock them held foam end tie eye cut	12
Accuracy	2	exit blew clam daft ever file zest quit jury kelp hung note	24
Numbers	3	dug 1 dug 2 dug 3 dug 4 dug 5 dug 6 dug 7 dug 8 dug 9 dug 0	36
Symbols	4	ff $ ff $ ff $ ll (ll (ll (;;) ;;) ;;) ;; / ;; / ;; /	48

PRETEST Take one 1-minute timing.

5	Ruth arranged for the brokers to order cranberries for	12
6	Harriet. There was an error in the order. Carriers sent our	24
7	barrel of herring to Roger who was recovering in a barrack.	36

| 1 | 2 | 3 | 4 | 5 | 6 | 7 | 8 | 9 | 10 | 11 | 12 |

PRACTICE Type lines for speed or accuracy. *Time—3 or 5 minutes.*

Key Review: R	8	frf rrr frf rrr frf rrr rug err fRf RfR rRr RrR Rex Rod rrr	12
	9	rare purr arrow arbor Barrel armory carrier Harriet arrange	24
	10	roar rear Jerry curry mirror orator Warrant forever sorrier	36
	11	burr curr Error order Morris narrow merrier furrier arrears	48
	12	Harris herring brokers earring disarray preferred Cranberry	60
	13	Ferris remarry forward borrows Orchards rearrange referring	72

⏱00.30 30-SECOND OKS Take a 30-second OK timing on each line. Repeat.

SPEED: 2 errors allowed

ACCURACY: 0 errors allowed

14	Rex enjoys playing with lazy farm ducks by the quiet river.	12
15	The bold majority was voting to equalize export of chicken.	12
16	Andrea and Carol quickly gave Jim two dozen boxes of chops.	12

| 1 | 2 | 3 | 4 | 5 | 6 | 7 | 8 | 9 | 10 | 11 | 12 |

TECHNIQUE CHECK Type for 30 seconds on each line.

Proper finger position and curve.

Feet on floor.

Space bar—thumb close.

17	radar Roger marry refer array riser juror Harry recur sorry	12
18	Ruth Ruhr razor racer artery dreary recruit barrack recover	12
19	r r r rrr r r r rrr ran war are raw Ray errs over purr Herr	12

⏱01.00 1-MINUTE OKS Take one 1-minute OK timing on each line.

SPEED: 3 errors allowed

ACCURACY: 1 error allowed

20	Morris ordered my narrow mirror from the brokers in Ferris.	12
21	Harris will rearrange the dreary barracks for the recruits.	12

| 1 | 2 | 3 | 4 | 5 | 6 | 7 | 8 | 9 | 10 | 11 | 12 |

POSTTEST Repeat the Pretest.

PROGRESS CHECK TIMINGS

WARMUP

Practice the following paragraph. *Time—2 minutes.*

Various people have developed many different keyboards over the years. The first changes were made to make typing faster and more accurate. Recent changes have been made to reduce injuries to hands and wrists.

`00.00` **TIMING**

(SI = 1.58)

What happens to your application package when it arrives at   13
the office of a prospective employer, and what will the person   26
doing the hiring look for? Answers to both of these questions   38
will give you insight on hiring practices and techniques.   50

Most companies require that all application materials be in   63
their hands by a set deadline. Your failure to meet any company   76
deadlines will usually exclude you from further consideration.   89
Therefore, always meet application deadlines. Someone will check   102
your papers to determine if everything you submitted meets the   115
minimum hiring requirements. If so, your application then will   128
be screened by a personnel officer or committee. This person or   141
group will scrutinize your application form, letter, and resume   154
to ascertain if you possess the qualifications necessary to do   167
the job. He or she will call or correspond with your references   180
to verify your job skills and the application data you supplied.   193

If you meet the requirements of the firm, you may be called   206
for an interview or, in some cases, asked for more information.   219
What happens if you do not secure an interview? Some firms will   232
destroy your application. Other firms will keep your papers on   245
file in the event that a different job you can undertake becomes   258
vacant. Still other firms will hold your files until they have   271
another job of the same type that you can fill.   280

| 1 | 2 | 3 | 4 | 5 | 6 | 7 | 8 | 9 | 10 | 11 | 12 | 13 |

WARMUP

Practice the following lines. *Time—2 minutes.*

Fluency	1	title eight forks vials heir lamb foam land dog rid pep sir	12
Accuracy	2	balk fuzz crux dove bury quit joke gale hems nods pier walk	24
Numbers	3	aid 1 aid 2 aid 3 aid 4 aid 5 aid 6 aid 7 aid 8 aid 9 aid 0	36
Symbols	4	ff % ff % ff % kk * kk * kk * ;; \ ;; \ ;; \ ;; | ;; | ;; |	48

PRETEST

Take one 1-minute timing.

5	The bossy hostess stressed to Burgess that success may	12
6	rest on issues like a shiny gloss on glasses and stupendous	24
7	desserts. Sara asserts the answer is to amass great assets.	36

| 1 | 2 | 3 | 4 | 5 | 6 | 7 | 8 | 9 | 10 | 11 | 12 |

PRACTICE

Type lines for speed or accuracy. *Time—3 or 5 minutes.*

Key Review: S

8	sss sas sss sds sss sfs sws sxs sSs SsS SsS Sas Sue Sal sss	12
9	saws sips Bossy sacks assets assess Assists assigns sensors	24
10	boss spas amiss Swiss assays Issues success possess glasses	36
11	sums skis bless shoes stress Misses asserts Burgess seasons	48
12	status scissor Dessert fossils assassin Sailboats satisfies	60
13	assert essence Hostess hassles Assessor savorless sawhorses	72

00.30 30-SECOND OKS

Take a 30-second OK timing on each line. Repeat.

SPEED: 2 errors allowed

ACCURACY: 0 errors allowed

14	Pam Burkey wished to listen to five exciting jazz quartets.	12
15	Jake Hanes gave away around forty bronze plaques in Mexico.	12
16	Zeke Poe was building exotic huts for Jim by a quiet river.	12

| 1 | 2 | 3 | 4 | 5 | 6 | 7 | 8 | 9 | 10 | 11 | 12 |

TECHNIQUE CHECK

Type for 30 seconds on each line.

Proper finger position and curve.

Back erect, lean forward.

Proper position at machine.

17	socks sagas sails gloss brass dress asset essay issue cases	12
18	sad she sap sat sea ash ask use bus gas has was yes sod gas	12
19	sags sassy shush sissy saints salads salons saddens sadness	12

01.00 1-MINUTE OKS

Take one 1-minute OK timing on each line.

SPEED: 3 errors allowed

ACCURACY: 1 error allowed

20	Sissy Burgess sacks the shoes and socks for her Swiss boss.	12
21	The hostess asserts her desserts satisfy the sassy gossips.	12

| 1 | 2 | 3 | 4 | 5 | 6 | 7 | 8 | 9 | 10 | 11 | 12 |

POSTTEST

Repeat the Pretest.

PROGRESS CHECK TIMINGS

WARMUP

Practice the following paragraph. *Time—2 minutes.*

Computer networks create electronic highways that you can explore. Companies can exchange information and conduct their business more efficiently and more profitably.

`00.00` **TIMING**

(SI = 1.57)

When you create a money plan, outline your expected income 13
and expenses like you did for your personal income statement. 25
Organize your plan on paper or use a computer. Either way, you 38
have a recorded plan and a place to keep track of your actual 50
income and expenses. 54

Include an income section and an expense section on your 66
plan. In the income section, list all your sources of income, 78
leaving nothing out. Then record your expected expenses in the 91
expenses section. Also, plan for unexpected expenses in case an 104
accident happens or special events come up. 113

In each section, make columns for your budgeted income and 126
expenses and columns for actual income or expenses. Record all 139
your budgeted income and expenses in the planned columns. You 151
should extend the planned dollar amount to all twelve months. 163

Each month, record all your actual income and expenses. At 176
the end of the month, figure the difference between your planned 189
and actual amounts. Look for items that you underestimated or 201
overestimated. Make adjustments and refine your plan to avoid 213
financial problems. 217

Over time, this plan, often called a budget, will help you 230
know your income history and spending habits. From this data, 242
you can formulate a sensible money plan to match your needs and 255
wants on the basis of fact, not fiction. 263

| 1 | 2 | 3 | 4 | 5 | 6 | 7 | 8 | 9 | 10 | 11 | 12 | 13 |

WARMUP

Practice the following lines. *Time—2 minutes.*

Fluency	1	tutor downs panel risks mend sick they and dye for me go by	12
Accuracy	2	post lazy exit oven bump kale jilt cove drug flow have quad	24
Numbers	3	bus 1 bus 2 bus 3 bus 4 bus 5 bus 6 bus 7 bus 8 bus 9 bus 0	36
Symbols	4	kk < kk < kk < ll > ll > ll > ;; { ;; { ;; { ;; } ;; } ;; }	48

PRETEST

Take one 1-minute timing.

5	Matthew tactfully asked the student about the test she	12
6	took on the eighth. Her attitude about this test was better	24
7	than her first attempt in Detroit ten or twelve weeks back.	36

| 1 | 2 | 3 | 4 | 5 | 6 | 7 | 8 | 9 | 10 | 11 | 12 |

PRACTICE

Type lines for speed or accuracy. *Time—3 or 5 minutes.*

Key Review: T			
	8	ftf ttt ftf ttt ftf ttt tat tot fTf TfT tTt TtT Tab Tom ttt	12
	9	tact text Betty start Otters street attract tactful student	24
	10	tent Tate twist tasty stitch turtle tatters tuition Battery	36
	11	trot test stout tenth better tattoo testate Stewart Estates	48
	12	status trotter Matthew cattail Attitude uttermost statistic	60
	13	detect Attempt fittest Detroit atwitter etiquette statuette	72

`00.30` 30-SECOND OKS

Take a 30-second OK timing on each line. Repeat.

SPEED: 2 errors allowed

ACCURACY: 0 errors allowed

14	Tom Knox quipped over how he could buy forty glazed jewels.	12
15	Six dozen quarters will buy joyful Kelli cheap video games.	12
16	A mock jury acquitted five publicized boxers in Washington.	12

| 1 | 2 | 3 | 4 | 5 | 6 | 7 | 8 | 9 | 10 | 11 | 12 |

TECHNIQUE CHECK

Type for 30 seconds on each line.

Control hand bounce.

Eyes on copy.

Arms quiet.

17	tan tow tub the toe tap ten tar too tie tab tot tag tin tax	12
18	that tilt attic theft attest tablet tattle twitter tourists	12
19	not bit let bat mat vet sit ate wet cat put hit net set yet	12

`01.00` 1-MINUTE OKS

Take one 1-minute OK timing on each line.

SPEED: 3 errors allowed

ACCURACY: 1 error allowed

20	The attempted theft of the otter left the tourist atwitter.	12
21	The statistics on that tenth test were better than thought.	12

| 1 | 2 | 3 | 4 | 5 | 6 | 7 | 8 | 9 | 10 | 11 | 12 |

POSTTEST

Repeat the Pretest.

PROGRESS CHECK TIMINGS

WARMUP

Practice the following paragraph. *Time—2 minutes.*

The home shopping industry via computers makes it easy to shop without leaving your home. Industry analysts expect this type of shopping to quintuple over the next few years.

00.00 TIMING

(SI = 1.56)

Voice mail is a popular and effective communication tool.	13
It automates the delivery of voice messages over the present	25
telephone networks. The hardware and software for voice mail	37
converts voice messages into synthesized speech patterns that	49
can be stored, sent, or heard by the receiver.	58
Voice mail augments or complements other mail services and	71
will often double as the means for dictation input to a word	83
processing operator. Further, it will provide the advantages of	96
electronic mail to those who may not keyboard effectively, such	109
as administrators and executives. An important use of voice mail	122
is to eliminate the unproductive game of telephone tag. If the	135
recipient is away from the desk, he or she can later recall the	148
stored message.	151
To use voice mail, you pick up your telephone and dial the	164
desired party. If you do not reach the person you are calling	176
after a certain number of rings, the voice mail system requests	189
that you leave a message. You then speak the message and hang	201
up. A light flashes on the receiving phone to indicate a message	214
is waiting. Your party can access the message at any time and	226
either store it for later use or delete it.	235
Major telephone companies are adding voice mail to their	247
services. A system for voice mail is expensive; however, as more	260
users subscribe to such services, the cost will decrease.	271

| 1 | 2 | 3 | 4 | 5 | 6 | 7 | 8 | 9 | 10 | 11 | 12 | 13 |

WARMUP — Practice the following lines. *Time—2 minutes.*

Fluency	1	chaps widow borne flaps owns fuel tidy lens nap air bow urn	12
Accuracy	2	body down evil hazy coax daft nail gale junk mope quip soar	24
Numbers	3	the 1 the 2 the 3 the 4 the 5 the 6 the 7 the 8 the 9 the 0	36
Symbols	4	ss @ ss @ ss @ jj & jj & jj & ;; = ;; = ;; = ;; + ;; + ;; +	48

PRETEST — Take one 1-minute timing.

5	Curtis and Lulu from Augusta will attend that luau and	12
6	try the hula to the strumming of authentic ukuleles. Curtis	24
7	usually refuses to eat my untidy and unusual sea cucumbers.	36

| 1 | 2 | 3 | 4 | 5 | 6 | 7 | 8 | 9 | 10 | 11 | 12 |

PRACTICE — Type lines for speed or accuracy. *Time—3 or 5 minutes.*

Key Review: U

8	juj uuu juj uuu juj uuu uni uno jUj UjU uUu UuU Una Urn uuu	12
9	luau guru uncut strum August Output unusual futures unlucky	24
10	hula Lulu sunup Fugue unique unglue unfurls suburbs ukulele	36
11	tutu Curt usury usurp Untidy unruly unplugs uranium surplus	48
12	Untied Auburn sutures tubular cucumbers unanimous furniture	60
13	autumn cumulus Augusta queuing usefully Luxurious unaccused	72

[00.30] 30-SECOND OKS — Take a 30-second OK timing on each line. Repeat.

SPEED: 2 errors allowed

ACCURACY: 0 errors allowed

14	Mary Kimmel joined us to explore big white caves of quartz.	12
15	Chad Maxwell quit serving pizza to Buff and my jovial kids.	12
16	Mixing home jobs with office tasks penalized my quiet Vera.	12

| 1 | 2 | 3 | 4 | 5 | 6 | 7 | 8 | 9 | 10 | 11 | 12 |

TECHNIQUE CHECK — Type for 30 seconds on each line.

Efficient use of shift keys.

Wrists low, not touching.

Smooth stroking, even pace.

17	uUu Useful Tutors Unplug Untrue Umlaut Upturn Audits Butler	12
18	cutup mucus usual unify upend urges under ulcer uncle undue	12
19	users unity until unpin umber ultra lupus urban union usage	12

[01.00] 1-MINUTE OKS — Take one 1-minute OK timing on each line.

SPEED: 3 errors allowed

ACCURACY: 1 error allowed

20	Curt will play an unusual fugue on his flute for his uncle.	12
21	The useful tutors were unanimous about buying that ukulele.	12

| 1 | 2 | 3 | 4 | 5 | 6 | 7 | 8 | 9 | 10 | 11 | 12 |

POSTTEST — Repeat the Pretest.

PROGRESS CHECK TIMINGS

WARMUP

Practice the following paragraph. *Time—2 minutes.*

Punctuation marks are a mechanical means to make writing more easily understood. They make the relationship between all words, phrases, and clauses clear.

00.00 TIMING

(SI = 1.55)

Safe driving benefits you, your friends, your family, and	13
society. The car has the potential to destroy you economically	26
and physically and do considerable damage to people around you.	39
To prevent accidents and to enjoy your automobile, drive safely.	52
Human error accounts for more than half of the automobile	65
accidents in the United States. You can significantly reduce	77
accidents by driving safely and defensively. In fact, you can	89
take safe driving classes, enroll in a defensive driving course,	102
or hire a personal driving tutor.	109
Safe driving means always wearing your seat belt, even for	122
short trips. Scores of accidents happen within a short distance	135
of home. Adjust your speed to the road conditions. On snow or	147
ice and in rain or fog, slow down even though others pass you.	160
Secure small children in approved safety seats.	170
Observe other drivers. Anticipate what they will do. Keep a	183
cautious distance behind cars in front of you, and indicate your	196
driving plans to others by using your turn signals and brake	208
lights. If you become sleepy, pull over to the side of the road	221
and take a nap or do something to reenergize yourself.	232
To help protect the environment, join a car pool, tune up	245
your car frequently, and conserve your speed. You will save fuel	258
as well as reduce carbon monoxide pollution.	267

| 1 | 2 | 3 | 4 | 5 | 6 | 7 | 8 | 9 | 10 | 11 | 12 | 13 |

LESSON 22   ALPHABET PRACTICE—LETTER V

WARMUP   Practice the following lines. *Time—2 minutes.*

Fluency	1	visible laughs shelf vigor right idle firm kept map pen bit	12
Accuracy	2	aqua zero want evil joke bite calf duck waxy gush move pier	24
Numbers	3	run 1 run 2 run 3 run 4 run 5 run 6 run 7 run 8 run 9 run 0	36
Symbols	4	dd # dd # dd # jj ^ jj ^ jj ^ ;; [;; [;; [;;] ;;] ;;]	48

PRETEST   Take one 1-minute timing.

5	Vivacious Velma and evasive Vera were involved in four	12
6	survival events near Vesuvius. Seven survivors were vividly	24
7	giving overviews to a savvy bevy in civvies from Vancouver.	36

| 1 | 2 | 3 | 4 | 5 | 6 | 7 | 8 | 9 | 10 | 11 | 12 |

PRACTICE   Type lines for speed or accuracy. *Time—3 or 5 minutes.*

Key Review: V

8	fvf vvv fvf vvv fvf vvv vet vim fVf VfV vVv VvV Vie Von vvv	12
9	avid Vera vivid savvy evolve votive Revival vacuums vending	24
10	vase vest valve verve Vivian vivify revived vanilla Revolve	36
11	Over bevy event Velma evolve velvet revving survive verdict	48
12	values Evasive vividly civvies Vesuvius vivacious inventive	60
13	vaults revolve Involve evolves overview survivors Vancouver	72

`00.30` 30-SECOND OKS   Take a 30-second OK timing on each line. Repeat.

SPEED: 2 errors allowed

ACCURACY: 0 errors allowed

14	Kevin Max writes prized journals of high quality for clubs.	12
15	Freda Hyke was giving six major bronze plaques for casting.	12
16	Quiet Mike plays goofy clarinet with five Dixie jazz bands.	12

| 1 | 2 | 3 | 4 | 5 | 6 | 7 | 8 | 9 | 10 | 11 | 12 |

TECHNIQUE CHECK   Type for 30 seconds on each line.

Space bar—thumb close.

Arms quiet.

Eyes on copy.

17	v v v vvv v v v vvv vat via vow vim Val vote vine vest Vane	12
18	veto gave halve views velvet values visible vividly vinegar	12
19	devil level gavel diver brave vault avail verge rival vapor	12

`01.00` 1-MINUTE OKS   Take one 1-minute OK timing on each line.

SPEED: 3 errors allowed

ACCURACY: 1 error allowed

20	Vera was on the verge of wearing vivid velvet to the event.	12
21	The savvy divers are evasive about involving the survivors.	12

| 1 | 2 | 3 | 4 | 5 | 6 | 7 | 8 | 9 | 10 | 11 | 12 |

POSTTEST   Repeat the Pretest.

PROGRESS CHECK TIMINGS

WARMUP

Practice the following paragraph. *Time—2 minutes.*

It is important to wear the appropriate clothing for a job interview. A business suit or other suitable clothing may be required. Whatever the attire, the clothing should be clean, neat, and attractive.

00.00 TIMING

(SI = 1.54)

One fact characterizes all records. Each record, no matter 13
what the origin or type, passes through defined stages from its 26
beginning to its destruction. To put it simply, all records have 39
a moment of birth and a time of death. Records progress through 52
stages called a life cycle. The stages in the life cycle are 64
explained as the creation, active use, inactive use and storage, 77
and final disposition. 82

A record is created when data are captured either on paper, 95
electronic media, or film. The record has a period of high use, 108
usually from one to three years, which is called the active 120
life. Once the frequent use of the record slows, a period of low 133
use begins. This second period, which can last from two to seven 146
years, is called its inactive life. The record is destroyed at 159
some point after its inactive life. In some cases the record may 172
be retained indefinitely. 177

As records move through their life cycles, the personnel, 190
methods, storage, and security needed to manage records might 202
change. These adjustments will occur because of new tools being 215
created to handle records. To manage records correctly, the 227
records manager must design a records system that recognizes 239
the stages in the life cycles of records and the new ways of 251
keeping those records. 255

| 1 | 2 | 3 | 4 | 5 | 6 | 7 | 8 | 9 | 10 | 11 | 12 | 13 |

LESSON 23   ALPHABET PRACTICE—LETTER W

WARMUP   Practice the following lines. *Time—2 minutes.*

Fluency	1	downtown bicycle antique dismay lapels tight blend burn vow	12
Accuracy	2	cafe axes jive bush plot quiz died fame gnat half ward keys	24
Numbers	3	sow 1 sow 2 sow 3 sow 4 sow 5 sow 6 sow 7 sow 8 sow 9 sow 0	36
Symbols	4	ff $ ff $ ff $ ll (ll (ll (;;) ;;) ;;) ;; / ;; / ;; /	48

PRETEST   Take one 1-minute timing.

5	Ward was waiting for the lowdown on the whirlwind trip	12
6	through Warsaw. Andrew was awkwardly swapping stories about	24
7	worldwide trips with Whitlow and a widow in yellow jewelry.	36

| 1 | 2 | 3 | 4 | 5 | 6 | 7 | 8 | 9 | 10 | 11 | 12 |

PRACTICE   Type lines for speed or accuracy. *Time—3 or 5 minutes.*

Key Review: W

8	sws www sws www sws www wet wow sWs WsW wWw WwW Web Win www	12
9	Away ewes widow sweep willow wallow Whitlow waxwork swallow	24
10	whew swap Wayne tweed wigwam window Powwows awkward wayworn	36
11	wade weep swamp Jewel twenty winnow Wiggins whipsaw wayward	48
12	Kowtow lowdown waxwing Winslow withdraw worldwide watchword	60
13	Warsaw windows wigwags walkway Snowplow waterways whirlwind	72

00.30 30-SECOND OKS   Take a 30-second OK timing on each line. Repeat.

SPEED: 2 errors allowed

ACCURACY: 0 errors allowed

14	Will gave a quick but zestful jab to my drum and xylophone.	12
15	William Dent quickly fixes the big jet and zips over there.	12
16	Jami quickly boxed wood and put logs on her very cozy fire.	12

| 1 | 2 | 3 | 4 | 5 | 6 | 7 | 8 | 9 | 10 | 11 | 12 |

TECHNIQUE CHECK   Type for 30 seconds on each line.

Back erect, lean forward.

Proper position at machine.

Efficient use of right shift key.

17	wow war wig who wag way was wed win wax why won wit woe wad	12
18	week wages wails waits waddle wadded waders waddled waddles	12
19	Wag sew vow Was caw Wig low raw Wax few dew Wed new Wet Win	12

01.00 1-MINUTE OKS   Take one 1-minute OK timing on each line.

SPEED: 3 errors allowed

ACCURACY: 1 error allowed

20	Winslow may withdraw his bid to plow and sweep my driveway.	12
21	The Warsaw widow will swap her jewels for a worldwide trip.	12

| 1 | 2 | 3 | 4 | 5 | 6 | 7 | 8 | 9 | 10 | 11 | 12 |

POSTTEST   Repeat the Pretest.

PROGRESS CHECK TIMINGS

WARMUP

Practice the following paragraph. *Time—2 minutes.*

When writing a report, a bibliography is often included at the end. It will list all of the works used in the preparation of the report as well as all of the works cited.

⌜00.00⌝ TIMING

(SI = 1.54)

Knowing how to listen is one of the most valuable skills   12
you possess. However, like any skill left idle or unpracticed,   25
it can be lost. In our world of fast computers and constantly   37
droning televisions, we expect huge amounts of information at   49
our fingertips. Many of us have stopped listening, and now we   61
function as filter systems, skimming through the clamor to look   74
for things that catch our attention.   81

To sharpen listening skills, you can begin by maintaining   94
eye contact with the speaker. This provides facial messages and   107
lessens the chance of being distracted by any noise. Another   119
technique is to visualize what a speaker is trying to say. This   132
places the listener in an active position and can help avoid the   145
mental vacation often taken while appearing to be listening. A   158
mental lapse is easy to take since the human being is able to   170
listen at three times the speed of the normal speaker.   181

It is very important to wait until the person speaking has   194
stopped before you reply. Do not guess the focus of the speaker   207
and interject with a response or answer. This is not only rude,   220
but may prove embarrassing if the response does not match the   232
point being made. A few seconds of quiet to actively think and   245
listen to what a speaker is saying can enrich the conversation.   258
Be an active and very considerate listener.   267

| 1 | 2 | 3 | 4 | 5 | 6 | 7 | 8 | 9 | 10 | 11 | 12 | 13 |

WARMUP		Practice the following lines. *Time—2 minutes.*	
Fluency	1	problems suspend surname autism orient chair field mama did	12
Accuracy	2	dome were quit leak gone club plus hazy rose vein join flex	24
Numbers	3	and 1 and 2 and 3 and 4 and 5 and 6 and 7 and 8 and 9 and 0	36
Symbols	4	ff % ff % ff % kk * kk * kk * ;; \ ;; \ ;; \ ;; | ;; | ;; |	48

PRETEST   Take one 1-minute timing.

	5	Dexter and Jinx were extremely eager to exit after the	12
	6	hoax on Alexis. Xavier had to overexert to get to Knoxville	24
	7	before Alexis examined the hoax and fixed an extra jukebox.	36

| 1 | 2 | 3 | 4 | 5 | 6 | 7 | 8 | 9 | 10 | 11 | 12 |

PRACTICE   Type lines for speed or accuracy. *Time—3 or 5 minutes.*

Key Review: X

	8	sxs xxx sxs xxx sxs xxx xsx xsx sXs XsX xXx XxX Xwa Xws xxx	12
	9	coax Hoax affix index exceed Dexter extreme exactly mixture	24
	10	Alex exit boxes relax influx Luxury complex jukebox overtax	36
	11	Jinx lynx epoxy Felix deluxe oxygen fixture maximum pretext	48
	12	Galaxy foxtrot texture hexagon textbook overexert Knoxville	60
	13	prefix examine mixture Taxable extremes Unexcused executrix	72

⏱ 00:30 30-SECOND OKS   Take a 30-second OK timing on each line. Repeat.

SPEED: 2 errors allowed
ACCURACY: 0 errors allowed

	14	Felix Vaughn met Becky Quid at jazz concerts in West Provo.	12
	15	Six jumpy girls won thirty prized books in five quick days.	12
	16	Pearl enjoys quoting crazy words from the five extra books.	12

| 1 | 2 | 3 | 4 | 5 | 6 | 7 | 8 | 9 | 10 | 11 | 12 |

TECHNIQUE CHECK   Type for 30 seconds on each line.

Feet on floor.
Arms quiet.
Efficient use of shift keys.

	17	exam axle sixty exact exotic excise expires example exhibit	12
	18	annex latex texts sixth expel exist exert extra taxes Sioux	12
	19	Exits Onyx Matrix Axis Mixes Boxes Next Exude Export Laxity	12

⏱ 01:00 1-MINUTE OKS   Take one 1-minute OK timing on each line.

SPEED: 3 errors allowed
ACCURACY: 1 error allowed

| | 20 | Felix overexerted and extra oxygen was needed to relax him. | 12 |
| | 21 | Alex will exit to Knoxville with the luxury jukebox for me. | 12 |

| 1 | 2 | 3 | 4 | 5 | 6 | 7 | 8 | 9 | 10 | 11 | 12 |

POSTTEST   Repeat the Pretest.

TIMING 23

PROGRESS CHECK TIMINGS

Practice the following paragraph. *Time—2 minutes.*

A new data and information highway, the Internet, allows you to access data and send it across town, into the next state, around the nation, or into foreign countries.

⌗00.00⌗ TIMING

(SI = 1.53)

Today, business managers must have sound information in 12
order to make wise, correct, and informed choices. An organized 25
plan to seek this information must be designed. Such a system 37
allows for the collection of data and then transforms this data 50
into useful formats. The processed data can then be used by the 63
women and men who must make business decisions. 73

These systems process data using many methods. A manual 85
system may use simple writing tools to record and process data, 98
while the more automated system uses many types of machines to 111
speed the flow of paper and work. These machines may include 123
typewriters, copying machines, and many others. You will find 135
that word processors are used often in such a plan. 145

While some business firms rely solely on a manual system, 158
most firms use a blend of both electronic and manual methods. 170
This mix might improve both the amount and the quality of the 182
information that can be made available to the business. It is 194
vital that all managers keep a good balance of methods to ensure 207
that their information is stable. A firm must have pertinent 219
information at the right place and the right time. This data 231
must also be obtained at a justifiable cost for it to be useful. 244
Good managers work hard to be sure this occurs. 253

| 1 | 2 | 3 | 4 | 5 | 6 | 7 | 8 | 9 | 10 | 11 | 12 | 13 |

WARMUP   Practice the following lines. *Time—2 minutes.*

Fluency	1	their foams usual fuels maid down with may jam own to he if	12
Accuracy	2	quit jinx zany bait draw deep fate gust hold yoke meat cave	24
Numbers	3	own 1 own 2 own 3 own 4 own 5 own 6 own 7 own 8 own 9 own 0	36
Symbols	4	kk < kk < kk < ll > ll > ll > ;; { ;; { ;; { ;; } ;; } ;; }	48

PRETEST   Take one 1-minute timing.

5   Young Jenny Kyle displayed your syrupy yellow dessert.   12

6   The mystery dessert typically brought in money to the youth   24

7   of Calgary who shyly sold the dessert yearly in old Sydney.   36

| 1 | 2 | 3 | 4 | 5 | 6 | 7 | 8 | 9 | 10 | 11 | 12 |

PRACTICE   Type lines for speed or accuracy. *Time—3 or 5 minutes.*

Key Review: Y

8   jyj yyy jyj yyy jyj yyy yam yea jYj YjY yYy YyY You Yes yyy   12

9   byte Your byway yummy byplay Payday mystify synergy loyalty   24

10   buoy Yale gypsy cycle yearly typify Tyranny yelling ability   36

11   Andy duty slyly Jenny syrupy yeasty dynasty yardage tyranny   48

12   heyday loyally mystery Calgary symphony dystrophy Lyrically   60

13   Sydney odyssey mystery display sympathy Mythology typically   72

`00.30` 30-SECOND OKS   Take a 30-second OK timing on each line. Repeat.

SPEED: 2 errors allowed

ACCURACY: 0 errors allowed

14   The panicky Queen of Cadiz was viewing onyx marble jewelry.   12

15   Kirby played mighty fine sax with the Victory Jazz Quartet.   12

16   The expert Bolivian jockey was jumping four unique hazards.   12

| 1 | 2 | 3 | 4 | 5 | 6 | 7 | 8 | 9 | 10 | 11 | 12 |

TECHNIQUE CHECK   Type for 30 seconds on each line.

Sharp, quick keystroking.

17   yum cry may pay dye day yet hay lay buy shy yak ray yew bye   12

Control hand bounce.

18   yucca today yours yearn yards yield youth dryly years shyly   12

Space bar—thumb close.

19   y y y yyy y y y yyy hey yank yelp yoke yell yarn yard young   12

`01.00` 1-MINUTE OKS   Take one 1-minute OK timing on each line.

SPEED: 3 errors allowed

20   Sydney may display your yellow mystery syrups at Yuba City.   12

ACCURACY: 1 error allowed

21   Kirby loyally attends the Calgary youth symphony every day.   12

| 1 | 2 | 3 | 4 | 5 | 6 | 7 | 8 | 9 | 10 | 11 | 12 |

POSTTEST   Repeat the Pretest.

PROGRESS CHECK TIMINGS

WARMUP

Practice the following paragraph. *Time—2 minutes.*

There is always a great deal for everyone to do during the holiday season. Many people are busy attending business and social functions, wrapping gifts, or preparing for gatherings.

00.00 TIMING

(SI = 1.52)

You invest a good deal of money in an automobile; thus, you 13
want to keep it in proper running order. Regular and frequent 25
inspections of the parts of your car help you spot any emerging 38
problems and minimize them before you have to arrange expensive 51
journeys to the repair shop. Also, you must schedule routine 63
maintenance to keep the car running. In addition to filling your 76
car with gasoline, you should schedule routine maintenance. 88

Regulate the air pressure in the tires. Over-inflated or 100
under-inflated tires cause abnormal wear and will force you to 113
buy new tires sooner than you expect. The battery needs water to 126
work. If the water in your battery is low, you may not get the 139
electrical current necessary to start your car or even use the 151
lights. Fill the battery with distilled water. Some batteries 163
are self-contained and do not require any additional water. 175

Without oil your engine will stop working. You must monitor 188
your oil level and add the right kind of oil to your engine when 201
it gets low. Also, you must change oil in your car as often as 214
the manufacturer recommends. Automatic transmission fluid makes 227
the transmission work. Check and change this transmission fluid 240
as often as recommended. 245

Your water pump circulates water through your radiator and 258
throughout the engine to cool it. Inspect the water level in the 271
radiator often, and test the fan belt to make sure it is tight. 284

| 1 | 2 | 3 | 4 | 5 | 6 | 7 | 8 | 9 | 10 | 11 | 12 | 13 |

WARMUP

Practice the following lines. *Time—2 minutes.*

Fluency	1	downtown penalty turkeys handle social slang blame coal bus	12
Accuracy	2	zeal apex hive bugs prey aqua comb damp foil jerk news true	24
Numbers	3	tie 1 tie 2 tie 3 tie 4 tie 5 tie 6 tie 7 tie 8 tie 9 tie 0	36
Symbols	4	ss @ ss @ ss @ jj & jj & jj & ;; = ;; = ;; = ;; + ;; + ;; +	48

PRETEST

Take one 1-minute timing.

5	Bold Buzz and Zizzi were caught in a dizzying blizzard	12
6	in northern Arizona while Ziggy sizzled in drizzly rains of	24
7	the Amazon River in Brazil. These zoologists were frazzled.	36

| 1 | 2 | 3 | 4 | 5 | 6 | 7 | 8 | 9 | 10 | 11 | 12 |

PRACTICE

Type lines for speed or accuracy. *Time—3 or 5 minutes.*

Key Review: Z

8	aza zzz aza zzz aza zzz zoo zip aZa ZaZ zZz ZzZ Zen Zoe zzz	12
9	fizz Buzz tizzy Pizza frizzy puzzle whizzed drizzle buzzard	24
10	zoos jazz Lizzy fuzzy dazzle zigzag pizzazz Quizzes gizzard	36
11	fuzz whiz Jazzy fizzy buzzes Brazil muzzled sizzled grizzly	48
12	Amazon bazaars buzzers Nozzles blizzard finalized zoologist	60
13	snazzy Arizona guzzled fizzles embezzle Haphazard magazines	72

⌗00.30⌗ 30-SECOND OKS

SPEED: 2 errors allowed

ACCURACY: 0 errors allowed

Take a 30-second OK timing on each line. Repeat.

14	A jury acquitted big Zane Koche of very weird tax problems.	12
15	Jinx gave a few marvelous banquets in cozy Hyde Park homes.	12
16	Hal Rex knows bicycling means prize views and joyful quiet.	12

| 1 | 2 | 3 | 4 | 5 | 6 | 7 | 8 | 9 | 10 | 11 | 12 |

TECHNIQUE CHECK

Proper position at machine.

Proper finger position.

Space bar—thumb close.

Type for 30 seconds on each line.

17	czar raze zebra zeros piazza fizzle zeroing nozzles zealous	12
18	mazes amaze dozes zones dizzy seize sizes unzip razed azure	12
19	zap zoo zip zinc zest zone zooms zippy zesty zonked zircons	12

⌗01.00⌗ 1-MINUTE OKS

SPEED: 3 errors allowed

ACCURACY: 1 error allowed

Take one 1-minute OK timing on each line.

20	There is no chance of blizzards or grizzlies in the Amazon.	12
21	Buzz and Ziggy whizzed through Arizona in a snazzy new car.	12

| 1 | 2 | 3 | 4 | 5 | 6 | 7 | 8 | 9 | 10 | 11 | 12 |

POSTTEST

Repeat the Pretest.

PROGRESS CHECK TIMINGS

WARMUP

Practice the following paragraph. *Time—2 minutes.*

Travel can be rewarding. Whether you travel overseas or around your own country, you can learn a great deal about the people and their customs. Enjoy your trip and learn as much as you can.

`00.00` **TIMING**

(SI = 1.51)

Once you have decided you need another car and that you can	13
afford to buy one, where do you shop? If you drive down almost	26
any main road in any city in the United States, you will notice	39
car dealers with new and used cars.	46
Dealers who specialize in new cars usually sell used cars	59
as well. They get new cars from the manufacturers and used cars	72
from people who trade in their old models for new ones. Dealers	85
selling new cars generally represent one principal manufacturer	98
and sell cars made just by that corporation. They service and	110
repair cars, especially those they sell that have a warranty.	122
Dealers who specialize in the sale of used cars normally do	135
not sell new cars; they sell only cars that are not new. Many of	148
these dealers do not have their own repair shop. Although they	161
frequently warrant their cars, they may offer a warranty for a	174
short period of time, usually three to six months.	184
Check the classified ads in your local newspaper for trade	197
advertisements. People who sell their cars through the paper	209
usually do not guarantee them. They sell the car as is. Caveat	222
emptor prevails; in other words, let the buyer beware.	233
Other sources worth checking for car purchases are people	246
you trust, television commercials, automobile trade magazines,	259
car rental agencies, and the Internet. Regardless of the source,	272
always evaluate the car thoroughly before purchasing it.	283

| 1 | 2 | 3 | 4 | 5 | 6 | 7 | 8 | 9 | 10 | 11 | 12 | 13 |

Individual Finger Practice

Lessons 27–31

CONTENT

Each of the five lessons in this section presents exercises emphasizing the use of specific fingers. These exercises allow the student with weak fingers to strengthen the reaches to proper keys.

OBJECTIVE

To improve stroking speed and accuracy on the keys controlled by each finger.

TECHNIQUE TIP

Keep eyes on copy most of the time.

TIMING 20

PROGRESS CHECK TIMINGS

Practice the following paragraph. *Time—2 minutes.*

The current trend for using capitalization in business writing is to use capitalization more sparingly--for emphasis, distinction, or to give importance.

`00.00` TIMING

(SI = 1.51)

Guarding the data that are stored in a computer system is	13
an item of major concern for the business world. The growing	25
number of men, women, and children who own computers or have	37
access to them at work or school has caused alarming increases	50
in crimes that range from bank fraud to spying. Students have	62
been caught stealing tests or changing grades. There have been a	75
huge number of reported cases of a young computer whiz caught	87
breaking into private business databanks.	95
Safeguarding data must be a major undertaking in the modern	108
office. It should be noted that no system will ever be perfect.	121
The goal is to limit risks. Both hardware and software must be	134
secured. This hardware includes all equipment. Only authorized	147
personnel should have access to highly sensitive software.	159
Computer crime has become so frequent that terms related to	172
this problem have become common jargon in the field. Trapdoors,	185
data diddling, and logic bomb are but a few of these terms. A	197
great deal of extra time and money will be spent trying to fight	210
any criminal actions. Business executives, office workers, law	223
officers, lawyers, and all others who are concerned are looking	236
for answers to the problems that computer crimes present. The	248
answers will not come easily or quickly or cheaply.	258

| 1 | 2 | 3 | 4 | 5 | 6 | 7 | 8 | 9 | 10 | 11 | 12 | 13 |

WARMUP

Practice the following lines. *Time—2 minutes.*

Fluency	1	The auditor may blame me for the dismal profit of the firm.	12
Accuracy	2	The quiet supervisor was vexed by crazy joking of my folks.	24
Numbers	3	The 1,204 men, 893 women, and 567 children will visit Ohio.	36
Symbols	4	dd # dd # dd # jj ^ jj ^ jj ^ ;; [;; [;; [;;] ;;] ;;]	48

PRETEST

Take one 1-minute timing.

5 My funny papa put my quart jar of peanuts in my gray buggy. 12

| 1 | 2 | 3 | 4 | 5 | 6 | 7 | 8 | 9 | 10 | 11 | 12 |

PRACTICE 1

Type lines for speed or accuracy. *Time—3 or 5 minutes.*

First Finger
and Fourth Finger

6 fff fgf frf ftf fvf fbf fff fjf jjj jhj juj jyj jmj jnj jjj 12

7 aaa aqa aza qaq aaa zaz aaa a;a ;;; ;p; ;/; p;p ;;; /;/ ;;; 24

8 pup buy may hum Papa lazy Ruby aqua tubby thumb funny truth 36

9 tub hub nut try Jury numb hung hurt Buggy gummy path; maze; 48

10 Jar put tan gab aunt bury Bart runt grave puppy punt/ gaze/ 60

11 vat tag fat tar jump pump many baby Happy yummy jumpy Quart 72

| 1 | 2 | 3 | 4 | 5 | 6 | 7 | 8 | 9 | 10 | 11 | 12 |

⏱ 00.30 30-SECOND OKS

SPEED: 2 errors allowed

ACCURACY: 0 errors allowed

Take a 30-second OK timing on each line. Repeat.

12 hung jury|hurt my thumb|my lazy aunt|bury my ruby|gummy tar 12

13 buy an urn|papa may hum|tubby baby|top my jump|a happy runt 12

14 furry puppy|a grave truth|a tan buggy|tag a quart|aqua opal 12

| 1 | 2 | 3 | 4 | 5 | 6 | 7 | 8 | 9 | 10 | 11 | 12 |

PRACTICE 2

Type for 30 seconds on each line.

15 fff fgf frf ftf fvf fbf fff fjf jjj jhj juj jyj jmj jnj jjj 12

16 aaa aqa aza qaq aaa zaz aaa a;a ;;; ;p; ;/; p;p ;;; /;/ ;;; 12

17 ant urn Pat bat navy bunt raft fury topaz rummy plaza Ozark 12

⏱ 01.00 1-MINUTE OKS

SPEED: 3 errors allowed

ACCURACY: 1 error allowed

Take one 1-minute OK timing on each line.

18 Happy Bart may buy an aqua topaz or a ruby for my Aunt Pat. 12

19 My tubby baby may jump on the puppy and may hurt his thumb. 12

| 1 | 2 | 3 | 4 | 5 | 6 | 7 | 8 | 9 | 10 | 11 | 12 |

POSTTEST

Repeat the Pretest.

PROGRESS CHECK TIMINGS

Practice the following paragraph. *Time—2 minutes.*

Many people enjoy traveling to foreign countries. Some prefer to travel by bus or car, and others prefer to travel by airplane or train. Another fine way to travel is by cruise ship.

`00.00` **TIMING**

(SI = 1.50)

Employers want to confirm your job skills, work habits, and	13
work history. Therefore, they may contact the references you	25
list on your resume. Carefully choose those people you include.	38
Employers prefer the names of past employers, schoolteachers,	50
and supervisors who can describe your job skills and abilities.	63
Unless the job application asks for character references, avoid	76
using friends, family, and the clergy.	84
Always be sure to get consent from those you want to use as	97
references. Write or call or speak to them in person. Tell them	110
where you are applying, the type of post you are considering,	122
and when they might be contacted. Obtain a correct address and	135
phone number from each person you list. This plan makes sure	147
the organization will be able to reach your contacts.	158
List your references last on your resume. Give the full	170
name, title, complete address, and phone number of each. Verify	183
numbers and the spelling of names. If you are using a college	195
placement service, state that references will be supplied upon	208
request or may be obtained from college placement staff.	219
Employers often call references and even may ask them to	231
complete a rating sheet. Answering the call or completing the	243
form takes time. After you secure a job, sending a short note to	256
extend thanks to your contacts for their help is in order.	268

| 1 | 2 | 3 | 4 | 5 | 6 | 7 | 8 | 9 | 10 | 11 | 12 | 13 |

WARMUP

Practice the following lines. *Time—2 minutes.*

Fluency	1	Helena is busy but may go to the show by the eighth of May.	12
Accuracy	2	Quiet Jody Kim won a lovely big cruise for the extra prize.	24
Numbers	3	These 1,579 men and 2,468 women receive diplomas on May 30.	36
Symbols	4	ff $ ff $ ff $ 11 (11 (11 (;;) ;;) ;;) ;; / ;; / ;; /	48

PRETEST

Take one 1-minute timing.

5 Eddie Eide locked six old cows on the low side of the deck. 12

| 1 | 2 | 3 | 4 | 5 | 6 | 7 | 8 | 9 | 10 | 11 | 12 |

PRACTICE 1

Second Finger and Third Finger

Type lines for speed or accuracy. *Time—3 or 5 minutes.*

6 ddd ded dcd ede ddd cdc ddd dkd kkk kik k,k iki kkk ,k, kkk 12
7 sss sws sxs wsw sss xsx sss sls lll lol l.l olo lll .l. lll 24
8 ewe Old eke did iced Wool cede weed diced kick, dock, cool. 36
9 die lox six oil deed Edie wood silk scold owls, Inc., code. 48
10 odd Kid wok low seed Doll dike kill decks slow, i.e., loll. 60
11 ice sow Sid cow lock wide died lick oiled socks wicks Eddie 72

00.30 30-SECOND OKS

SPEED: 2 errors allowed

ACCURACY: 0 errors allowed

Take a 30-second OK timing on each line. Repeat.

12 wide oiled dock|old silk dolls|did kill weeds|six oil deeds 12
13 wood owls|cows lick|slow ewes|odd wool socks|old wood decks 12
14 kid did kick|Elle licked ice|sow seeds|Edie liked wild rice 12

| 1 | 2 | 3 | 4 | 5 | 6 | 7 | 8 | 9 | 10 | 11 | 12 |

PRACTICE 2

Type for 30 seconds on each line.

15 ddd ded dcd ede ddd cdc ddd dkd kkk kik k,k iki kkk ,k, kkk 12
16 sss sws sxs wsw sss xsx sss sls lll lol l.l olo lll .l. lll 12
17 lie wed sew Wes dew side wild Eide will solos slide decided 12

01.00 1-MINUTE OKS

SPEED: 3 errors allowed

ACCURACY: 1 error allowed

Take one 1-minute OK timing on each line.

18 Edie decided to deed her wood dolls and silk socks to Elle. 12
19 The six cows and ewes will kick and slide on the iced dock. 12

| 1 | 2 | 3 | 4 | 5 | 6 | 7 | 8 | 9 | 10 | 11 | 12 |

POSTTEST

Repeat the Pretest.

PROGRESS CHECK TIMINGS

WARMUP

Practice the following paragraph. *Time—2 minutes.*

> Optic fibers enable the transmission of data at the speed of light. The fiber itself is the same size as a strand of human hair. Numerous fibers are wrapped in a plastic tube, which then are placed underground.

`00.00` **TIMING**

(SI = 1.50)

The computer, when used as a word processor, permits the	12
keyboard operator to produce memos, letters, reports, and tables	25
quickly, precisely, and neatly. Word processing software allows	38
the user to format, edit, correct, delete, and move text with	50
greater ease.	53
With the power of spreadsheet software, the computer can	65
help the user solve many types of math and business problems.	77
These problems and their solutions can be the base for making	89
sound judgments as economic and fiscal states change.	100
Graphics software allows the user to present data in the	112
form of pictures, charts, and graphs. Employees often need to	124
change raw data into pie charts, bar graphs, and line graphs.	136
They may need such charts and graphs to present their views to	149
peers and upper management. The result is not only factual but	162
also very attractive.	166
Database software allows data to be typed, organized, and	179
used in many different ways. For example, a client database can	192
be sorted by name, city, state, or the street address. Such a	204
database can be used to prepare mailing labels or to arrange	216
data in tables that will be included in a report.	226
More and more computers are being used in firms, homes, and	239
schools today. Through the surge of software programs designed	252
to meet user needs, the computer has become a valuable tool in	265
our world.	267

| 1 | 2 | 3 | 4 | 5 | 6 | 7 | 8 | 9 | 10 | 11 | 12 | 13 |

WARMUP		Practice the following lines. *Time—2 minutes.*	
Fluency	1	Diane may wish to roam by bus and then go to work for them.	12
Accuracy	2	Hazel found the aqua oxygen mask which I sent over by jeep.	24
Numbers	3	The 57 children gave 268 gifts to 140 families for 39 days.	36
Symbols	4	ff % ff % ff % kk * kk * kk * ;; \ ;; \ ;; \ ;; | ;; | ;; |	48

PRETEST   Take one 1-minute timing.

5   Ike and Eddie Eide iced a cake and Papa packed a pizza pie.   12

| 1 | 2 | 3 | 4 | 5 | 6 | 7 | 8 | 9 | 10 | 11 | 12 |

PRACTICE 1   Type lines for speed or accuracy. *Time—3 or 5 minutes.*

Second Finger
and Fourth Finger

6   ddd ded dcd ede ddd cdc ddd dkd kkk kik k,k iki kkk ,k, kkk   12

7   aaa aqa aza qaq aaa zaz aaa a;a ;;; ;p; ;/; p;p ;;; /;/ ;;;   24

8   Ice did eke die ices Deck dike iced acid, pipe, died, kick,   36

9   Ike pea zap Ada pica dice papa pike pack; daze/ cake; peek/   48

10   pie dip pep pad deed Dick pick paid dice, Eide/ deep, keep;   60

11   ace kid ape Zip peck pipe peek cape paced Pizza cede, peak;   72

[00.30] 30-SECOND OKS   Take a 30-second OK timing on each line. Repeat.

SPEED: 2 errors allowed

ACCURACY: 0 errors allowed

12   pick a pea|pack a pie|iced deck|zip a pad|ice a cake|a pipe   12

13   Dick Eide paid|Pepe paced|deep dike|keep deeds|Ada did peek   12

14   kick a pipe|zip a cape|pick a pack|did zap papa|Ada did ace   12

| 1 | 2 | 3 | 4 | 5 | 6 | 7 | 8 | 9 | 10 | 11 | 12 |

PRACTICE 2   Type for 30 seconds on each line.

15   ddd ded dcd ede ddd cdc ddd dkd kkk kik k,k iki kkk ,k, kkk   12

16   aaa aqa aza qaq aaa zaz aaa a;a ;;; ;p; ;/; p;p ;;; /;/ ;;;   12

17   dad cap add cad pad aced pace adze Eddie dazed diced zapped   12

[01.00] 1-MINUTE OKS   Take one 1-minute OK timing on each line.

SPEED: 3 errors allowed

ACCURACY: 1 error allowed

18   Ada picked a peck of peas while Dad and Dick diced a quail.   12

19   Eddie aced a test; Dad paid for a zippy plaid cap and cape.   12

| 1 | 2 | 3 | 4 | 5 | 6 | 7 | 8 | 9 | 10 | 11 | 12 |

POSTTEST   Repeat the Pretest.

PROGRESS CHECK TIMINGS

WARMUP

Practice the following paragraph. *Time—2 minutes.*

The field of interior design is growing. Many clients are taking advantage of the expertise that an interior designer can provide. Designers hope to make the rooms more comfortable and attractive.

`00.00` **TIMING**

(SI = 1.50)

A money plan must match your goals and means. Once you have   13
set your goals, you must assess your current money position to   26
see how much money you have, where it comes from, and where it   39
is going. The answers to these questions will help to describe   52
your present fiscal condition.   58

First, gather all the data on what you own and what you   70
owe. Collect your paycheck stubs, expense records, debt history,   83
and savings and investment data. Then, categorize these items   95
into assets and liabilities. Assets are the things you own, such   108
as your cash on hand and savings, home and interior furnishings,   121
and bike or car. Liabilities include any items on which you owe,   134
such as loans and taxes and other debts.   142

Second, from this data create a personal balance sheet and   155
figure your net worth. Net worth is the difference between what   168
you own and what you owe. Thus, subtract your liabilities from   181
your assets to prepare your balance sheet yearly.   191

Third, draft a personal income statement. This statement   203
lists all your income, such as your wages and interest earned on   216
savings accounts. It also includes your expenses, such as rent   229
or mortgage payments, utilities, insurance payments, food and   241
clothing, and any other daily living expenses and entertainment.   254
Compute any difference between your total income and your total   267
expenses. If they are equal, your budget is on target. If you   279
spend more than you earn, make adjustments. Draft your income   291
statement monthly.   295

| 1 | 2 | 3 | 4 | 5 | 6 | 7 | 8 | 9 | 10 | 11 | 12 | 13 |

WARMUP   Practice the following lines. *Time—2 minutes.*

Fluency	1	Do the work and then amend this title for the antique auto.	12
Accuracy	2	Jim quickly fixed a big Lopez house against winter vandals.	24
Numbers	3	Sara needs 312 plums, 45 oranges, 68 pears, and 907 grapes.	36
Symbols	4	kk < kk < kk < 11 > 11 > 11 > ;; { ;; { ;; { ;; } ;; } ;; }	48

PRETEST   Take one 1-minute timing.

     5   Rob and Ruth Oslo slowly turn my gummy wool sox inside out.   12

     | 1 | 2 | 3 | 4 | 5 | 6 | 7 | 8 | 9 | 10 | 11 | 12 |

PRACTICE 1   Type lines for speed or accuracy. *Time—3 or 5 minutes.*

First Finger
and Third Finger

6	fff fgf frf ftf fvf fbf fff fjf jjj jhj juj jyj jmj jnj jjj	12
7	sss sws sxs wsw sss xsx sss sls lll lol l.l olo lll .l. lll	24
8	for hug soy try rug tuft wool Oslo ruby bury turn solo U.S.	36
9	out sox tub box Rob wows ours Bros. hours bowls burns Lolly	48
10	fry bum lox fox sow Ruth loom Mrs. gummy solos buggy slowly	60
11	tug hum sol won now bug Nov. only Holly furry Thurs. unfurl	72

`00.30` 30-SECOND OKS   Take a 30-second OK timing on each line. Repeat.

SPEED: 2 errors allowed

ACCURACY: 0 errors allowed

12	furry wool sox|buy the wooly bunny|you now mow slowly|a rug	12
13	only Holly won|tug a buggy|try my solo|slowly turn|this tub	12
14	turn my loom|only Sol may run|Ruth Oslo burns my lox|my rug	12

     | 1 | 2 | 3 | 4 | 5 | 6 | 7 | 8 | 9 | 10 | 11 | 12 |

PRACTICE 2   Type for 30 seconds on each line.

15	fff fgf frf ftf fvf fbf fff fjf jjj jhj juj jyj jmj jnj jjj	12
16	sss sws sxs wsw sss xsx sss sls lll lol l.l olo lll .l. lll	12
17	my run you holy jolly lobby yummy bunny funny grubby slowly	12

`01.00` 1-MINUTE OKS   Take one 1-minute OK timing on each line.

SPEED: 3 errors allowed

ACCURACY: 1 error allowed

18	Jolly Sol won a ruby bowl and you won the box in the lobby.	12
19	Put my grubby yellow bunny and the furry fox with the rugs.	12

     | 1 | 2 | 3 | 4 | 5 | 6 | 7 | 8 | 9 | 10 | 11 | 12 |

POSTTEST   Repeat the Pretest.

PROGRESS CHECK TIMINGS

WARMUP	Practice the following paragraph. *Time—2 minutes.*

Changes in the computer industry really are amazing. More and more business travelers are using their laptop computers and taking them wherever they go. This new generation of laptops is stronger, lighter, smaller, and more powerful.

00.00 **TIMING**

(SI = 1.49)

The next time you stay at an extravagant hotel, do not be — 13
surprised if you cannot find a menu, the city guide, or anything — 26
else printed on paper. With a keyboard in every room, and using — 39
the television set as a monitor, you will have instant access to — 52
the main computer in the hotel. Through the computer, you can — 64
quickly view all of the services of the hotel and the telephone — 77
extensions of the various departments. — 85

In addition to accessing teletext services, you can tune in — 98
the national news, review the scores of any ball games, and find — 111
the latest stock market quotations. You can even check out. — 123

When you want to eat dinner, the system will provide you — 135
with a complete list of quality restaurants, along with their — 147
addresses, phone numbers, and prices. You can also review the — 159
entire menu to see if there is anything you might like to eat. — 172
The same type of information is available for entertainment. In — 185
addition, if you do not want to leave the hotel, video games, — 197
such as chess and bridge, are available. — 205

Convention guests will be able to view schedules, meeting — 218
times, and locations of activities at the touch of a button. In — 231
fact, guest speakers from all around the globe can be brought to — 244
the convention via laser cables or satellite. The computer has — 257
modernized the way we do things at home, on the job, and even at — 270
a hotel. — 272

| 1 | 2 | 3 | 4 | 5 | 6 | 7 | 8 | 9 | 10 | 11 | 12 | 13 |

WARMUP

Practice the following lines. *Time—2 minutes.*

Fluency	1	The neighbor cut an eye on the ivory handle of the antique.	12
Accuracy	2	Mickey Powers boxed the five big jugs of liquid antifreeze.	24
Numbers	3	Mary paid $4,706 for the boat and $1,382.59 for the motors.	36
Symbols	4	ss @ ss @ ss @ jj & jj & jj & ;; = ;; = ;; = ;; + ;; + ;; +	48

PRETEST

Take one 1-minute timing.

5   Papa and Opal wax tall sloops as Lola slaps and zaps wasps.   12

| 1 | 2 | 3 | 4 | 5 | 6 | 7 | 8 | 9 | 10 | 11 | 12 |

PRACTICE 1

Third Finger
and Fourth Finger

Type lines for speed or accuracy. *Time—3 or 5 minutes.*

6   sss sws sxs wsw sss xsx sss sls lll lol l.l olo lll .l. lll   12
7   aaa aqa aza qaq aaa zaz aaa a;a ;;; ;p; ;/; p;p ;;; /;/ ;;;   24
8   Al all sox Sal slop loss Oslo spool walls sows; pals/ saps.   36
9   low pap pox lop was Opal solo sloop papaw wool; zips/ awls.   48
10 sow pop paw lap sap Lola Papa oozes plows pool; paws/ owls.   60
11 saw owl pal Sol wax loop wows Swoop polls soap; wasp/ pass.   72

`00.30` 30-SECOND OKS

SPEED: 2 errors allowed

ACCURACY: 0 errors allowed

Take a 30-second OK timing on each line. Repeat.

12 saw an owl|pass wool sox|a loss|a poll|slow laps|low walls.   12
13 pool polo|saw an opal|Papa slaps a wasp|saw Sal sow|Pop was   12
14 saw low Alps|a slow loop|Opal saw a wax zoo|pass Sol a soap   12

| 1 | 2 | 3 | 4 | 5 | 6 | 7 | 8 | 9 | 10 | 11 | 12 |

PRACTICE 2

Type for 30 seconds on each line.

15 sss sws sxs wsw sss xsx sss sls lll lol l.l olo lll .l. lll   12
16 aaa aqa aza qaq aaa zaz aaa a;a ;;; ;p; ;/; p;p ;;; /;/ ;;;   12
17 zap wow pal lox sax pow lass pope squall lope/ walls; zoos.   12

`01.00` 1-MINUTE OKS

SPEED: 3 errors allowed

ACCURACY: 1 error allowed

Take one 1-minute OK timing on each line.

18 Wally Oslo swims slow pool laps as a lass plays a solo sax.   12
19 A lass saw my pal Sol slowly pass an opal to Papa at a zoo.   12

| 1 | 2 | 3 | 4 | 5 | 6 | 7 | 8 | 9 | 10 | 11 | 12 |

POSTTEST

Repeat the Pretest.

PROGRESS CHECK TIMINGS

WARMUP

Practice the following paragraph. *Time—2 minutes.*

To improve the quality of your study time, consider some basic ideas. Set up a study pattern and conscientiously follow it. You might study for fifty minutes and then relax for ten minutes. You will be glad you did.

`00.00` TIMING

(SI = 1.49)

When you make an appointment to interview for a job, plan	13
to arrive a few minutes early. When you arrive at the office,	25
tell the assistant who you are, whom you are to meet, and the	37
reason for your visit. As you wait, review your resume or read a	50
magazine or sit quietly; above all, avoid nervous motions. Be	62
polite and make good eye contact with everyone you meet. You may	75
offer a copy of your resume to the interviewer even though he or	88
she should have a copy. Reviewing your document may serve as an	101
icebreaker to introduce you.	107
Follow the lead of the interviewer. Some people prefer a	119
direct approach, in which the interviewer will ask you questions	132
that you will answer. This type of interview is more relaxed and	145
less stressful on you. Other people use an indirect approach. In	158
this case the interviewer will allow you to lead the session.	170
Listen carefully before answering questions. Then answer them	182
directly and accurately, giving an adequate explanation. On the	195
other hand, avoid giving long answers that are drawn out; you	207
do not want to lead the listener astray.	215
When you are taking the lead in the interview, begin by	227
stating your perception of the job and then matching your job	239
skills, abilities, and personal qualities to the requirements	251
of the job. When the interview is over, thank the person for	263
the interview. Send a note that same day and state your interest	276
in the post.	278

| 1 | 2 | 3 | 4 | 5 | 6 | 7 | 8 | 9 | 10 | 11 | 12 | 13 |

Word-Level Keystroking Practice

Lessons 32–36

CONTENT

When you learn to type, you begin by stroking individual letters. As you become more fluent, you type entire words rather than separating them into individual keystrokes. You will practice word-level responses in this section.

OBJECTIVE

To improve stroking speed and accuracy by typing at the word-response level.

TECHNIQUE TIP

Center your body opposite the J Key and lean forward slightly.

PROGRESS CHECK TIMINGS

WARMUP

Practice the following paragraph. *Time—2 minutes.*

Research evidence tells us that you most likely will change your career at least three times during your life. Often career change means that you will need to continue your education, either during the day or during the night.

[00.00] TIMING

(SI = 1.48)

Upon graduation, one of your first principal decisions will   13
be whether to buy a new car. To make such a decision, you must   26
determine whether your existing car is reliable and adequate,   38
whether you need a new car, and if so, whether to purchase or   50
lease the car. Perhaps you live in a zoned area that has good   62
mass transit, including buses, trains, and taxis, and therefore,   75
you do not require a car.   80

To resolve whether or not you need a car, you must consider   93
the economics of owning a car as well as the ecological impact   106
of driving your vehicle. The cost of owning your car includes   118
the purchase price and the expenses of insurance, maintenance,   131
and depreciation. To determine the purchase price from the final   144
bill, add the base price, options, fees, and taxes.   154

Your insurance costs will vary depending upon the insurance   167
coverage you want. The more insurance you procure, the more it   180
will cost per month. As you drive the car, you will consume gas,   193
oil, and other indispensable fluids. You will need to replace   205
the oil, buy new tires, tune up the car, and do other repairs.   218
Parking costs must also be included in these other extensive   230
maintenance costs.   234

Your car will wear out from driving and, to some degree,   246
from just being parked in your garage. This wear and tear is   258
labeled depreciation. Over time the car will have reduced value.   271
Think of depreciation as the difference between the purchase   283
price for the car and the selling price after it is depreciated.   296

| 1 | 2 | 3 | 4 | 5 | 6 | 7 | 8 | 9 | 10 | 11 | 12 | 13 |

LESSON 32   WORD-LEVEL KEYSTROKING

LESSON 32

WARMUP

Practice the following lines. *Time—2 minutes.*

Fluency	1	toe wish laugh pay maid shape cut lame autos lay also turns	12
Accuracy	2	cod yolk super jaw high vigor mix bone quote zip furs never	24
Numbers	3	zip 1 zip 2 zip 3 zip 4 zip 5 zip 6 zip 7 zip 8 zip 9 zip 0	36
Symbols	4	dd # dd # dd # jj ^ jj ^ jj ^ ;; [;; [;; [;;] ;;] ;;]	48

PRETEST

Take one 1-minute timing.

5   Dean and I will go to the park to play. We will see my   12

6   niece who works there; she sells hot dogs with soda pop. We   24

7   have to leave the park at three to catch the bus. Dean will   36

8   go home after we dine. We enjoy the times we spend at play.   48

     | 1 | 2 | 3 | 4 | 5 | 6 | 7 | 8 | 9 | 10 | 11 | 12 |

PRACTICE 1

Type lines for speed or accuracy. *Time—3 or 5 minutes.*

9   to the and for Dogs home boat times three Leave guest board   12

10   my see bus dad Park when sale After glass horse there women   24

11   at who eat Hot sold play went Catch spend plate their today   36

12   in ate she ice will Wait game niece sells house Movie salad   48

13   On pop men our must dine show enjoy guess sodas Coast glove   60

⌨ 00.12 12-SECOND TIMINGS

Total words typed × 5 = wpm

Take three 12-second timings on each line.

14   The glass and plate will go on sale when the house is sold.

15   Men and women wait in line to board the boat for the coast.

16   My dad and I went to a game show after we ate our hot dogs.

    5   10   15   20   25   30   35   40   45   50   55   60

PRACTICE 2

Type for 30 seconds on each line.

17   boats for sale|at their house|this is our guess|who will go   12

18   be my guest|catch the horse|play today|enjoy the good movie   12

19   we ate the salad|park my bus|after the game|there is a home   12

00.30 30-SECOND TIMINGS

Total words typed × 2 = wpm

Take two 30-second timings on each line.

20   The glass and plate will go on sale when the house is sold.   12

21   Men and women wait in line to board the boat for the coast.   12

22   My dad and I went to a game show after we ate our hot dogs.   12

     | 1 | 2 | 3 | 4 | 5 | 6 | 7 | 8 | 9 | 10 | 11 | 12 |

POSTTEST

Repeat the Pretest.

PROGRESS CHECK TIMINGS

WARMUP

Practice the following paragraph. *Time—2 minutes.*

More and more people are continuing their education during their career. They are attending day or night classes. Many are choosing to change their careers entirely. More schooling can open the door for job opportunities.

`00.00` TIMING

(SI = 1.48)

When someone introduces you to another person, you will	12
want to give some thought to the impression you will make after	25
the meeting. Your appearance and your conduct impact the first	38
impression you make. Your clothes should be clean, correctly	50
fitted, and proper for the occasion. Consider your approach to	63
the person you are meeting. Assuming that you wish to make an	75
agreeable impression, acknowledge the other person with good eye	88
contact, a smile, and a friendly response. Use the name of the	101
person in your greeting. If the occasion warrants it, shake the	114
hand of the person confidently and firmly. Be sure your hands	126
are clean and manicured.	131
The way that you exit is just as important as the first	143
greeting. Sometimes a parting handshake and kind comment are	155
wise. At the very least, avoid insincerity; try to leave the	167
notion that your day is a little richer for having met this new	180
person. Each of us likes to assume that we are worthy of the	192
kindness of another. Developing a friendship deserves zealous	204
effort and practice. A new friendship could get off to a great	217
start through friendly greetings and partings. With effort and	230
over a period of time, quite a number of new friendships will	242
form. Always cultivate your new friends with continued sincerity	255
and courtesy.	258

| 1 | 2 | 3 | 4 | 5 | 6 | 7 | 8 | 9 | 10 | 11 | 12 | 13 |

LESSON 33   WORD-LEVEL KEYSTROKING

WARMUP   Practice the following lines. *Time—2 minutes.*

Fluency	1	row when eight and roam forms dig bowl title but dish right	12
Accuracy	2	vex cage white joy like paper fun home storm bad quit zebra	24
Numbers	3	jam 1 jam 2 jam 3 jam 4 jam 5 jam 6 jam 7 jam 8 jam 9 jam 0	36
Symbols	4	ff $ ff $ ff $ ll (ll (ll (;;) ;;) ;;) ;; / ;; / ;; /	48

PRETEST   Take one 1-minute timing.

5   Sam and I hope to go on a hike in the old woods by the   12
6   lake. The trails are steep and rough. It will take us three   24
7   hours to reach the top. We will hide in the green grass and   36
8   watch the deer. We will have our lunch and start back down.   48

| 1 | 2 | 3 | 4 | 5 | 6 | 7 | 8 | 9 | 10 | 11 | 12 |

PRACTICE 1   Type lines for speed or accuracy. *Time—3 or 5 minutes.*

9   it top the Old hats back lake hours trail Quick depot grass   12
10   we car our big cool hope hike reach rough Party seven Ranch   24
11   Us Sam and one swim deer take watch start shoes night purse   36
12   go Two top her will each down Lunch clear train woods socks   48
13   Is his new eat tall hide best steep spots leave three Sarah   60

⎡00.12⎤ 12-SECOND TIMINGS

Total words typed × 5 = wpm

Take three 12-second timings on each line.

14   The old train will leave the big depot at seven each night.
15   Sarah and I will go to the party in our new shoes and hats.
16   A clear lake is one of the best spots to take a quick swim.

| 5 | 10 | 15 | 20 | 25 | 30 | 35 | 40 | 45 | 50 | 55 | 60 |

PRACTICE 2   Type for 30 seconds on each line.

17   two deer|in the car|watch my purse|hide the hat|at one time   12
18   on his ranch|three old socks|to the lake|take a quick lunch   12
19   clear night|train depot|new start|old shoes|by the top hats   12

⎡00.30⎤ 30-SECOND TIMINGS

Total words typed × 2 = wpm

Take two 30-second timings on each line.

20   The old train will leave the big depot at seven each night.   12
21   Sarah and I will go to the party in our new shoes and hats.   12
22   A clear lake is one of the best spots to take a quick swim.   12

| 1 | 2 | 3 | 4 | 5 | 6 | 7 | 8 | 9 | 10 | 11 | 12 |

POSTTEST   Repeat the Pretest.

PROGRESS CHECK TIMINGS

WARMUP

Practice the following paragraph. *Time—2 minutes.*

At one time, desktop publishing software was essential to merge text and graphics to create a professional newsletter. However, many word processing software packages available have all the requirements needed to create any type of document.

`00.00` **TIMING**

(SI = 1.47)

There is an old adage about all work and no play, and it is   13
full of truth. Certainly our work life is important to us. It   25
not only earns money for daily living, but it also carries with   38
it individual satisfaction. Too much work without some type of   51
offsetting play does not lead to a healthy existence. Recreation   64
is one of the answers to a balanced and happy life. Focusing   76
your interests on an activity outside of work can breathe fresh   89
air back into your life. Recreation can rejuvenate, refresh, and   102
challenge your mind and body.   108

Recreation can take a variety of forms just as long as it   121
differs from your daily work. It might be something passive like   134
reading or watching sports, or it can be zealous. Some examples   147
are cycling, running, and swimming. Recreation can be a solo   159
event or it can take place in a group. Whatever the setting or   172
the sort of involvement, recreation is quite central to your   184
sound mental health and good physical health. It can reap value   197
for you in all aspects of your life.   204

New technology now allows some workers the chance to work   217
with a personal computer at home. The line between professional   230
and personal time is blurred when you work at home because you   243
do not physically go to or come home from the office. The office   256
is always there. Therefore, the need for planned relaxation is   269
even more important when working at home.   277

| 1 | 2 | 3 | 4 | 5 | 6 | 7 | 8 | 9 | 10 | 11 | 12 | 13 |

LESSON 34   WORD-LEVEL KEYSTROKING

WARMUP   Practice the following lines. *Time—2 minutes.*

Fluency	1	fog goal ivory wow firm blame sir idle audit irk fish rotor	12
Accuracy	2	two done grove jar hoax miles kit quip stove cub zany frame	24
Numbers	3	vex 1 vex 2 vex 3 vex 4 vex 5 vex 6 vex 7 vex 8 vex 9 vex 0	36
Symbols	4	ff % ff % ff % kk * kk * kk * ;; \ ;; \ ;; \ ;; | ;; | ;; |	48

PRETEST   Take one 1-minute timing.

5   The party must board the ship at seven today. The ship   12
6   will leave port at eight and set sail for the warm water of   24
7   the South Seas. The group on board this ship will enjoy the   36
8   fine food for each and every meal they share on their trip.   48

| 1 | 2 | 3 | 4 | 5 | 6 | 7 | 8 | 9 | 10 | 11 | 12 |

PRACTICE 1   Type lines for speed or accuracy. *Time—3 or 5 minutes.*

9   at set ask his Must sale they party water every Quiet trees   12
10   Of for fly run ship warm trip Board shops share pools south   24
11   on and Jet win four seas fine Today group chair cabin close   36
12   in buy gum the port Each food leave study wants water Paper   48
13   Bo New car job help meal desk seven enjoy order plane party   60

⎣00.12⎦ 12-SECOND TIMINGS   Take three 12-second timings on each line.

Total words typed × 5 = wpm

14   The new desk and chair will help keep their study in order.
15   Mark and Bo like to wade in the quiet pools near the cabin.
16   He wants to fly the jet plane over the trees on their farm.

| 5 | 10 | 15 | 20 | 25 | 30 | 35 | 40 | 45 | 50 | 55 | 60 |

PRACTICE 2   Type for 30 seconds on each line.

17   he may buy it|hot wax your car|ask the|near his farm|we run   12
18   close the shops|wade in|deep water|mark my paper|win a gift   12
19   go over|their order|find the gum|study the job|to the cabin   12

⎣00.30⎦ 30-SECOND TIMINGS   Take two 30-second timings on each line.

Total words typed × 2 = wpm

20   The new desk and chair will help keep their study in order.   12
21   Mark and Bo like to wade in the quiet pools near the cabin.   12
22   He wants to fly the jet plane over the trees on their farm.   12

| 1 | 2 | 3 | 4 | 5 | 6 | 7 | 8 | 9 | 10 | 11 | 12 |

POSTTEST   Repeat the Pretest.

TIMING 11

PROGRESS CHECK TIMINGS

Practice the following paragraph. *Time—2 minutes.*

The new changes occurring in the telephone industry really are amazing. Just think: a shopper can buy a cordless or memory telephone for a few dollars. In addition, the videophone will soon impact homes and industry.

00.00 TIMING

(SI = 1.47)

When you consider the personnel, keyboarding, and research	13
time it takes to create and store business files, the loss of	25
important files can be extremely costly. It is vital that these	38
files be protected from unintentional losses.	47
The protection of vital files can be done in several ways.	60
The first way, and perhaps the quickest way, is to set up the	72
application software to create an automatic backup file. This	84
method ensures that you always have a second copy of a file.	96
The second way is to create a manual backup of the file.	108
This process requires the user to make a duplicate file of the	121
original file and save it in another location. For example, a	133
file saved on the hard disk can be saved on a floppy disk or a	146
zip disk or to a network disk.	152
A third method requires the user to make a backup of all	164
the files on the original storage medium to a second storage	176
medium. For example, a zip disk containing your important files	189
can be copied to a second zip disk. This method can be used with	202
duplicate floppy disks, hard drives, compact digital discs, and	215
magnetic tape cassettes.	220
If you are working on a networked system, you often have a	233
distinct advantage for protecting files because most network	245
systems have nightly backup routines. A backup of files saved on	258
the network disks is created automatically.	267
To be extra secure, it is wise to use more than one method	280
to backup your files. You do not want to find that important	292
data on a file has been lost when no backup exists. Be safe;	304
protect your files.	308

| 1 | 2 | 3 | 4 | 5 | 6 | 7 | 8 | 9 | 10 | 11 | 12 | 13 |

WARMUP

Practice the following lines. *Time—2 minutes.*

Fluency	1	yen duty shame tow name handy aid land field apt sock their	12
Accuracy	2	zoo work quiet vat jump flyer wax code hives yet bags never	24
Numbers	3	cob 1 cob 2 cob 3 cob 4 cob 5 cob 6 cob 7 cob 8 cob 9 cob 0	36
Symbols	4	kk < kk < kk < ll > ll > ll > ;; { ;; { ;; { ;; } ;; } ;; }	48

PRETEST

Take one 1-minute timing.

5   The yard crew will come to weed and mow the grass. The   12

6   team will prune the rose bush and edge the grass. The noise   24

7   from the mower will scare the cat. We must hide her in that   36

8   small shed in the back. One of the crew will let her loose.   48

| 1 | 2 | 3 | 4 | 5 | 6 | 7 | 8 | 9 | 10 | 11 | 12 |

PRACTICE 1

Type lines for speed or accuracy. *Time—3 or 5 minutes.*

9   to the her buy come Yard must prune small Rodeo truck shove   12

10   we and one new Weed crew Hide grass loose north store shelf   24

11   in mow Can mud lawn edge shed Noise bring arena black tires   36

12   of May let his from rose back mower ropes drove table Stand   48

13   by cat her Ban team bush your scare spurs lamps Place wagon   60

`00.12` 12-SECOND TIMINGS

Total words typed × 5 = wpm

Take three 12-second timings on each line.

14   Bring your ropes and spurs to the rodeo in the north arena.

15   Cara drove their black truck to the store to buy new tires.

16   Place the lamps on the wood table and shove the shelf back.

     5   10   15   20   25   30   35   40   45   50   55   60

PRACTICE 2

Type for 30 seconds on each line.

17   stand by|his wagon|weed the lawn|mud on tires|ban the noise   12

18   come back|drove a truck|new mower|may scare|my cat|in place   12

19   black lamps|your team|in the yard|from the north|small bush   12

`00.30` 30-SECOND TIMINGS

Total words typed × 2 = wpm

Take two 30-second timings on each line.

20   Bring your ropes and spurs to the rodeo in the north arena.   12

21   Cara drove their black truck to the store to buy new tires.   12

22   Place the lamps on the wood table and shove the shelf back.   12

| 1 | 2 | 3 | 4 | 5 | 6 | 7 | 8 | 9 | 10 | 11 | 12 |

POSTTEST

Repeat the Pretest.

PROGRESS CHECK TIMINGS

WARMUP

Practice the following paragraph. *Time—2 minutes.*

An appropriate place to study is very important. Sitting upright at a desk or table keeps you alert and in the mood to study. Distracting objects or things that might cause your mind to wander should be hidden away.

00.00 TIMING

(SI = 1.46)

The terms used by individuals who extend credit often are	13
unfamiliar to most persons. If you are not acquainted with the	26
meaning of a term, it may cost you money; or, at least, you may	39
be embarrassed. Here are some of the terms you should know.	51
When you borrow money, you receive a sum of money called	63
the principal or the amount financed. You pay interest on this	76
amount. The interest rate is the percent of interest you pay on	89
the principal. The period of time for which you borrow the money	102
is called the term. The amount that you owe, which decreases as	115
you make payments, is your outstanding balance. The total amount	128
you repay, interest and principal, is the maturity value.	140
If you are late in making your payments or if you fail to	153
make your payments regularly, you will be assessed penalties or	166
default charges. If you are often late or if you stop making	178
payments altogether, you are considered to be in default. The	190
creditor can take back, or repossess, any of the products you	202
purchased and take you to court to recover lost payments.	214
As you use credit, you establish a history called a credit	227
rating. This rating, if it is good, helps you secure more credit	240
when you need it. Protect your credit rating by making all your	253
payments on time and by paying your debts in their entirety. If	266
you get into financial trouble, ask for advice from your credit	279
counselor to minimize jeopardizing your credit rating and your	292
ability to obtain credit in the future.	300

| 1 | 2 | 3 | 4 | 5 | 6 | 7 | 8 | 9 | 10 | 11 | 12 | 13 |

WARMUP

Practice the following lines. *Time—2 minutes.*

Fluency	1	sob such goals cod keys vigor rob both theme pen melt panel	12
Accuracy	2	job evil zebra put king squab hug soap exact fed awry miles	24
Numbers	3	men 1 men 2 men 3 men 4 men 5 men 6 men 7 men 8 men 9 men 0	36
Symbols	4	ss @ ss @ ss @ jj & jj & jj & ;; = ;; = ;; = ;; + ;; + ;; +	48

PRETEST

Take one 1-minute timing.

5   The new swim team was the very best the coach had ever   12
6   been able to teach. She was very proud of this great group.   24
7   Each of these boys and girls would win many races when they   36
8   went to meets. Their new relay team would also place first.   48

| 1 | 2 | 3 | 4 | 5 | 6 | 7 | 8 | 9 | 10 | 11 | 12 |

PRACTICE 1

Type lines for speed or accuracy. *Time—3 or 5 minutes.*

9   to the Was she swim been bear coach group Meets pitch beige   12
10 of New win sit team Able blue teach these relay tells watch   24
11 at was bay led mall this drug Proud girls Teams story stars   36
12 in had buy Met best boys tent Great would place giant stamp   48
13 my she see Jim ever many Card young races first brown store   60

00.12 **12-SECOND TIMINGS**

Total words typed × 5 = wpm

Take three 12-second timings on each line.

14   We will pitch my beige tent by the bay and watch the stars.
15   Jim tells a story about a giant brown bear and a blue fish.
16   We will buy a stamp for a card at a drug store in the mall.

| 5 | 10 | 15 | 20 | 25 | 30 | 35 | 40 | 45 | 50 | 55 | 60 |

PRACTICE 2

Type for 30 seconds on each line.

17   group meets|the girls sit|watch the teams|great young bears   12
18   led many boys|able to coach|met the group|see the new place   12
19   buy a watch|best story|Jim would win|she was proud|buy many   12

00.30 **30-SECOND TIMINGS**

Total words typed × 2 = wpm

Take two 30-second timings on each line.

20   We will pitch my beige tent by the bay and watch the stars.   12
21   Jim tells a story about a giant brown bear and a blue fish.   12
22   We will buy a stamp for a card at a drug store in the mall.   12

| 1 | 2 | 3 | 4 | 5 | 6 | 7 | 8 | 9 | 10 | 11 | 12 |

POSTTEST

Repeat the Pretest.

PROGRESS CHECK TIMINGS

WARMUP

Practice the following paragraph. *Time—2 minutes.*

Revise your study time if you need to spend more time on one subject than on other subjects. If you focus better at a certain time of the day, then study your most difficult subject during that time.

00.00 TIMING

(SI = 1.46)

When communicating through electronic mail, you may choose | 13
from many options to scan incoming messages or to send outgoing | 26
messages. Some of these options are to print the messages, store | 39
them for later use, route them to other people, or erase them | 51
because they are not needed or you want to maintain privacy. | 63

After writing a message, the writer can store it quickly | 75
for later use or send it promptly. If stored, it may be saved on | 88
either a disk or the hard drive. Messages can be sent to just | 100
one individual or to many people. | 107

An electronic mail system provides users with a list of the | 120
messages to be read. Depending on the capability of the system, | 133
a recipient can examine all messages fully or skim through the | 146
list and read only those that appear to be most urgent. Once a | 159
message is read, the user can save it, delete it, print it, or | 172
route it to someone else. Wise users emphasize deleting messages | 185
that have been read; the old ones take up a lot of space. | 197

Printing makes a paper copy, often called a hard copy, of | 210
the message on a local or remote printer. A local printer is the | 223
one attached to your computer. A remote printer is one that is | 236
located away from your computer. The printed message could be | 248
filed for reviewing later. It could be destroyed when action has | 261
been taken on it or when it no longer has any worth. | 271

| 1 | 2 | 3 | 4 | 5 | 6 | 7 | 8 | 9 | 10 | 11 | 12 | 13 |

CONTENT

Research indicates that certain English words are used more often than others. This section provides practice on some of the most frequently used words.

OBJECTIVE

To improve stroking speed and accuracy by typing the most frequently used English words.

TECHNIQUE TIP

Keep elbows alongside the body in a relaxed position.

TIMING 8

PROGRESS CHECK TIMINGS

WARMUP

Practice the following paragraph. *Time—2 minutes.*

Mail merge is a tool that takes the same letter but changes names, addresses, and other specific information. Mail merge would be helpful when you are sending out your cover letters to various companies.

00.00 TIMING

(SI = 1.45)

Part of money management is the wise use of credit. While	13
saving money to buy something you want is best, often you cannot	26
wait until your savings have accrued. For example, you may need	39
a reliable car to get you to work. If you have not saved enough	52
money to purchase the car, you will need to finance it; that is,	65
you must acquire credit.	70
To get credit, you must show you justly deserve it. Those	83
who extend credit use three tests to determine if they will give	96
you credit. They look at your character, capital, and capacity.	109
Character means your personal integrity and credit history. They	122
check to see whether you pay other obligations, are honest, and	135
are reliable. The assets you own are your capital. The lender	147
may ask you to provide a personal balance sheet to confirm that	160
you have enough capital to back your credit. Capacity means your	173
earning power or having enough income to make the payments now	186
and in the future. If you meet the checks of character, capital,	199
and capacity, probably you will be given credit.	209
The steps in getting credit are simple. Visit the bank, a	222
savings and loan institution, or even a private lending firm;	234
then complete a loan application. On the form provide all the	246
data the loan officer will need to judge whether or not to give	259
you credit. If you get credit, you will be asked to sign the	271
credit contract, which establishes the terms of the credit, such	284
as the size of the loan, the total interest to be paid, monthly	297
payment amounts, the due dates, and fees for late payments.	309

| 1 | 2 | 3 | 4 | 5 | 6 | 7 | 8 | 9 | 10 | 11 | 12 | 13 |

LESSON 37   FREQUENTLY USED WORDS

WARMUP

Practice the following lines. *Time—2 minutes.*

Fluency	1	box tot sir toe worn foam them fish gland rocks angle bowls	12
Accuracy	2	bay fig elf keg aqua calm hive joke waltz blind piers waxed	24
Numbers	3	big 1 big 2 big 3 big 4 big 5 big 6 big 7 big 8 big 9 big 0	36
Symbols	4	dd # dd # dd # jj ^ jj ^ jj ^ ;; [;; [;; [;;] ;;] ;;]	48

PRETEST

Take one 1-minute timing.

5   The national dealer supported the request for training   12
6   of the school planning department. He issued the orders and   24
7   money for the original training several weeks ago. Three of   36
8   our local dealers will meet with him to plan that training.   48

| 1 | 2 | 3 | 4 | 5 | 6 | 7 | 8 | 9 | 10 | 11 | 12 |

PRACTICE 1

Type lines for speed or accuracy. *Time—3 or 5 minutes.*

9   am Ask meet Long place again dealer course percent contract   12
10   My may send hand basis Field before copies several division   24
11   of Our Take sent weeks items please having through national   36
12   he Now Will what their other issued reason without original   48
13   by the many wish Value which school second because Planning   60

`00.12` 12-SECOND TIMINGS

Total words typed × 5 = wpm

Take three 12-second timings on each line.

14   He will reply now to our national school planning division.
15   People request money and support services for the training.
16   Cash was given for local property and other items of value.

| 5 | 10 | 15 | 20 | 25 | 30 | 35 | 40 | 45 | 50 | 55 | 60 |

PRACTICE 2

Type for 30 seconds on each line.

17   for able even given order people request property questions   12
18   way back does local taken report support services therefore   12
19   new cash form money since within whether training available   12

`00.30` 30-SECOND TIMINGS

Total words typed × 2 = wpm

Take two 30-second timings on each line.

20   He will reply now to our national school planning division.   12
21   People request money and support services for the training.   12
22   Cash was given for local property and other items of value.   12

| 1 | 2 | 3 | 4 | 5 | 6 | 7 | 8 | 9 | 10 | 11 | 12 |

POSTTEST

Repeat the Pretest.

PROGRESS CHECK TIMINGS

WARMUP

Practice the following paragraph. *Time—2 minutes.*

There is an old adage about all work and no play. This adage is full of truth. Our work life is important to us. It not only provides income for everyday living, but it also carries with it much personal satisfaction.

00.00 TIMING

(SI = 1.44)

Your resume profiles your job skills, work history, school	13
record, personal interests, honors, and awards. It also gives	25
the names of people who will vouch for you. This document is an	38
essential summary that will reflect you and your experiences for	51
a prospective employer.	56
Before you write your resume, gather all the required data.	69
Acquire three or four books that show sample resumes; then study	82
the format of these resumes. Choose one design and format your	95
resume in the same way. Of course, you can change the layout to	108
fit your taste and needs before you type your resume or have it	121
prepared by a professional.	127
After you state your employment objective, describe each	139
job that you have held. Then list your most recent job first,	151
followed by the job you held prior to that, and so forth, until	164
you have given your full job history. State the position titles,	177
periods of employment, job tasks, and skills you used.	188
Give a summary of your education, including the schools you	201
attended, the diplomas or degrees you received, the grades you	214
earned, the activities you took part in, the clubs you joined,	227
the courses you took that relate to the job, plus your major and	240
minor. Firms may want to scrutinize the job skills you learned.	253
So, you will want to be sure to list any computer hardware and	266
software you have used.	271

| 1 | 2 | 3 | 4 | 5 | 6 | 7 | 8 | 9 | 10 | 11 | 12 | 13 |

WARMUP

Practice the following lines. *Time—2 minutes.*

Fluency	1	due pep spa apt land oboe keys paid vials works usury firms	12
Accuracy	2	pen bat let fur quit hold duck jobs zones misty weave exact	24
Numbers	3	fix 1 fix 2 fix 3 fix 4 fix 5 fix 6 fix 7 fix 8 fix 9 fix 0	36
Symbols	4	ff $ ff $ ff $ 11 (11 (11 (;;) ;;) ;;) ;; / ;; / ;; /	48

PRETEST

Take one 1-minute timing.

5	The recent bank inquiry about the charge account shows	12
6	no one has paid for any of the merchandise for the past two	24
7	years. This bank should continue to address its development	36
8	of a quality system to collect those general credit claims.	48

| 1 | 2 | 3 | 4 | 5 | 6 | 7 | 8 | 9 | 10 | 11 | 12 |

PRACTICE 1

Type lines for speed or accuracy. *Time—3 or 5 minutes.*

9	at and Bank hope being Large better direct between continue	12
10	If can call each about Shall number future general enclosed	24
11	in any just Fact check above annual states However material	36
12	me One must past offer Where system charge account recently	48
13	no has paid Year those claim Advise letter inquiry addition	60

`00.12` 12-SECOND TIMINGS

Total words typed × 5 = wpm

Take three 12-second timings on each line.

14	The inquiry states the annual costs for the charge account.	
15	The employees will offer the quality merchandise to my men.	
16	You must call each person for any possible future meetings.	

| 5 | 10 | 15 | 20 | 25 | 30 | 35 | 40 | 45 | 50 | 55 | 60 |

PRACTICE 2

Type for 30 seconds on each line.

17	going income various address benefits community convenience	12
18	happy little quality further possible employees development	12
19	sales matter meeting letters schedule important merchandise	12

`00.30` 30-SECOND TIMINGS

Total words typed × 2 = wpm

Take two 30-second timings on each line.

20	The inquiry states the annual costs for the charge account.	12
21	The employees will offer the quality merchandise to my men.	12
22	You must call each person for any possible future meetings.	12

| 1 | 2 | 3 | 4 | 5 | 6 | 7 | 8 | 9 | 10 | 11 | 12 |

POSTTEST

Repeat the Pretest.

PROGRESS CHECK TIMINGS

WARMUP

Practice the following paragraph. *Time—2 minutes.*

If you are going to school, it is very important that you study the subject matter of your courses. Studying is a diligent effort at learning. Learn how to study effectively, and practice good study habits.

`00.00` TIMING

(SI = 1.42)

The paperwork is done. Your application documents have been 13
presented to the correct person or office. Now you must wait for 26
a reply. This is one of the most difficult times during the job 39
search. Nonetheless, use this time well. Learn whatever you can 52
about the firm so that if you do get an interview, you will be 65
prepared to ask and to respond to questions. Talk with people 77
who work for the firm and with people who do business with the 90
firm. If the firm is a corporation, obtain a copy of the annual 103
report. Know what the company produces, find out the names of 115
the officers of the company, and then learn how the company is 128
organized. To get a general feeling of the business, visit the 141
job site. 143

Now is also a good time to look over your wardrobe. Decide 156
on the clothing you will wear to the interview. Make sure your 169
clothes are clean, pressed, and in good repair. 179

After a week or two, you may follow up with a short letter 192
that expresses your continued interest in the firm. Restate your 205
primary qualifications and that you would like an interview. A 218
telephone call may be used in place of this letter. 228

Anticipate a return telephone call or letter that grants 240
you an interview. When you receive the call or letter, you must 253
respond immediately to set the time and place for the interview. 266

| 1 | 2 | 3 | 4 | 5 | 6 | 7 | 8 | 9 | 10 | 11 | 12 | 13 |

WARMUP　　　　Practice the following lines. *Time—2 minutes.*

Fluency	1	big man cod rid both duty make melt slept forks dial burns	12
Accuracy	2	bat cot van gab quiz drum jerk help zebra wharf fixes lowly	24
Numbers	3	pay 1 pay 2 pay 3 pay 4 pay 5 pay 6 pay 7 pay 8 pay 9 pay 0	36
Symbols	4	ff % ff % ff % kk * kk * kk * ;; \ ;; \ ;; \ ;; | ;; | ;; |	48

PRETEST　　　　Take one 1-minute timing.

5　　　　　　Today the building committee of the church completed a　12
6　　purchase for office insurance. A member of the office staff　24
7　　shows the rates for protection might increase. The question　36
8　　about the price of this policy returned when the bill came.　48

| 1 | 2 | 3 | 4 | 5 | 6 | 7 | 8 | 9 | 10 | 11 | 12 |

PRACTICE 1　　　Type lines for speed or accuracy. *Time—3 or 5 minutes.*

9　　be but card feel been Needs small Church delivery committee　12
10　on Had date Give book after board cannot building education　24
11　so law keep last made great Visit family Industry insurance　36
12　we get part only show Rates might member personal Operation　48
13　us two them when than Price staff office Question reference　60

`00.12` 12-SECOND TIMINGS　　Take three 12-second timings on each line.

Total words typed × 5 = wpm

14　The staff returned a personal insurance card and date book.
15　The administration needs the total figure on every receipt.
16　Writing down that invoice price offers complete protection.

　　5　　10　　15　　20　　25　　30　　35　　40　　45　　50　　55　　60

PRACTICE 2　　　Type for 30 seconds on each line.

17　down today figure writing increase protection approximately　12
18　bill month either invoice purchase completed administration　12
19　care every policy receipt students following representative　12

`00.30` 30-SECOND TIMINGS　　Take two 30-second timings on each line.

Total words typed × 2 = wpm

20　The staff returned a personal insurance card and date book.　12
21　The administration needs the total figure on every receipt.　12
22　Writing down that invoice price offers complete protection.　12

| 1 | 2 | 3 | 4 | 5 | 6 | 7 | 8 | 9 | 10 | 11 | 12 |

POSTTEST　　　Repeat the Pretest.

PROGRESS CHECK TIMINGS

Practice the following paragraph. *Time—2 minutes.*

New technology now allows some people to work at home on a personal computer via the phone lines and a modem. Even when you are working at home, the need for some relaxation is important.

00.00 TIMING

(SI = 1.42)

The letter of application is an essential part of the job	13
application process. This letter, which should be accompanied by	26
your resume, must sell you to the firm. Write it with that plan	39
in mind, and write it so the employer feels that you can do the	52
job that has to be done.	57
Application letters are three to four paragraphs in length.	70
The first paragraph states you are applying for the job. Keep	82
your opening short. State that you are applying for a certain	94
position, giving its exact title. You need to say nothing more.	107
The middle paragraph describes your job skills and shows	119
that they match those skills the firm seeks. Specifically, tell	132
how your skills and expertise fit the job skills required; show	145
what you can do for the firm. Your letter should zero in on your	158
work background, your education, and your personal traits. Use	171
brief sentences that convey your understanding of the needs of	184
the firm and how you are best suited to meet them.	194
The last paragraph is a request for an interview. Be direct	207
and politely ask for an interview. It is a good idea to list the	220
phone number or numbers at which you can be reached during the	233
day and evening hours.	238
The application letter must be produced on a computer, word	251
processor, or typewriter. It must be free of errors, with no	263
mistakes in spelling, grammar, or punctuation. Print the letter	276
on clean paper.	279

| 1 | 2 | 3 | 4 | 5 | 6 | 7 | 8 | 9 | 10 | 11 | 12 | 13 |

WARMUP Practice the following lines. *Time—2 minutes.*

Fluency	1	dog fix dig hay torn lamb bowl lame wicks roams eight bland	12
Accuracy	2	axe cab lay jaw czar jinx drum figs hours pilot ivory quick	24
Numbers	3	sub 1 sub 2 sub 3 sub 4 sub 5 sub 6 sub 7 sub 8 sub 9 sub 0	36
Symbols	4	kk < kk < kk < 11 > 11 > 11 > ;; { ;; { ;; { ;; } ;; } ;; }	48

PRETEST Take one 1-minute timing.

5	The copy machine dealers requested the company manager	12
6	and president make public a list of customers interested in	24
7	doing business for different districts. These dealers think	36
8	the interest for orders would cover the cost of production.	48

| 1 | 2 | 3 | 4 | 5 | 6 | 7 | 8 | 9 | 10 | 11 | 12 |

PRACTICE 1 Type lines for speed or accuracy. *Time—3 or 5 minutes.*

9	as ago due Case done also books first agency Should already	12
10	do box let good four copy While right change Months believe	24
11	is day low Kind cost fill never sheet Desire public company	36
12	it set Oil name more plan cover There period orders forward	48
13	or him put page Room said Under think toward prices manager	60

`00.12` 12-SECOND TIMINGS Take three 12-second timings on each line.

Total words typed × 5 = wpm

14	I think the company should plan to make the records public.	
15	A college president requested payment covering four months.	
16	The customer probably has an interest in the copy business.	

| 5 | 10 | 15 | 20 | 25 | 30 | 35 | 40 | 45 | 50 | 55 | 60 |

PRACTICE 2 Type for 30 seconds on each line.

17	well college another business district different interested	12
18	city dealers machine interest customer requested management	12
19	real members payment covering probably president production	12

`00.30` 30-SECOND TIMINGS Take two 30-second timings on each line.

Total words typed × 2 = wpm

20	I think the company should plan to make the records public.	12
21	A college president requested payment covering four months.	12
22	The customer probably has an interest in the copy business.	12

| 1 | 2 | 3 | 4 | 5 | 6 | 7 | 8 | 9 | 10 | 11 | 12 |

POSTTEST Repeat the Pretest.

PROGRESS CHECK TIMINGS

Practice the following paragraph. *Time—2 minutes.*

As a computer user who is familiar with the Internet, you may one day wish to create your own home page. Your home page may include data about you, your schooling, and your hobbies and interests.

00.00 TIMING

(SI = 1.38)

When you prepare your resume, keep your future employer in	13
mind. List all the information your employer will find useful.	26
In addition to your work history and your education, you will	38
want to include any honors and awards you have earned. You also	51
will want to list any clubs you joined, sports you played, and	64
hobbies or interests you have.	70
A list of honors and awards shows that you have earned the	83
acclaim of others, that you have excelled in certain things, and	96
that you have worked hard. Give the name of the award or honor,	109
the date it was received, and the group that sponsored it. Your	122
list provides the employer with a record of your achievements,	135
so be sure it is exact and accurate.	142
Active work in clubs and sports shows that you are willing	155
to work with people, you can direct others, and you can follow	168
directions. These characteristics often carry over to your work	181
traits. Employers want people who can fit into their companies	194
by working with and for others. If you have special interests or	207
hobbies, be sure to list them on your resume; they might aid an	220
employer in finding the right location for you in the company.	233
A resume should be one page in length, but two pages may be	246
used if needed. Once you have finished your resume, scrutinize	259
it for errors and correct any you find. Print the final copy on	272
paper of good quality, and be sure that it is clean and neat.	284
Make extra copies for your files.	291

| 1 | 2 | 3 | 4 | 5 | 6 | 7 | 8 | 9 | 10 | 11 | 12 | 13 |

WARMUP

Practice the following lines. *Time—2 minutes.*

Fluency	1	fit fir box pal heir such dish corn focus world girls title	12
Accuracy	2	fog war zap hex baby jaws opal cats dozen valid mixed quake	24
Numbers	3	bus 1 bus 2 bus 3 bus 4 bus 5 bus 6 bus 7 bus 8 bus 9 bus 0	36
Symbols	4	ss @ ss @ ss @ jj & jj & jj & ;; = ;; = ;; = ;; + ;; + ;; +	48

PRETEST

Take one 1-minute timing.

5	The opportunity to provide five products to individual	12
6	departments of the government is certainly my pleasure. All	24
7	additional assistance required will immediately be given by	36
8	our companies. We are pleased to supply this new equipment.	48

| 1 | 2 | 3 | 4 | 5 | 6 | 7 | 8 | 9 | 10 | 11 | 12 |

PRACTICE 1

Type lines for speed or accuracy. *Time—3 or 5 minutes.*

9	all out most Ever five along Plans amount working effective	12
10	ten pay Once both Glad dated power return defense companies	24
11	was are from Area have thank Issue supply federal equipment	36
12	its not over name Know some would control pleased Certainly	48
13	own His sale rate into with forms Receive present necessary	60

`00.12` 12-SECOND TIMINGS

Total words typed × 5 = wpm

Take three 12-second timings on each line.

14	He may contact the present service companies from the area.	
15	We need additional assistance with ten individual products.	
16	The membership department required information immediately.	

| 5 | 10 | 15 | 20 | 25 | 30 | 35 | 40 | 45 | 50 | 55 | 60 |

PRACTICE 2

Type for 30 seconds on each line.

17	current pleasure required department individual immediately	12
18	provide products attached government membership information	12
19	problem shipment received assistance additional opportunity	12

`00.30` 30-SECOND TIMINGS

Total words typed × 2 = wpm

Take two 30-second timings on each line.

20	He may contact the present service companies from the area.	12
21	We need additional assistance with ten individual products.	12
22	The membership department required information immediately.	12

| 1 | 2 | 3 | 4 | 5 | 6 | 7 | 8 | 9 | 10 | 11 | 12 |

POSTTEST

Repeat the Pretest.

TIMING 3

PROGRESS CHECK TIMINGS

WARMUP

Practice the following paragraph. *Time—2 minutes.*

Recreation can take many forms as long as it is different from your daily work. Some passive activities include reading or watching television. Some very active forms include playing racquetball or gardening.

`00.00` TIMING

(SI = 1.37)

All of us need money to acquire goods and services, to save 13
and invest, to take a vacation, or to give to a worthy cause. 25
When your paycheck arrives, you notice that part of it goes for 38
taxes, part for social security, and the remainder is yours. How 51
do you manage the money you earn? The time to think about that 64
is before you get too immersed in debt and before you spend your 77
money on things you want rather than things you need. You need a 90
strategy to help you make good decisions on how and where and 102
when to spend and invest your money. 109

Money experts agree that a money plan is essential. A plan 122
allows you to establish income and spending goals. The plan 134
provides you with a gauge for measuring income and all expenses. 147
However, no plan is permanent. You will adjust your plan as you 160
progress through life and earn more money or change your style 173
of living. 175

A good plan is practical and is matched to your personal 187
values, goals, and income. You must think ahead one, five, ten, 200
and even twenty years. What do you want, or even need, over that 213
period of time? You may need to consider family goals and needs 226
such as a house, a car, medical and life insurance, and planning 239
for retirement. Of course, you must expect some emergencies and 252
include an amount for savings in your plan. 261

Money, like any other resource, must be managed. Develop an 274
organized plan now; it will help you achieve your goals in life. 287

| 1 | 2 | 3 | 4 | 5 | 6 | 7 | 8 | 9 | 10 | 11 | 12 | 13 |

SECTION 6

Horizontal/Vertical Reaches Practice

Lessons 42–51

CONTENT

The ten lessons in this section are devoted to improving your stroking on reaches that require your fingers to move sideways on the rows of the keyboard or to move from one row of keys to another.

OBJECTIVE

To improve stroking speed and accuracy on horizontal and vertical reaches.

TECHNIQUE TIP

Make quick, snappy strokes using the correct fingers.

TIMING 2

PROGRESS CHECK TIMINGS

WARMUP

Practice the following paragraph. *Time—2 minutes.*

Your voice is important to your business. Although your words are important, your tone of voice conveys the attitude of the company. Customers build an immediate image of your firm.

`00.00` TIMING

(SI = 1.30)

When you apply for a job, you may be asked to fill out a	12
job application form. The task will be easy if you have taken	24
the time to organize and prepare your resume.	33
First, read the directions. You may be asked to fill out	45
the form in your own handwriting, or you may be asked to use a	58
typewriter. If you are asked to write, check to see if you are	71
to print or to use a cursive style of writing. Be sure to form	84
clear, sharp letters and use a pen. If you use a typewriter,	96
be sure the type will be crisp and clear. Be sure to align the	109
form properly so that the copy is straight and does not print	121
over any lines.	124
The application form must be filled out in full. Examine	136
all questions and give full answers. If you need more space for	149
answers, attach a sheet with the extra data to the application	162
form. Do not omit any vital information or give poor responses.	175
If you have no response to a query or if a question does not	187
apply, insert a dash.	191
Just before you return the form, proofread your answers,	203
check the accuracy of dates, and attach any essential papers.	215
Keep the papers clean and neat with no frayed edges or eraser	227
smears. When you are sure the form is correct, sign and date it,	240
and return the form.	244

| 1 | 2 | 3 | 4 | 5 | 6 | 7 | 8 | 9 | 10 | 11 | 12 | 13 |

LESSON 42 HORIZONTAL/VERTICAL REACHES

WARMUP Practice the following lines. *Time—2 minutes.*

Fluency	1	The downtown firm got the authentic bowl for Glen and Ruby.	12
Accuracy	2	Suz quickly jumped to wax rough floors in a dark vestibule.	24
Numbers	3	run 1 run 2 run 3 run 4 run 5 run 6 run 7 run 8 run 9 run 0	36
Symbols	4	dd # dd # dd # jj ^ jj ^ jj ^ ;; [;; [;; [;;] ;;] ;;]	48

PRETEST Take one 1-minute timing.

5	Ladd shall add flags to the gala at the hall. Ask Alda	12
6	to dash for the tall glass and half the salad or the kasha.	24

| 1 | 2 | 3 | 4 | 5 | 6 | 7 | 8 | 9 | 10 | 11 | 12 |

PRACTICE 1 Type lines for speed or accuracy. *Time—3 or 5 minutes.*

All Home Row Keys	7	ash dad jag Ada fad adds glad alas dash fall flag gala Lash	12
	8	lad ask add gas Hal lags gash hall half lass Saga sash gags	24
	9	sad slag Sal had all lags dads Alda halls falls kasha flags	36
	10	gag has Dag sags slags glass slash Flash flask shall salads	48
In Reaches	11	sat fat ate flat seat aft afar Dear ark arm Hard area arena	60
Out Reaches	12	gab gap gaze gaff Tap tag tax tan tall task bag bar ban bad	72

00.30 30-SECOND OKS Take a 30-second OK timing on each line. Repeat.

SPEED: 2 errors allowed

ACCURACY: 0 errors allowed

13	a glad lad|Dag shall fall|a gag|Ada adds gas|Al has a glass	12
14	a slag falls|had cash|Hal has a flag|sad saga|Sal had salad	12
15	glass flask|all dash|a sad fad|ask a lass|tap a glass|a lad	12

| 1 | 2 | 3 | 4 | 5 | 6 | 7 | 8 | 9 | 10 | 11 | 12 |

PRACTICE 2 Type for 30 seconds on each line.

16	oh ohm coho cohort aloha alcohol mohair prohibit incoherent	12
17	how hot hold honk hour homes honor holly jodhpur toothpaste	12
18	Al Ada Ladd Dag Hal Sal Allan Fay Art Sara Gar Gay Pat John	12

01.00 1-MINUTE OKS Take one 1-minute OK timing on each line.

SPEED: 3 errors allowed

ACCURACY: 1 error allowed

19	Sad Allan has had half a salad and Hal has had all lasagna.	12
20	A glad dad shall ask the lad and lass to add a glass flask.	12

| 1 | 2 | 3 | 4 | 5 | 6 | 7 | 8 | 9 | 10 | 11 | 12 |

POSTTEST Repeat the Pretest.

TIMING 1

PROGRESS CHECK TIMINGS

Practice the following paragraph. *Time—2 minutes.*

Microchips can fit on the head of a pin. They have the amazing ability to store thousands and thousands of pieces of information called bits. These chips begin as thin slices of strong silicon.

00.00 TIMING

(SI = 1.27)

Finding a new job in the job market today requires a lot of   13
time and hard work. You must first locate a firm with a job and   26
then sell yourself to the firm to get the job. Once you are on   39
the job, you must strive to do your job well to advance or to   51
earn a wage increase.   55

Firms put want ads in newspapers in order to attract new   67
employees. Most ads tell what type of job is open, what skills   80
are required, and whom to contact. Read the ad with care to see   93
if your job skills match the skills listed in the ad. If you   105
feel you can do the job, apply to the person or office given in   118
the job ad.   120

Some firms post job openings on the bulletin boards in the   133
personnel office. Check these listings often as part of your   145
job search. When a new job is posted, read the ad to see if you   158
have the job skills the firm expects. If you qualify, ask how to   171
apply for the job.   175

Firms often send job listings to schools. The school staff   188
posts the ads and maintains files on current job openings. Many   201
schools often have an office that specializes in job placement.   214
People in the office will help you find job openings that match   227
your skills. They will help you write your resume, fill out the   240
application form, and write your letter of application.   251

Some placement offices hold special classes on skills for   264
the job search. Some companies send agents to schools to find   276
new employees. Check with your local schools to find out when   288
the agents will be in your area.   294

| 1 | 2 | 3 | 4 | 5 | 6 | 7 | 8 | 9 | 10 | 11 | 12 | 13 |

LESSON 43 HORIZONTAL/VERTICAL REACHES

PRETEST

Take one 1-minute timing.

5   Teddy sews a perfect aqua butterfly on the side of the   12

6 frilly sweater. Marge used a needle on the fragile pillows.   24

| 1 | 2 | 3 | 4 | 5 | 6 | 7 | 8 | 9 | 10 | 11 | 12 |

PRACTICE 1

Type lines for speed or accuracy. *Time—3 or 5 minutes.*

Home Row to Third Row

7 aqua Opaque swam swan swat sway swell answer sweeps Sweater   12

8 side Cadet debit under Yodel deacon mildew thunder altitude   24

9 fry free frame frost Afraid frilly fragile freckle Carefree   36

Third Row to Home Row

10 laws sews crews Views allows elbows borrows Pillows windows   48

11 bed red fed Wed aged bled edge feed owed used editor Needle   60

12 surf Dwarf curfew perfect surface Perfume tearful butterfly   72

`00.30` **30-SECOND OKS**

Take a 30-second OK timing on each line. Repeat.

SPEED: 2 errors allowed

ACCURACY: 0 errors allowed

13 owed the aged deacon|free swims|fragile pillows|used frames   12

14 tearful editor|perfect perfumes|carefree answer|swell crews   12

15 mildewy window surface|led cadets|borrows needles|few yodel   12

| 1 | 2 | 3 | 4 | 5 | 6 | 7 | 8 | 9 | 10 | 11 | 12 |

PRACTICE 2

Type for 30 seconds on each line.

16 gift left lift raft sift soft after craft fifty often swift   12

17 urge argue merge barge organ charge energy forget emergency   12

18 Edgar Frank Marge Teddy Debbie France Argentina Yellowstone   12

`01.00` **1-MINUTE OKS**

Take one 1-minute OK timing on each line.

SPEED: 3 errors allowed

ACCURACY: 1 error allowed

19 Fifty carefree cadets often swim swiftly in that aqua surf.   12

20 Debbie borrows that frilly sweater and perfume from Margie.   12

| 1 | 2 | 3 | 4 | 5 | 6 | 7 | 8 | 9 | 10 | 11 | 12 |

POSTTEST

Repeat the Pretest.

Progress Check Timings

Timings 1–35

CONTENT

The lesson materials in this *Skillbuilding* program are heavily weighted with special features to assist in developing speed and accuracy. Therefore, they are inappropriate for assessing overall keyboarding skill. The Progress Check Timings, on the other hand, provide realistic copy of normal difficulty for measuring speed and accuracy on 3- or 5-minute timings at regular intervals during the course.

OBJECTIVE

To measure overall skill development at regular intervals throughout the *Skillbuilding* course.

LESSON 44 HORIZONTAL/VERTICAL REACHES

WARMUP

Practice the following lines. *Time—2 minutes.*

Fluency	1	The rich girls laugh and cycle with vigor to the giant oak.	12
Accuracy	2	Jake may analyze car power quotas or exhibit vast findings.	24
Numbers	3	get 1 get 2 get 3 get 4 get 5 get 6 get 7 get 8 get 9 get 0	36
Symbols	4	ff % ff % ff % kk * kk * kk * ;; \ ;; \ ;; \ ;; | ;; | ;; |	48

PRETEST

Take one 1-minute timing.

5	Suzanne told anecdotes about the handcrafted lizard at	12
6	that greenhouse. She was also amazed by offbeat surfboards.	24

| 1 | 2 | 3 | 4 | 5 | 6 | 7 | 8 | 9 | 10 | 11 | 12 |

PRACTICE 1

Type lines for speed or accuracy. *Time—3 or 5 minutes.*

Home Row to First Row

7	gaze hazy Jazz amaze craze crazy topaz Azalea bazaar hazard	12
8	madcap Redcaps redcoat wildcat handcuff broadcast Handcraft	24
9	Offbeat halfback Woodcraft grandchild surfboards broadcloth	36

First Row to Home Row

10	czar Zany pizza plaza Lizard stanza wizard sizable blizzard	48
11	anecdotes Crabgrass webfoot subgroups Subfloors subfreezing	60
12	enhance Inherit manhole pinhole unhitch Downhill greenhouse	72

`00.30` 30-SECOND OKS

Take a 30-second OK timing on each line. Repeat.

SPEED: 2 errors allowed

ACCURACY: 0 errors allowed

13	wizards amazed|sizable surfboards|inherits crazy handcrafts	12
14	greenhouse azaleas|broadcast anecdotes|subfreezing blizzard	12
15	woodcraft bazaars|zany halfbacks|hazy topaz|manhole hazards	12

| 1 | 2 | 3 | 4 | 5 | 6 | 7 | 8 | 9 | 10 | 11 | 12 |

PRACTICE 2

Type for 30 seconds on each line.

16	back, dark, deck, milk, check, frock, prank, quick, remark,	12
17	banjo enjoy inject injure unjust injury conjure conjunction	12
18	Dunham Mozart Brazil Suzanne Elizabeth Manhattan Eisenhower	12

`01.00` 1-MINUTE OKS

Take one 1-minute OK timing on each line.

SPEED: 3 errors allowed

ACCURACY: 1 error allowed

19	Our grandchild inherited a sizable hazy topaz from Suzanne.	12
20	That subfreezing blizzard in Manhattan amazed a crazy czar.	12

| 1 | 2 | 3 | 4 | 5 | 6 | 7 | 8 | 9 | 10 | 11 | 12 |

POSTTEST

Repeat the Pretest.

WARMUP

Type the digits in columns. Press ENTER after the final digit of each number.

1									
425	692	904	500	374	646	630	480	856	123
250	891	275	908	432	784	303	779	581	918
608	946	236	624	373	213	404	814	117	641
159	878	208	165	229	455	275	791	396	579
936	712	578	916	504	757	893	100	603	823

PRETEST

Type the digits in columns. Press ENTER after the final digit of each number. Do not type the commas.

2					
6,241.45	4,289.84	1,128.81	9,451.90	8,949.63	6,671.83
4,525.98	7,029.02	2,036.59	7,829.00	7,143.08	1,930.36
5,140.67	6,928.12	7,545.69	3,308.62	5,072.35	4,286.37
4,389.00	8,594.78	7,091.20	2,947.36	7,165.07	4,863.05
8,756.67	7,135.15	6,003.71	1,433.67	1,849.94	5,132.25

PRACTICE 1

Complete this Practice 3 times.

Type the digits in columns. Press ENTER after the final digit of each number. Do not type the commas.

3					
4,748.78	4,352.63	7,181.93	1,718.39	4,050.60	4,326.01
5,869.47	5,263.41	8,291.72	2,819.27	1,020.33	5,089.70
6,958.49	6,352.43	8,913.73	1,389.37	7,080.90	3,790.56
4,479.57	4,153.61	9,372.81	3,927.18	4,004.40	2,581.08
5,658.79	4,162.13	8,182.91	1,828.19	5,005.50	1,670.49

PRACTICE 2

Complete this Practice 3 times.

Type the digits in columns. Press ENTER after the final digit of each number. Do not type the commas.

4					
2,608.68	6,431.86	4,178.80	7,636.04	1,751.20	5,237.05
2,071.53	6,491.37	7,714.29	5,540.96	9,975.75	1,912.31
3,112.19	7,913.04	8,562.00	5,134.00	3,075.68	9,583.40
4,389.50	4,895.42	6,083.99	1,379.04	2,629.34	3,649.72
7,182.62	7,859.80	6,347.42	8,273.51	5,248.62	5,868.69

PRACTICE 3

Complete this Practice 3 times.

Type the digits in columns. Press ENTER after the final digit of each number. Do not type the commas.

5					
4,247.63	1,568.69	6,123.08	6,552.36	4,763.20	9,832.02
9,638.45	7,501.67	7,473.56	3,121.59	6,841.84	5,142.05
4,083.95	8,289.20	7,895.45	3,687.39	8,465.39	5,871.10
7,427.31	2,009.94	1,776.11	4,801.83	2,389.76	6,006.39
2,128.45	2,357.90	4,917.00	5,390.19	5,071.24	1,684.92

POSTTEST

Repeat the Pretest.

WARMUP

Practice the following lines. *Time—2 minutes.*

Fluency	1	Ryan got the icy land and the ancient bicycle as a memento.	12
Accuracy	2	The few big extra frozen squid make the picnics very jolly.	24
Numbers	3	put 1 put 2 put 3 put 4 put 5 put 6 put 7 put 8 put 9 put 0	36
Symbols	4	kk < kk < kk < ll > ll > ll { ;; { ;; { ;; } ;; } ;; }	48

PRETEST

Take one 1-minute timing.

5 The nervous folks of Fairbanks were doubtful about the 12

6 access to brief electric service in the suburbs in January. 24

| 1 | 2 | 3 | 4 | 5 | 6 | 7 | 8 | 9 | 10 | 11 | 12 |

PRACTICE 1

Type lines for speed or accuracy. *Time—3 or 5 minutes.*

First Row to Third Row

7 dice face nice cease cedar juice Ulcer access cancel Decent 12

8 brag brat Brace brand break brief bring broom Abrupt fabric 24

9 debt doubt Obtain subtle bobtail Subteens subtitle doubtful 36

Third Row to First Row

10 deck Neck check elect piece become Collect because electric 48

11 Carve nerve harvest nervous Observe service starves survive 60

12 curb Verb derby forbid harbor Marble suburb disturb sherbet 72

[00.30] 30-SECOND OKS

SPEED: 2 errors allowed

ACCURACY: 0 errors allowed

Take a 30-second OK timing on each line. Repeat.

13 subtle service|brings juice|cancels access|nervous subteens 12

14 obtain checks|nice harvest|survive doubt|carve marble faces 12

15 doubtful subtitles|observe breaks|decent fabric|cedar decks 12

| 1 | 2 | 3 | 4 | 5 | 6 | 7 | 8 | 9 | 10 | 11 | 12 |

PRACTICE 2

Type for 30 seconds on each line.

16 nut menu numb bonus minus nurse annual minute number peanut 12

17 hatbox outbid cutback setbacks softball footballs textbooks 12

18 Brad Alice Aztec Brazil Brian Cecil Joyce January Fairbanks 12

[01.00] 1-MINUTE OKS

SPEED: 3 errors allowed

ACCURACY: 1 error allowed

Take one 1-minute OK timing on each line.

19 Joyce was disturbed by abrupt annual cutbacks in textbooks. 12

20 An ulcer setback ceased when a nice nurse canceled peanuts. 12

| 1 | 2 | 3 | 4 | 5 | 6 | 7 | 8 | 9 | 10 | 11 | 12 |

POSTTEST

Repeat the Pretest.

WARMUP

Type the digits in columns. Press ENTER after the final digit of each number.

1
426	582	673	678	811	923	308	619	523	346
130	623	597	440	593	406	517	248	789	409
550	269	373	825	491	651	172	485	396	715
789	840	487	348	907	789	549	539	401	283
925	671	152	863	529	201	106	276	362	506

PRETEST

Type the digits in columns. Press ENTER after the final digit of each number.

2
5.04	9.85	6.04	5.75	1.23	16.57	16.80	16.12
4.71	4.17	1.89	6.27	4.56	27.46	72.39	42.73
8.92	6.89	5.03	8.05	7.89	49.39	85.34	58.10
6.10	1.26	6.19	4.90	1.00	20.03	68.14	94.96
2.33	3.78	7.23	3.83	2.48	91.38	95.87	70.58

PRACTICE 1

Complete this Practice 3 times.

Type the digits in columns. Press ENTER after the final digit of each number.

3
5.78	5.12	7.29	1.83	5.05	18.72	46.81	12.68
4.97	4.31	8.18	2.72	4.00	92.01	32.59	67.79
6.79	6.13	9.27	3.81	6.10	83.39	75.76	39.58
5.87	5.21	9.19	1.73	7.09	45.70	28.30	44.01
6.97	6.31	8.38	2.82	2.03	56.46	10.94	21.50

PRACTICE 2

Complete this Practice 3 times.

Type the digits in columns. Press ENTER after the final digit of each number.

4
6.87	5.21	7.92	1.38	6.05	93.40	28.93	85.76
5.78	4.12	8.81	2.27	5.00	70.58	10.14	27.49
4.87	6.21	9.72	3.18	4.01	82.96	52.36	32.00
5.97	5.61	7.91	1.37	3.90	57.63	75.41	41.15
6.88	6.22	8.83	2.28	2.30	41.21	96.70	68.39

PRACTICE 3

Complete this Practice 3 times.

Type the digits in columns. Press ENTER after the final digit of each number.

5
5.05	5.00	8.08	8.00	2.02	37.09	79.18	47.03
4.04	4.00	7.07	7.00	1.01	20.81	22.01	83.54
6.06	6.00	9.09	9.00	3.03	59.04	56.34	16.15
5.04	4.04	8.07	7.07	2.00	60.17	57.48	92.26
2.05	5.05	9.07	8.08	3.00	20.63	39.60	70.89

POSTTEST

Repeat the Pretest.

WARMUP

Practice the following lines. *Time—2 minutes.*

Fluency	1	Nancy Burke may blame the neighbor for the sick field hand.	12
Accuracy	2	Joseph whispered quietly as Marv fixed the broken zoo cage.	24
Numbers	3	fix 1 fix 2 fix 3 fix 4 fix 5 fix 6 fix 7 fix 8 fix 9 fix 0	36
Symbols	4	ss @ ss @ ss @ jj & jj & jj & ;; = ;; = ;; = ;; + ;; + ;; +	48

PRETEST

Take one 1-minute timing.

5   A ragtag jury judged the strength of offbeat halfbacks   12

6   at a springtime jubilee for that snazzy hardcover magazine.   24

| 1 | 2 | 3 | 4 | 5 | 6 | 7 | 8 | 9 | 10 | 11 | 12 |

PRACTICE 1

Home Row to Third Row

Type lines for speed or accuracy. *Time—3 or 5 minutes.*

7   grab Gram gray ogre angry grade grass degree Regret engrave   12

8   length ragtag Pigtail lengthen Ringtail strength springtime   24

9   jugs jump judo jury just Judge juice Adjust jubilee juggler   36

Home Row to First Row

10   hazy lazy Maze razz azure dazed razor blazer Gazebo gazelle   48

11   glaze Ablaze snazzy dazzling Magazines hardcover bedclothes   60

12   madcap redcap offbeat halfback Hoofbeat puffball Surfboards   72

`00.30` 30-SECOND OKS

SPEED: 2 errors allowed

ACCURACY: 0 errors allowed

Take a 30-second OK timing on each line. Repeat.

13   juice jugs|lengthen blazers|dazzling gazelle|judo magazines   12

14   springtime grass|angry judge|dazed juggler|ragtag halfbacks   12

15   adjust grade|gray razor|hazy jury|engrave snazzy surfboards   12

| 1 | 2 | 3 | 4 | 5 | 6 | 7 | 8 | 9 | 10 | 11 | 12 |

PRACTICE 2

Type for 30 seconds on each line.

16   kit ski kick kind king skip biking huskies walking kitchens   12

17   bowl. coal. deal. earl. fuel. girl. howl. idol. nail. will.   12

18   Grey June Aztec Grace Grant Grable Greece Juneau Washington   12

`01.00` 1-MINUTE OKS

SPEED: 3 errors allowed

ACCURACY: 1 error allowed

Take one 1-minute OK timing on each line.

19   Dazzling Grace Grant just likes to judge skiing and biking.   12

20   The judge graded offbeat magazines and ragtag gray blazers.   12

| 1 | 2 | 3 | 4 | 5 | 6 | 7 | 8 | 9 | 10 | 11 | 12 |

POSTTEST

Repeat the Pretest.

WARMUP

Type the digits in columns. Press ENTER after the final digit of each number.

1	737	747	757	767	777	284	395	406	510	623
	174	468	500	932	239	107	284	392	406	917
	896	152	981	656	428	399	602	120	283	396
	578	853	894	514	405	162	239	840	951	602
	100	680	459	154	113	849	505	626	133	848

PRETEST

Type the digits in columns. Press ENTER after the final digit of each number. Do not type the commas.

2	19	2,084	3,195	4,216	5,317	642	75	8,638
	7	100	20	31	42	5,310	6,421	753
	9,864	9,753	868	975	6,094	5	8,668	9,701
	208	219	4,203	314	2,534	9,635	4,537	5,857
	796	7,709	801	231	9	40	982	60

PRACTICE 1

Complete this Practice 3 times.

Type the digits in columns. Press ENTER after the final digit of each number. Do not type the commas.

3	569	4,152	71	173	7,089	1,470	1,258	3,692
	48	6,621	822	2,918	304	3,600	914	5,081
	667	53	9,371	737	6,208	420	7,036	47
	5,748	1	73	3,719	310	8,051	925	8,630
	675	415	7,382	78	5	471	9	275

PRACTICE 2

Complete this Practice 3 times.

Type the digits in columns. Press ENTER after the final digit of each number. Do not type the commas.

4	58	536	778	1,623	20	301	8,112	7,232
	474	5,342	86	255	415	250	434	354
	49	6,521	549	161	7,066	4,370	9,653	576
	6,759	6,142	49	2	1,008	90	870	4,298
	489	614	8,765	1,453	80	2,031	109	60

PRACTICE 3

Complete this Practice 3 times.

Type the digits in columns. Press ENTER after the final digit of each number. Do not type the commas.

5	4,004	600	707	90	101	30	50	1,430
	5,050	4,044	80	7,077	20	1,011	3	209
	5,006	5,000	9,009	8,008	2,003	2,000	2,013	5,678
	400	500	700	800	200	20	479	27
	505	6,006	808	909	303	300	8,686	1

POSTTEST

Repeat the Pretest.

LESSON 47 HORIZONTAL/VERTICAL REACHES

WARMUP Practice the following lines. *Time—2 minutes.*

Fluency	1	Kay may bid for the worn mementos she got for the big firm.	12
Accuracy	2	Zoe found the six quiet cats on a swampy jungle river bank.	24
Numbers	3	sew 1 sew 2 sew 3 sew 4 sew 5 sew 6 sew 7 sew 8 sew 9 sew 0	36
Symbols	4	dd # dd # dd # jj ^ jj ^ jj ^ ;; [;; [;; [;;] ;;] ;;]	48

PRETEST Take one 1-minute timing.

5   Those postgraduates sought employment with the dynamic   12

6   symphony which played hymns on a platform in the playhouse.   24

| 1 | 2 | 3 | 4 | 5 | 6 | 7 | 8 | 9 | 10 | 11 | 12 |

PRACTICE 1 Type lines for speed or accuracy. *Time—3 or 5 minutes.*

Third Row to Home Row

7   Fitful outfits restful doubtful platform outfield Portfolio   12

8   Catgut outgoing outgrows Mortgages nightgowns postgraduates   24

9   anyhow mayhem boyhood Keyhole cubbyhole Greyhound playhouse   36

Third Row to First Row

10   cynic dynamo syntax dryness dynamic Dynasty Keynote shyness   48

11   Hymns lymph Rhyme thyme symbol sympathy symphony employment   60

12   bump drum album crumb Forum human Humid stump assume autumn   72

[00.30] 30-SECOND OKS Take a 30-second OK timing on each line. Repeat.

SPEED: 2 errors allowed
ACCURACY: 0 errors allowed

13   dynamic symbol|outgoing human|boyhood shyness|drum platform   12

14   assume mortgages|dynamo symphony|restful album|fitful cynic   12

15   autumn employment|doubtful postgraduates|outgrows playhouse   12

| 1 | 2 | 3 | 4 | 5 | 6 | 7 | 8 | 9 | 10 | 11 | 12 |

PRACTICE 2 Type for 30 seconds on each line.

16   like pike sheik spike hiking strike dislike paprika manikin   12

17   bun gun pun sun aunt dune junk lung noun rung begun account   12

18   Ike Wayne Carolyn Marilyn Olympia Raymond Brooklyn Columbia   12

[01.00] 1-MINUTE OKS Take one 1-minute OK timing on each line.

SPEED: 3 errors allowed
ACCURACY: 1 error allowed

19   Outgoing Aunt Marilyn was doubtful of employment by autumn.   12

20   Ike and Raymond dislike crumbs in their platform playhouse.   12

| 1 | 2 | 3 | 4 | 5 | 6 | 7 | 8 | 9 | 10 | 11 | 12 |

POSTTEST Repeat the Pretest.

WARMUP

Type the digits in columns. Press ENTER after the final digit of each number.

1	580	530	192	631	438	456	268	709	497	956
	923	364	367	847	651	147	904	812	267	756
	154	287	549	329	295	258	186	308	358	456
	267	149	651	874	103	329	753	651	140	411
	103	270	802	509	782	710	158	902	789	600

PRETEST

Type the digits in columns. Press ENTER after the final digit of each number. Do not type the commas.

2	5,805	4,926	3,143	4,562	6,870	4,049	9,705	7,319
	9,233	3,678	6,476	1,409	9,048	8,122	2,677	2,495
	1,542	5,493	3,291	2,581	1,863	3,083	3,584	8,346
	2,761	6,518	8,746	3,297	7,536	6,511	1,400	2,407
	1,032	8,025	5,097	7,105	1,589	9,027	7,696	8,980

PRACTICE 1

Complete this Practice 3 times.

Type the digits in columns. Press ENTER after the final digit of each number. Do not type the commas.

3	5,588	5,522	7,182	1,728	5,017	6,002	2,174	8,713
	4,477	4,411	9,372	3,927	4,230	8,030	5,662	2,694
	6,699	6,633	8,391	3,819	6,100	4,170	1,200	7,640
	5,858	5,263	7,291	2,719	9,605	7,048	8,984	8,938
	4,747	4,163	9,182	1,928	4,088	9,300	5,735	4,185

PRACTICE 2

Complete this Practice 3 times.

Type the digits in columns. Press ENTER after the final digit of each number. Do not type the commas.

4	4,769	4,163	7,182	1,728	5,061	1,230	7,532	6,061
	5,867	5,261	9,372	6,927	7,410	4,708	9,801	3,750
	4,958	4,352	7,391	3,819	8,520	9,200	4,697	2,984
	5,749	5,143	9,172	1,729	9,630	6,013	2,332	4,009
	4,477	5,361	9,911	2,287	4,900	3,402	1,095	9,821

PRACTICE 3

Complete this Practice 3 times.

Type the digits in columns. Press ENTER after the final digit of each number. Do not type the commas.

5	4,004	6,060	7,007	9,090	1,002	3,030	2,300	1,010
	5,005	4,050	8,008	7,080	2,002	1,020	4,501	2,039
	6,006	5,060	9,009	8,090	3,003	2,030	5,908	3,502
	4,040	4,005	7,070	7,008	1,010	1,005	6,020	4,880
	5,050	6,004	8,080	9,007	2,020	3,001	7,004	6,040

POSTTEST

Repeat the Pretest.

LESSON 48 HORIZONTAL/VERTICAL REACHES

Practice the following lines. *Time—2 minutes.*

Fluency	1	The six rich men may go to the giant social by the old oak.	12
Accuracy	2	Parke Wold quit boxing just before things became very hazy.	24
Numbers	3	add 1 add 2 add 3 add 4 add 5 add 6 add 7 add 8 add 9 add 0	36
Symbols	4	ff $ ff $ ff $ 11 (11 (11 (;;) ;;) ;;) ;; / ;; / ;; /	48

PRETEST

Take one 1-minute timing.

5	I must amuse myself by gazing at the muzzled mules and	12
6	the quick, crazy ebony pony from the balcony of that hotel.	24

| 1 | 2 | 3 | 4 | 5 | 6 | 7 | 8 | 9 | 10 | 11 | 12 |

PRACTICE 1

Type lines for speed or accuracy. *Time—3 or 5 minutes.*

First Row to Third Row

7	any deny Pony Ebony nylon rainy sunny anyone canyon balcony	12
8	much Mule must smug amuse mural Demure mumble murmur muzzle	24
9	myth enemy Filmy mummy creamy Myself stormy academy anatomy	36

Home Row to First Row

10	hazy Maze amaze blaze crazy graze plaza topaz Bazaar gazing	48
11	ask, back, blink, chalk, flank, Kayak, prank, Quick, shark,	60
12	all. Bail. angel. canal. decal. equal. final. Hotel. motel.	72

`00.30` 30-SECOND OKS

SPEED: 2 errors allowed

ACCURACY: 0 errors allowed

Take a 30-second OK timing on each line. Repeat.

13	sunny balcony|stormy plaza|filmy nylon|muzzle an ebony pony	12
14	anyone mumble|amuse myself|smug enemy|any mummy|hazy murals	12
15	mules graze|murmur lazily|must deny myth|any academy bazaar	12

| 1 | 2 | 3 | 4 | 5 | 6 | 7 | 8 | 9 | 10 | 11 | 12 |

PRACTICE 2

Type for 30 seconds on each line.

16	cell lace mice dance twice ulcer voice accept celery cellar	12
17	madcap redcoat wildcat hardcover offbeat halfback surfboard	12
18	Amy Tiny Tony Alice Jimmy Kenya Albany Johnny Murphy Samuel	12

`01.00` 1-MINUTE OKS

SPEED: 3 errors allowed

ACCURACY: 1 error allowed

Take one 1-minute OK timing on each line.

19	Tony Samuels uses his creamy surfboard when rainy or sunny.	12
20	Tiny is amazed by a mule and ebony pony grazing in a plaza.	12

| 1 | 2 | 3 | 4 | 5 | 6 | 7 | 8 | 9 | 10 | 11 | 12 |

POSTTEST

Repeat the Pretest.

WARMUP

Type the digits in columns. Press ENTER after the final digit of each number.

1	555	444	474	585	696	414	525	636	500	303
	444	456	474	585	696	414	525	636	400	707
	666	654	747	858	969	141	252	363	600	606
	456	655	747	858	969	141	252	363	101	808
	654	665	774	885	996	114	225	336	202	909

PRETEST

Type the digits in columns. Press ENTER after the final digit of each number.

2	580	920	154	267	103	560	364	687	149	270
	192	367	549	651	802	631	847	329	874	509
	651	295	438	103	782	310	762	541	239	805
	702	194	872	649	803	596	637	820	461	459
	790	847	239	874	136	827	130	348	295	561

PRACTICE 1

Complete this Practice 3 times.

Type the digits in columns. Press ENTER after the final digit of each number.

3	474	699	414	633	712	882	189	128	456	130
	585	489	525	423	831	729	277	317	404	680
	696	578	636	512	932	818	398	239	505	702
	477	678	411	623	813	738	279	129	606	209
	588	489	522	412	721	919	387	237	707	600

PRACTICE 2

Complete this Practice 3 times.

Type the digits in columns. Press ENTER after the final digit of each number.

4	447	525	719	721	183	388	505	600	811	673
	569	416	993	823	272	279	504	237	900	159
	584	662	872	912	391	199	780	891	359	852
	677	415	781	723	228	397	920	735	248	409
	584	634	738	911	191	279	300	203	107	700

PRACTICE 3

Complete this Practice 3 times.

Type the digits in columns. Press ENTER after the final digit of each number.

5	400	606	700	909	100	303	100	303	300	190
	500	550	800	880	200	220	200	220	220	370
	600	440	900	770	303	110	300	110	200	968
	505	660	808	990	202	330	202	330	350	540
	504	500	707	800	101	200	101	200	598	202

POSTTEST

Repeat the Pretest.

LESSON 49 HORIZONTAL/VERTICAL REACHES

WARMUP		Practice the following lines. *Time—2 minutes.*	
Fluency	1	Nancy and Diana may halt their fight for the giant antique.	12
Accuracy	2	Six black jets flew quickly in the damp nights over Zurich.	24
Numbers	3	eat 1 eat 2 eat 3 eat 4 eat 5 eat 6 eat 7 eat 8 eat 9 eat 0	36
Symbols	4	ff % ff % ff % kk * kk * kk * ;; \ ;; \ ;; \ ;; | ;; | ;; |	48

PRETEST Take one 1-minute timing.

5	Ed Oliver enjoyed the colorful bazaar at the wharf. He	12
6	sold a perfectly wonderful banjo and a sizeable old red bed.	24

```
|  1  |  2  |  3  |  4  |  5  |  6  |  7  |  8  |  9  | 10  | 11  | 12  |
```

PRACTICE 1 Type lines for speed or accuracy. *Time—3 or 5 minutes.*

First Row to Home Row	7	Zap bazaars buzzard cadenza gizzard Organza sizable bonanza	12
	8	inhales manhole manhood unhappy Unhooks inhabits Evenhanded	24
	9	banjo enjoy enjoin Inject unjust conjure injures Conjecture	36
Third Row to Home Row	10	old golf polo role sold wool wolf yolk Policy solemn Volume	48
	11	bows brews brows crows Meows allows Widows curfews swallows	60
	12	red beds Deed edit fled lied redo seed shed sled tied Needs	72

`00.30` 30-SECOND OKS

SPEED: 2 errors allowed

ACCURACY: 0 errors allowed

Take a 30-second OK timing on each line. Repeat.

13	need sleds|crows swallow|wolf fled|redo beds|solemn cadenza	12
14	enjoy banjo|unjust policy|edit volume|sold wool|widows lied	12
15	mules graze|murmur lazily|must deny myth|any academy bazaar	12

```
|  1  |  2  |  3  |  4  |  5  |  6  |  7  |  8  |  9  | 10  | 11  | 12  |
```

PRACTICE 2 Type for 30 seconds on each line.

16	armhole drumhead farmhand farmhouse customhouse warmhearted	12
17	wharf forfeit perfect airfares colorful imperfect wonderful	12
18	Ed Adolph Oliver Tarzan Toledo Benjamin Gonzales Copenhagen	12

`01.00` 1-MINUTE OKS

SPEED: 3 errors allowed

ACCURACY: 1 error allowed

Take one 1-minute OK timing on each line.

19	Old Eddie Benjamin sold perfect red wool to unhappy widows.	12
20	The wolf unjustly injured my solemn farmhand and then fled.	12

```
|  1  |  2  |  3  |  4  |  5  |  6  |  7  |  8  |  9  | 10  | 11  | 12  |
```

POSTTEST Repeat the Pretest.

Keypad Practice

Lessons 112–116

CONTENT

The five lessons in this section will help you build your skill in using the keypad on computers and calculators. In addition, the correlated software provides an introduction to the keypad and additional practice exercises.

Keypad Practice Lessons 112–116 are structured to increase your speed and improve your accuracy. Each lesson should be completed as follows:

6-week course: each lesson 3 times
9-week course: each lesson 4 times
12-week course: each lesson 5 times
18-week course: each lesson 5 times

Repeat these lessons as often as needed to develop an appropriate skill level.

OBJECTIVE

To improve speed and accuracy in using a numeric keypad.

SUPPLEMENTARY SOFTWARE EXERCISES

INTRODUCTORY LESSONS

If you are not familiar with the keypad on your computer, or if you would like to review specific keys or proper finger position, do the Introductory Lessons in the correlated software for this program. These lessons are *not* printed in this textbook.

POWER PRACTICE

After you have completed your assignments for Lessons 112–116, work on the Power Practice drills in the correlated software program. The Power Practice will help you to maintain and increase your number keypad skills. Each Power Practice is given in a set of three; your most accurate attempt will be recorded. These drills are *not* printed in this textbook.

LESSON 50 HORIZONTAL/VERTICAL REACHES

WARMUP   Practice the following lines. *Time—2 minutes.*

Fluency	1	Jay and Andy may go to the giant world title fight with me.	12
Accuracy	2	Pam felt joy while gold zircon boxes quickly rose in value.	24
Numbers	3	use 1 use 2 use 3 use 4 use 5 use 6 use 7 use 8 use 9 use 0	36
Symbols	4	kk < kk < kk < ll > ll > ll > ;; { ;; { ;; { ;; } ;; } ;; }	48

PRETEST   Take one 1-minute timing.

5   Julie served the urban barbers thrifty meatballs while   12

6   Lon was drafted to serve fresh gravy to starving lumbermen.   24

   | 1 | 2 | 3 | 4 | 5 | 6 | 7 | 8 | 9 | 10 | 11 | 12 |

PRACTICE 1   Type lines for speed or accuracy. *Time—3 or 5 minutes.*

Home Row to Third Row

7   log lot low flop lock long look lost plow Bloom clock Igloo   12

8   plaque swat Dean frost drift gravy lengthy Just skies globe   24

9   Opaque swear deal fresh thrift agree strength adjust liking   36

Third Row to First Row

10   Echo nerve orbit meatball slyness symbolic Jump pump amount   48

11   wreck marvel Barber softball cynical Payment lumber fortune   60

12   Piece starve Verb outbid spryness anymore fume trunk secund   72

[00.30] 30-SECOND OKS   Take a 30-second OK timing on each line. Repeat.

SPEED: 2 errors allowed

ACCURACY: 0 errors allowed

13   echoes anymore|cynical slyness|low payment amount|real deal   12

14   clock piece|orbit globe|thrifty meatball gravy|return plows   12

15   just look lost|wreck trunk|opaque plaque|urban barber locks   12

   | 1 | 2 | 3 | 4 | 5 | 6 | 7 | 8 | 9 | 10 | 11 | 12 |

PRACTICE 2   Type for 30 seconds on each line.

16   aqua swing code fresh draft great springtime justice unkind   12

17   because serve urban outburst lynch enjoyment alumni sum sun   12

18   Herb Juan Julie Alfred Friday Greece Jackie Barbara Francis   12

[01.00] 1-MINUTE OKS   Take one 1-minute OK timing on each line.

SPEED: 3 errors allowed

ACCURACY: 1 error allowed

19   Lengthy springtime skies bring enjoyment to Julie and Herb.   12

20   On Friday the thrifty dean served the fresh meatball gravy.   12

   | 1 | 2 | 3 | 4 | 5 | 6 | 7 | 8 | 9 | 10 | 11 | 12 |

POSTTEST   Repeat the Pretest.

WARMUP   Practice the following lines. *Time—2 minutes.*

Fluency	1	Three busy men cut the ham and turkeys for the city social.	12
Accuracy	2	Janet expelled Quincy for his vigor in wrecking my bazaars.	24
Numbers	3	Invite 58 or 60 children, 379 women, and 214 men for lunch.	36
Symbols	4	kk < kk < kk < ll > ll > ll > ;; { ;; { ;; { ;; } ;; } ;; }	48

PRETEST   Take one 1-minute timing.

5   Find these files (page 6): (1) \con.lsn, (2) \mor.lsn,   12

6   and (3) \alth.lsn; then use the commands | more and | sort.   24

| 1 | 2 | 3 | 4 | 5 | 6 | 7 | 8 | 9 | 10 | 11 | 12 |

PRACTICE   Type lines for speed or accuracy. *Time—3 or 5 minutes.*

Key Review: (

7   l9l l(l l(l (l(l(l 19(l 19(l (l (2 (3 (4 (5 (6 (7 (8 (9 (0   12

)   8   ;0; ;); ;););) ;); ;0); ;0); 1) 2) 3) 4) 5) 6) 7) 8) 9) 0)   24

\   9   ;\; ;\; ;\; \;\ ;\; ;\\; ;\\; \1 \2 \3 \4 \5 \6 \7 \8 \9 \0   36

| 10   ;\; ;|; ;|; |;| ;|; ;||; ;||; 1| 2| 3| 4| 5| 6| 7| 8| 9| 0| 48

11   if (if (if (if) if) if) if \ if \ if \ if | if | if | 60

12   (page 6) \filename | more (review table 3) \database | sort   72

`00.30` 30-SECOND OKS   Take a 30-second OK timing on each line. Repeat.

SPEED: 2 errors allowed

13   We (Ed and I) gave a party for her (Jo) at the shop (Kidz).   12

ACCURACY: 0 errors allowed

14   Find the following filenames: \alpha, \number, or \symbols.   12

15   When looking in your files, use | more, | sort, and | find.   12

| 1 | 2 | 3 | 4 | 5 | 6 | 7 | 8 | 9 | 10 | 11 | 12 |

TECHNIQUE CHECK   Type for 30 seconds on each line.

Efficient use of shift keys.

16   (1) shoes, (2) socks, and (3) shirts (a) pants and (b) hats   12

Back erect, lean forward.

17   \filename \alpha.lsn \numbers.lsn \symbols.lsn \wp51\skb\ce   12

Smooth stroking, even pace.

18   Type | more and | sort. Use | find. Type | more and | sort.   12

`01.00` 1-MINUTE OKS   Take one 1-minute OK timing on each line.

SPEED: 3 errors allowed

19   That filename \Data (our database) is now called \Databank.   12

ACCURACY: 1 error allowed

20   The pipe symbol (|) is used with | more, | sort, or | find.   12

| 1 | 2 | 3 | 4 | 5 | 6 | 7 | 8 | 9 | 10 | 11 | 12 |

POSTTEST   Repeat the Pretest.

LESSON 51 HORIZONTAL/VERTICAL REACHES

WARMUP Practice the following lines. *Time—2 minutes.*

Fluency	1	The downtown firm of Rodney and Durham may audit the widow.	12
Accuracy	2	Quin Kamp brazenly ate five or six big jars of bad cashews.	24
Numbers	3	hit 1 hit 2 hit 3 hit 4 hit 5 hit 6 hit 7 hit 8 hit 9 hit 0	36
Symbols	4	ss @ ss @ ss @ jj & jj & jj & ;; = ;; = ;; = ;; + ;; + ;; +	48

PRETEST Take one 1-minute timing.

5   That warmhearted bride gave a sizable boxwood cello to   12
6 an unhappy greenhorn who plays funny harmony at a farmyard.   24

| 1 | 2 | 3 | 4 | 5 | 6 | 7 | 8 | 9 | 10 | 11 | 12 |

PRACTICE 1 Type lines for speed or accuracy. *Time—3 or 5 minutes.*

First Row to Third Row
7 boxwood Cello chevron algebra debt avenue Penny munch foamy   12
8 waxwing cent Brass thumbtack continue funny smudges Mystery   24
9 Waxwork cement bride doubt coconut Harmony formula farmyard   36

First Row to Home Row
10 blizzard anecdote subfloor crabgrass Unhappy enjoy Drumhead   48
11 Zap wizard sizable webfoot inherit greenhorn Injury armhole   60
12 zany Pizza hazard subfreezing hobgoblin unhitch Warmhearted   72

`00.30` 30-SECOND OKS Take a 30-second OK timing on each line. Repeat.

SPEED: 2 errors allowed
ACCURACY: 0 errors allowed

13 unhappy bride|brass thumbtack|mystery smudges|enjoy harmony   12
14 funny anecdotes|blizzards continue|inherit sizable farmyard   12
15 zap a zany wizard|warmhearted greenhorn|munch coconut pizza   12

| 1 | 2 | 3 | 4 | 5 | 6 | 7 | 8 | 9 | 10 | 11 | 12 |

PRACTICE 2 Type for 30 seconds on each line.

16 center zebra subtenant aluminum botany muggy academy gloomy   12
17 influenza dumbfounded subgroup enhanced injects customhouse   12
18 Brazil Bermuda January Suzanne Benjamin Elizabeth Manhattan   12

`01.00` 1-MINUTE OKS Take one 1-minute OK timing on each line.

SPEED: 3 errors allowed
ACCURACY: 1 error allowed

19 We enjoyed the funny anecdote the bride told of her injury.   12
20 Those warmhearted greenhorns continue to cement the avenue.   12

| 1 | 2 | 3 | 4 | 5 | 6 | 7 | 8 | 9 | 10 | 11 | 12 |

POSTTEST Repeat the Pretest.

WARMUP   Practice the following lines. *Time—2 minutes.*

Fluency	1	Glen is to go to town to visit and work for the rich widow.	12
Accuracy	2	Cliff jumps high as squishy mud oozes over a new bank exit.	24
Numbers	3	Go to 8240 South 97th before 5 p.m. to meet the 613 guests.	36
Symbols	4	ff % ff % ff % kk * kk * kk * ;; \ ;; \ ;; \ ;; | ;; | ;; |	48

PRETEST   Take one 1-minute timing.

5	"She [Sally] can fix the program [Addup]. (She is from	12
6	Boise [Idaho].) Addup should read {this program will add}."	24

| 1 | 2 | 3 | 4 | 5 | 6 | 7 | 8 | 9 | 10 | 11 | 12 |

PRACTICE   Type lines for speed or accuracy. *Time—3 or 5 minutes.*

Key Review: [	7	;[; ;[; ;[; [;[;[; ;[[; ;[[; [1 [2 [3 [4 [5 [6 [7 [8 [9 [0	12
]	8	;]; ;]; ;];];] ;]; ;]]; ;]]; 1] 2] 3] 4] 5] 6] 7] 8] 9] 0]	24
{	9	;[; ;{; ;{; {;{ ;{; ;{{; ;{{; {1 {2 {3 {4 {5 {6 {7 {8 {9 {0	36
}	10	;]; ;}; ;}; };} ;}; ;}}; ;}}; 1} 2} 3} 4} 5} 6} 7} 8} 9} 0}	48
	11	if [if [if [if] if] if] if { if { if { if } if } if }	60
	12	[page 613] {read and alphabetize} [pause] {loop} [applause]	72

⏱ 00.30 30-SECOND OKS   Take a 30-second OK timing on each line. Repeat.

SPEED: 2 errors allowed

ACCURACY: 0 errors allowed

13	(She [Gail] can go to the show in Elma [Washington] today.)	12
14	"If we can, [pause] we will fix it. [Applause.] Start now."	12
15	Math expressions are written like this: {(10, 11, 12, 13)}.	12

| 1 | 2 | 3 | 4 | 5 | 6 | 7 | 8 | 9 | 10 | 11 | 12 |

TECHNIQUE CHECK   Type for 30 seconds on each line.

Feet on floor.

Space bar—thumb close.

Control hand bounce.

16	[William] [Alabama] [pause] [page 9] [Applause] [Louisiana]	12
17	{(-1, 2, 3)} {loop} {(6, 7, 8)} {This program sorts names.}	12
18	[George] {(2, 4, 6)} [Oregon] {print} [see page 3] {(6, 7)}	12

⏱ 01.00 1-MINUTE OKS   Take one 1-minute OK timing on each line.

SPEED: 3 errors allowed

ACCURACY: 1 error allowed

19	(We do not know if she [Marian] is going to Nome [Alaska].)	12
20	{This program [Plus] averages grades and sorts last names.}	12

| 1 | 2 | 3 | 4 | 5 | 6 | 7 | 8 | 9 | 10 | 11 | 12 |

POSTTEST   Repeat the Pretest.

SECTION 7

Word Family Practice

Lessons 52–56

CONTENT

This section provides practice on some of the most commonly used word beginnings and endings in the English language.

OBJECTIVE

To improve stroking speed and accuracy by typing words with common English word beginnings and endings.

TECHNIQUE TIP

Return fingers immediately to the home position.

WARMUP

Practice the following lines. *Time—2 minutes.*

Fluency	1	The tidy maid lent the six keys to the men of the fur firm.	12
Accuracy	2	A jury awarded Mona Clark prizes for exhibiting aqua vases.	24
Numbers	3	Give Al 367 letters, 89 cards, 24 memos, and 150 envelopes.	36
Symbols	4	ff $ ff $ ff $ 11 (11 (11 (;;) ;;) ;;) ;; / ;; / ;; /	48

PRETEST

Take one 1-minute timing.

5   This problem said a < > b and a < b and b > a. Knowing   12

6   that a + 1 = 24 and a + b = 53, Karla can find that b = 30.   24

| 1 | 2 | 3 | 4 | 5 | 6 | 7 | 8 | 9 | 10 | 11 | 12 |

PRACTICE

Type lines for speed or accuracy. *Time—3 or 5 minutes.*

Key Review: =   7   ;=; ;=; ;=; =;= ;=; ;=;= ;=;= =1 =2 =3 =4 =5 =6 =7 =8 =9 =0   12

+   8   ;+; ;+; ;+; +;+ ;+; ;+;+ ;+;+ +1 +2 +3 +4 +5 +6 +7 +8 +9 +0   24

<   9   k,k k<k k<k <k< k<k k,<k k,<k <1 <2 <3 <4 <5 <6 <7 <8 <9 <0   36

>   10   l.l l>l l>l >l> l>l l.>l l.>l >1 >2 >3 >4 >5 >6 >7 >8 >9 >0   48

11   if = if = if = if + if + if + if < if < if < if > if > if >   60

12   2 + 22 = 24 3 + 33 = 36 Is x + y < 7 or x + y > 17? x < > y   72

00.30 30-SECOND OKS

Take a 30-second OK timing on each line. Repeat.

SPEED: 2 errors allowed

ACCURACY: 0 errors allowed

13   Irene said 64 + 46 = 110 and 100 + 46 = 146; we all agreed.   12

14   A > means greater than, < less than, and < > means unequal.   12

15   Millie knows x + y = 10 and x > y and x < > y; maybe x = 6.   12

| 1 | 2 | 3 | 4 | 5 | 6 | 7 | 8 | 9 | 10 | 11 | 12 |

TECHNIQUE CHECK

Type for 30 seconds on each line.

Wrists low, not touching.

Arms quiet.

Proper finger position and curve.

16   Does 6 + 6 = 12? Kelsie knows 23 + 14 = 37. Can 8 + 8 = 16?   12

17   Is x > 8 and y < 20? Kay knows 9 > n and w < 8. Is x < > y?   12

18   Denise figures a < > b. Brandon said a + b = 144. Is a < b?   12

01.00 1-MINUTE OKS

Take one 1-minute OK timing on each line.

SPEED: 3 errors allowed

ACCURACY: 1 error allowed

19   Henry concluded that x < > y and x < y, then x + y = 2 + 3.   12

20   Gary wrote to explain that c + d = e and c < d and c < > d.   12

| 1 | 2 | 3 | 4 | 5 | 6 | 7 | 8 | 9 | 10 | 11 | 12 |

POSTTEST

Repeat the Pretest.

LESSON 52   WORD FAMILIES

WARMUP   Practice the following lines. *Time—2 minutes.*

Fluency	1	Toby and Maud rush to town to fix ham and turkey for Henry. 12
Accuracy	2	Gary equipped the six with affordable mauve chintz jackets. 24
Numbers	3	The address for Jo is 1249 65th Street, not 8703 15th Road. 36
Symbols	4	dd # dd # dd # jj ^ jj ^ jj ^ ;; [;; [;; [;;] ;;] ;;] 48

PRETEST   Take one 1-minute timing.

     5   Stunned Constance was on probation for misfiling her disks.   12

       | 1 | 2 | 3 | 4 | 5 | 6 | 7 | 8 | 9 | 10 | 11 | 12 |

PRACTICE 1   Type lines for speed or accuracy. *Time—3 minutes.*

Word Beginnings: con	6	con con conk condo Conch cones confer convey Connie confuse 12
dis	7	dis dis Disc dish disks disbar disuse dismay dismal Discuss 24
mis	8	mis mis mist Miser misty misdo mishap Mister misery misdeed 36
pro	9	pro pro prom prod Prop probe profit Protect promote problem 48

PRACTICE 2   Type lines for speed or accuracy. *Time—3 minutes.*

Word Endings: ing	10	ing ing ring Bring aging being acting biting Filing dialing 12
ion	11	ion ion lion onion Union Action lotion nation ration motion 24
nce	12	nce nce once dance Ounce fence bounce chance Glance absence 36
ned	13	ned ned boned fined Lined owned dined earned loaned Stunned 48

PRACTICE 3   Type for 30 seconds on each line.

Combinations	14	confusing Distance misfiling conference Probation misgiving 12
	15	disowned Mistaking Providing confusion promotion discussion 12
	16	misaligned pronounce Constance disjoined Condition mistuned 12

⏱00.30 30-SECOND OKS   Take a 30-second OK timing on each line. Repeat.

SPEED: 2 errors allowed   17   Missy loaned her condo to Bing and dined at the conference.   12

ACCURACY: 0 errors allowed   18   Connie will discuss an action which will protect the union.   12

       19   Ned was confusing the discussion about dismal prom profits.   12

       | 1 | 2 | 3 | 4 | 5 | 6 | 7 | 8 | 9 | 10 | 11 | 12 |

POSTTEST   Repeat the Pretest.

LESSON 108   SYMBOLS

WARMUP   Practice the following lines. *Time—2 minutes.*

Fluency	1	The girl paid for the ivory forks when she got to the city.	12
Accuracy	2	Zeke Bendford will quote exact prices every night to Jamie.	24
Numbers	3	Our bills totaled $4,513, $920, and $6,817 over four weeks.	36
Symbols	4	dd # dd # dd # jj ^ jj ^ jj ^ ;; [;; [;; [;;] ;;] ;;]	48

PRETEST   Take one 1-minute timing.

5	Mike did 3^9 and 10^7 before his meeting with Klemin &	12
6	Rogers Co. on 8/31 and 9/1. He also read Math & Men/Women*.	24

| 1 | 2 | 3 | 4 | 5 | 6 | 7 | 8 | 9 | 10 | 11 | 12 |

PRACTICE   Type lines for speed or accuracy. *Time—3 or 5 minutes.*

Key Review: *	7	k8k k*k k*k *k* k*k k8*k k8*k *1 *2 *3 *4 *5 *6 *7 *8 *9 *0	12
&	8	j7j j&j j&j &j& j&j j7&j j7&j &1 &2 &3 &4 &5 &6 &7 &8 &9 &0	24
^	9	j6j j^j j^j ^j^ j^j j6^j j6^j ^1 ^2 ^3 ^4 ^5 ^6 ^7 ^8 ^9 ^0	36
/	10	;/; ;/; ;/; /;/ ;/; ;/;/ ;/;/ /1 /2 /3 /4 /5 /6 /7 /8 /8 /0	48
	11	if * if * if * if & if & if & if ^ if ^ if ^ if / if / if /	60
	12	*See page 3 Smith & Jones R^2 *See Table 3 Black & Blue X^3	72

00.30 30-SECOND OKS   Take a 30-second OK timing on each line. Repeat.

SPEED: 2 errors allowed

ACCURACY: 0 errors allowed

13	The books* are listed below. *Reviewed on 1/9. *See page 4.	12
14	A & C billed him on 6/29 and 7/30. D & K billed us on 8/29.	12
15	Use ^ to raise any variable to a power: x^3 or y^r or r^15.	12

| 1 | 2 | 3 | 4 | 5 | 6 | 7 | 8 | 9 | 10 | 11 | 12 |

TECHNIQUE CHECK   Type for 30 seconds on each line.

Eyes on copy.

Control hand bounce.

Sharp, quick keystroking.

16	*Review page 7 on 8/17. *Edit the map on 9/22. *Pay by 3/3.	12
17	Jerry & Andy|March & Neff|night & day|up & down|hide & seek	12
18	Find x^2 or x^3. Use y^4 or y^5. Explain 12^12 and/or 13^3.	12

01.00 1-MINUTE OKS   Take one 1-minute OK timing on each line.

SPEED: 3 errors allowed

ACCURACY: 1 error allowed

19	B & G* and T & C* paid a May/June bill for fall/winter ads.	12
20	Students taking the BC & CD* math test on 6/29 missed 26^3.	12

| 1 | 2 | 3 | 4 | 5 | 6 | 7 | 8 | 9 | 10 | 11 | 12 |

POSTTEST   Repeat the Pretest.

WARMUP		Practice the following lines. *Time—2 minutes.*	
Fluency	1	A neighbor pays Diana to do the work so he can go downtown.	12
Accuracy	2	The next big delivery cart may stop quickly for Zack Jewel.	24
Numbers	3	Ed bought 415 lamps and 803 tables for 267 people on May 9.	36
Symbols	4	ff $ ff $ ff $ 11 (11 (11 (;;) ;;) ;;) ;; / ;; / ;; /	48

PRETEST Take one 1-minute timing.

5 Honest Tess can change those five reports on that computer. 12

| 1 | 2 | 3 | 4 | 5 | 6 | 7 | 8 | 9 | 10 | 11 | 12 |

PRACTICE 1 Type lines for speed or accuracy. *Time—3 minutes.*

Word Beginnings: cha 6 cha cha chap Chalk chain chaos chairs Chalet change chatter 12

com 7 com com come coma Comb comic common compare company Compute 24

ove 8 ove ove Over oven overt ovens overdo Overly overage oversee 36

rep 9 rep rep reps Repay reply repel repair report repeat Replied 48

PRACTICE 2 Type lines for speed or accuracy. *Time—3 minutes.*

Word Endings: ess 10 ess ess less Tess mess Jess bless chess dress access excess 12

est 11 est est Best west test Nest pest guest invest digest honest 24

ive 12 ive ive hive give Dive five live Olive strive arrive native 36

ter 13 ter ter after Alter cater cuter Peter center letter lobster 48

PRACTICE 3 Type for 30 seconds on each line.

Combinations 14 changeless Computer overactive Reporter character repossess 12

15 Oversensitive chapter compress Repulsive comforter commuter 12

16 repetitive overinvest Competitive repressive Overprotective 12

00.30 30-SECOND OKS Take a 30-second OK timing on each line. Repeat.

SPEED: 2 errors allowed 17 Bess will arrive after five and strive to repair her chair. 12

ACCURACY: 0 errors allowed 18 Tess invested in olives after Peter replied to the company. 12

19 Ester and her comic guest will oversee the native lobsters. 12

| 1 | 2 | 3 | 4 | 5 | 6 | 7 | 8 | 9 | 10 | 11 | 12 |

POSTTEST Repeat the Pretest.

WARMUP   Practice the following lines. *Time—2 minutes.*

Fluency	1	She may wish to make a pale gown for the big formal social.	12
Accuracy	2	Excited parrots quiver as fighting jackals watch my zebras.	24
Numbers	3	My payroll is $8,745 for 30 days for 62 folks in 19 states.	36
Symbols	4	ss @ ss @ ss @ jj & jj & jj & ;; = ;; = ;; = ;; + ;; + ;; +	48

PRETEST   Take one 1-minute timing.

5   The 25% increase in 20# paper means an increase of $10   12

6   per ream. Please order color #4738 @ $220 a box for Debbie.   24

| 1 | 2 | 3 | 4 | 5 | 6 | 7 | 8 | 9 | 10 | 11 | 12 |

PRACTICE   Type lines for speed or accuracy. *Time—3 or 5 minutes.*

Key Review: @	7	s2s s@s s@s @s@ s@s s2@s s2@s @1 @2 @3 @4 @5 @6 @7 @8 @9 @0	12
#	8	d3d d#d d#d #d# d#d d3#d d3#d #1 #2 #3 #4 #5 #6 #7 #8 #9 #0	24
$	9	f4f f$f f$f f f$f f4$f f4$f $1 $2 $3 $4 $5 $6 $7 $8 $9 $0	36
%	10	f5f f%f f%f %f% f%f f5%f f5%f 1% 2% 3% 4% 5% 6% 7% 8% 9% 0%	48
	11	if @ if @ if @ if # if # if # if $ if $ if $ if % if % if %	60
	12	use #3 for $4 at 5% @ $2 use $4 for $5 at 33% @ $22 @ # $ %	72

⏱ 00.30 30-SECOND OKS   Take a 30-second OK timing on each line. Repeat.

SPEED: 2 errors allowed   13 She bought 2 boxes @ $22, 3 boxes @ $33, and 4 boxes @ $44. 12

ACCURACY: 0 errors allowed 14 Buy 26# of #2 potatoes and 32# of #3 potatoes or #1 onions. 12

                 15 David bought 25%, sold 18%, gained 32%, and lost 24% today. 12

| 1 | 2 | 3 | 4 | 5 | 6 | 7 | 8 | 9 | 10 | 11 | 12 |

TECHNIQUE CHECK   Type for 30 seconds on each line.

Arms quiet.   16 buy @ $2|bid @ $3|pay @ $4|sell @ $5|lose @ $6|invest @ $78 12

Smooth stroking, even pace. 17 #3 clips|#1 goal|#10 envelope|lost 129#|a 39# gain|7# steak 12

Proper finger position and curve. 18 buy 45%|get 123%|lose 78%|gains 76%|spends 32%|demands 100% 12

⏱ 01.00 1-MINUTE OKS   Take one 1-minute OK timing on each line.

SPEED: 3 errors allowed   19 Send Jon to get 35% more or 36# of #3 sweet potatoes @ $25. 12

ACCURACY: 1 error allowed 20 Our lands increased 24%, and we bought 236# of seed @ $989. 12

| 1 | 2 | 3 | 4 | 5 | 6 | 7 | 8 | 9 | 10 | 11 | 12 |

POSTTEST   Repeat the Pretest.

WARMUP

Practice the following lines. *Time—2 minutes.*

Fluency	1	Lena paid the big city firm to make an authentic ivory dog.	12
Accuracy	2	Maxine and Jenny Becks quickly dived for huge topaz jewels.	24
Numbers	3	Al changed 830 locks in 476 rooms in 125 hotels in 9 towns.	36
Symbols	4	ff % ff % ff % kk * kk * kk * ;; \ ;; \ ;; \ ;; | ;; | ;; |	48

PRETEST

Take one 1-minute timing.

5   Recently our anxious parents intended to press for answers.   12

| 1 | 2 | 3 | 4 | 5 | 6 | 7 | 8 | 9 | 10 | 11 | 12 |

PRACTICE 1

Type lines for speed or accuracy. *Time—3 minutes.*

Word Beginnings: int	6	int int into Intend intact intent intense Interim integrity	12
par	7	par par Part park pare parka Paris parades parents paradise	24
pre	8	pre pre prey Prep preen press prefer preach pretty Previews	36
rec	9	rec rec Recap recur recess recall Receipt recently reckless	48

PRACTICE 2

Type lines for speed or accuracy. *Time—3 minutes.*

Word Endings: ble	10	ble ble able Liable bubble capable affable Crumble bearable	12
ers	11	ers ers Peers asters alters Answers banners bankers boaters	24
ous	12	ous ous pious famous Joyous anxious jealous Curious furious	36
ted	13	ted ted dated Opted hated rated Basted lifted quoted wanted	48

PRACTICE 3

Type for 30 seconds on each line.

Combinations	14	interested Pardonable preamble Recorders intimidated parted	12
	15	prefabricated Receivable intravenous parameters Interlopers	12
	16	recited Precious preferable Recyclable prefers intelligible	12

`00.30` 30-SECOND OKS

Take a 30-second OK timing on each line. Repeat.

SPEED: 2 errors allowed

ACCURACY: 0 errors allowed

17   Affable boaters recalled those banners in the pretty parks.   12

18   A reckless press quoted curious bankers and famous parents.   12

19   Ted recited the precious preamble to many interested peers.   12

| 1 | 2 | 3 | 4 | 5 | 6 | 7 | 8 | 9 | 10 | 11 | 12 |

POSTTEST

Repeat the Pretest.

Symbol Practice

Lessons 107–111

CONTENT

The five lessons in this section provide practice on all the symbols on computer keyboards.

OBJECTIVE

To improve stroking speed and accuracy on the symbol keys.

TECHNIQUE TIP

Keep feet apart and flat on the floor.

WARMUP		Practice the following lines. *Time—2 minutes.*	
Fluency	1	Jay and Dick may fix their ivory chair by the sixth of May.	12
Accuracy	2	Jameson fixed unique carvings on the lovely parkway gazebo.	24
Numbers	3	Joe counted 765 flies, 340 bees, and 129 spiders on June 8.	36
Symbols	4	kk < kk < kk < 11 > 11 > 11 > ;; { ;; { ;; { ;; } ;; } ;; }	48

PRETEST

Take one 1-minute timing.

5   Ford should create quality tiled subways in cities in Peru.   12

| 1 | 2 | 3 | 4 | 5 | 6 | 7 | 8 | 9 | 10 | 11 | 12 |

PRACTICE 1

Type lines for speed or accuracy. *Time—3 minutes.*

Word Beginnings: for   6   for for fore fork form Ford forty forum Force forbid forget   12

imp   7   imp imp Imply impart impose impact impend impedes Impartial   24

per   8   per per pert perk Peru perch period Perform percent perfect   36

sub   9   sub sub subdue Submit suburb subtle Subway submits subjects   48

PRACTICE 2

Type lines for speed or accuracy. *Time—3 minutes.*

Word Endings: ate   10   ate ate Kate date gate fate state plate crate Create donate   12

ies   11   ies ies dies lies Pies ties cries flies Tries babies cities   24

ity   12   ity ity city pity Unity cavity entity sanity quality Vanity   36

led   13   led led bled fled sled tiled filed Oiled piled Ruled cycled   48

PRACTICE 3

Type for 30 seconds on each line.

Combinations   14   fortunate implies Personality sublimate formulate Implicate   12

15   perjuries Subsidies forties perforate subtitled Forestalled   12

16   impurities Forgeries impersonate permeate sublimity Periled   12

`00.30` 30-SECOND OKS

Take a 30-second OK timing on each line. Repeat.

SPEED: 2 errors allowed

17   Kate imposed a forty percent tax on the city subway system.   12

ACCURACY: 0 errors allowed

18   This state will formally donate quality pies to the cities.   12

19   That forum submitted forty perfect forgeries to this state.   12

| 1 | 2 | 3 | 4 | 5 | 6 | 7 | 8 | 9 | 10 | 11 | 12 |

POSTTEST

Repeat the Pretest.

LESSON 106 NUMBER PRACTICE—THE 0 KEY

PRETEST Take one 1-minute timing.

Do not use the capital letter O for the number 0 (zero).

5 I golfed 100 rounds scoring less than 100 a game while   12
6 playing with 10 pros for 10 hours or 10 rounds on April 10.   24

| 1 | 2 | 3 | 4 | 5 | 6 | 7 | 8 | 9 | 10 | 11 | 12 |

PRACTICE Type lines for speed or accuracy. *Time—3 or 5 minutes.*

Key Review: 0

7 ;;; ;p; ;;; ;p; ;0; ;0; ;p; ;;; ;0; ;0; ;00 ;00 ;0; 0;0 0;0   12
8 ;p;p ;pp; ;p0; ;p0; ;00; ;00; ;p;p ;p0; ;p0; ;00; ;00; ;0;0   24
9 0 sat 0 match 0 acres 10 hours 10 tails 100 jokes 100 rakes   36
10 0 sue 0 moths 0 agree 10 horns 10 teeth 100 jerks 100 reefs   48
11 ;;; ;p; ;0; ;00 ;00 ;pp; ;00; ;00; ;0;0 ;0;0 0;0; 0;0; 00;0   60
12 I walked 100 miles in 10 days while Kyle ran only 10 miles.   72

⏱ 00.30 30-SECOND OKS Take a 30-second OK timing on each line. Repeat.

SPEED: 2 errors allowed

ACCURACY: 0 errors allowed

13 I took 20 girls to see 405 birds and 360 snakes in 10 zoos.   12
14 Robin moved 690 loads 870 miles in 50 days to 210 counties.   12
15 He sailed on 10 seas on 690 boats for 704 days with 80 men.   12

| 1 | 2 | 3 | 4 | 5 | 6 | 7 | 8 | 9 | 10 | 11 | 12 |

TECHNIQUE CHECK Type for 30 seconds on each line.

Feet on floor.

Eyes on copy.

Arms quiet.

16 0 run|10 classic cars|100 more cups|10 events|10 need forks   12
17 10 row boats|30 ride trains|405 buy tickets|920 own|10 swim   12
18 902 sew gowns|360 lift weights|580 bake beans|701 have mats   12

⏱ 01.00 1-MINUTE OKS Take one 1-minute OK timing on each line.

SPEED: 3 errors allowed

ACCURACY: 1 error allowed

19 Al buys 100 bushes and 100 trees to plant in 10 fine yards.   12
20 The 10 skiers go 100 miles in 10 days staying in 10 cabins.   12

| 1 | 2 | 3 | 4 | 5 | 6 | 7 | 8 | 9 | 10 | 11 | 12 |

POSTTEST Repeat the Pretest.

WARMUP

Practice the following lines. *Time—2 minutes.*

Fluency	1	Bob and Henry make a big profit when they work by the lake.	12
Accuracy	2	Gus will quickly drive the bronze jeep back from the annex.	24
Numbers	3	We drove 8,259 miles to 147 cities on our trip of 360 days.	36
Symbols	4	ss @ ss @ ss @ jj & jj & jj & ;; = ;; = ;; = ;; + ;; + ;; +	48

PRETEST

Take one 1-minute timing.

5	Red Kelly insists on train reservations for a staid client.	12

| 1 | 2 | 3 | 4 | 5 | 6 | 7 | 8 | 9 | 10 | 11 | 12 |

PRACTICE 1

Type lines for speed or accuracy. *Time—3 minutes.*

Word Beginnings: ins	6	ins ins Inset insert Insect insane inside inspects inspired	12
res	7	res res rest Reset resin resent Reside rescue resort result	24
sta	8	sta sta stab stag Star stay staff stamp staid Stages states	36
tra	9	tra tra Trap tray trace trash Track trains tractor trailers	48

PRACTICE 2

Type lines for speed or accuracy. *Time—3 minutes.*

Word Endings: ent	10	ent ent bent tent lent Cent agent event Spent absent client	12
lly	11	lly lly jolly Kelly silly Sally chilly frilly really wholly	24
ons	12	ons ons dons Sons tons cons Irons lions moons aprons melons	36
red	13	red red bred Fred bored cared fired cured Hired shred tired	48

PRACTICE 3

Type for 30 seconds on each line.

Combinations	14	inspired resistant statement Traditions insertions Stations	12
	15	Restfully stallions Transparent insolvent staggered insured	12
	16	transpired reservations Insistent restored stammered Resent	12

00.30 30-SECOND OKS

Take a 30-second OK timing on each line. Repeat.

SPEED: 2 errors allowed

ACCURACY: 0 errors allowed

17	Fred and Sons fired Kelly who inspected trains or tractors.	12
18	Sally was tired and chilly when she hired the staff agents.	12
19	Star inspired the recent rescue from the lions at a resort.	12

| 1 | 2 | 3 | 4 | 5 | 6 | 7 | 8 | 9 | 10 | 11 | 12 |

POSTTEST

Repeat the Pretest.

LESSON 105   NUMBER PRACTICE—THE 9 KEY

WARMUP

Practice the following lines. *Time—2 minutes.*

Fluency	1	Alan may risk a fight with the panel to aid the city audit.	12
Accuracy	2	Shawn examined five large zippers to baste for Queen Jacky.	24
Numbers	3	Plant 9,876 fir, 3,402 pine, and 15 yew trees in my forest.	36
Symbols	4	ff % ff % ff % kk * kk * kk * ;; \ ;; \ ;; \ ;;	;;	;;		48

PRETEST

Take one 1-minute timing.

5   The 99 ministers married 999 couples from 99 cities in   12

6 9 months and 9 weeks using 99 wedding chapels since June 9.   24

| 1 | 2 | 3 | 4 | 5 | 6 | 7 | 8 | 9 | 10 | 11 | 12 |

PRACTICE

Type lines for speed or accuracy. *Time—3 or 5 minutes.*

Key Review: 9

7 lll lol lll lol l9l l9l lol lll l9l l9l l99 l99 l9l 9l9 9l9   12

8 lolo lool lo9l lo9l l99l l99l lolo lo9l lo9l l99l l99l l9l9   24

9 9 old 9 gates 9 odors 99 forms 99 piers 999 drugs 999 nails   36

10 9 ivy 9 goats 9 ovals 99 firms 99 piles 999 dolls 999 notes   48

11 lll lol l9l l99 l99 lool l99l l99l l9l9 l9l9 9l9l 9l9l 99l9   60

12 He picked 999 nuts from 9 trees of 9 different types May 9.   72

00.30 30-SECOND OKS

Take a 30-second OK timing on each line. Repeat.

SPEED: 2 errors allowed

13 Watch 913 kites in 29 shapes and 94 colors soar on March 9.   12

ACCURACY: 0 errors allowed

14 She played 859 games with 196 folks in 79 hours for 9 wins.   12

15 Ed returned 489 items over 96 hours to 19 stores for 9 men.   12

| 1 | 2 | 3 | 4 | 5 | 6 | 7 | 8 | 9 | 10 | 11 | 12 |

TECHNIQUE CHECK

Type for 30 seconds on each line.

Proper finger position and curve.

16 99 play ball|999 had tickets|99 cry aloud|9 busy days|9 sew   12

Back erect, lean forward.

17 967 fresh eggs|892 are used|95 seek help|913 run|49 go back   12

Proper position at machine.

18 957 mailed cards|912 wear red|394 can skate|968 are nervous   12

01.00 1-MINUTE OKS

Take one 1-minute OK timing on each line.

SPEED: 3 errors allowed

19 Bruce scored 99 points in 9 plays and 99 yards on August 9.   12

ACCURACY: 1 error allowed

20 Transport 999 tons to 99 markets in 99 cities and 9 states.   12

| 1 | 2 | 3 | 4 | 5 | 6 | 7 | 8 | 9 | 10 | 11 | 12 |

POSTTEST

Repeat the Pretest.

Concentration Practice

Lessons 57–66

CONTENT

The ten lessons in Concentration Practice are divided into two sets of five lessons.

Lessons 57–61: Accuracy is the primary goal of these first five concentration lessons, which focus on some commonly transposed letters.

Lessons 62–66: Accuracy also is the primary goal of these additional five lessons, which focus on such problem areas as transposition on adjacent-key reaches, opposite-finger reaches, and vertical-key reaches. To achieve the maximum benefit from the second set of concentration lessons, you should do one or more other skillbuilding sections *before* you do Lessons 62 through 66.

OBJECTIVE

To improve stroking accuracy by working to eliminate transposition and other errors that result from the lack of concentration.

TECHNIQUE TIP

Keep forearms horizontal to the keyboard.

LESSON 104 NUMBER PRACTICE—THE 8 KEY

WARMUP

Practice the following lines. *Time—2 minutes.*

Fluency	1	Six of the eight firms make a profit if they work with Tod.	12
Accuracy	2	The lively squads rejected few examples for keeping zebras.	24
Numbers	3	We need 208 pencils, 49 staplers, 163 desks, and 57 rulers.	36
Symbols	4	ff $ ff $ ff $ 11 (11 (11 (;;) ;;) ;;) ;; / ;; / ;; /	48

PRETEST

Take one 1-minute timing.

5	Hal cleaned 888 rooms in 88 hours for 8 bosses while I	12
6	painted 888 doors and 88 windows in 88 mansions in 8 weeks.	24

| 1 | 2 | 3 | 4 | 5 | 6 | 7 | 8 | 9 | 10 | 11 | 12 |

PRACTICE

Type lines for speed or accuracy. *Time—3 or 5 minutes.*

Key Review: 8

7	kkk kik kkk kik k8k k8k kik kkk k8k k8k k88 k88 k8k 8k8 8k8	12
8	kiki kiik ki8k ki8k k88k k88k kiki ki8k ki8k k88k k88k k8k8	24
9	8 kin 8 bowls 8 lumps 88 veils 88 coats 888 units 888 zeros	36
10	8 kid 8 bales 8 locks 88 vases 88 crops 888 unite 888 zones	48
11	kkk kik k8k k88 k88 kiik k88k k88k k8k8 k8k8 8k8k 8k8k 88k8	60
12	Mark ran 88 miles in 8 days and biked 888 miles in 88 days.	72

`00.30` **30-SECOND OKS**

Take a 30-second OK timing on each line. Repeat.

SPEED: 2 errors allowed

ACCURACY: 0 errors allowed

13	We saw 768 sites and did 584 digs for 328 items in 18 days.	12
14	They sewed 78 dresses and fixed 658 hems for 182 customers.	12
15	Rob dove 873 times in 186 bays and 284 coves for 583 items.	12

| 1 | 2 | 3 | 4 | 5 | 6 | 7 | 8 | 9 | 10 | 11 | 12 |

TECHNIQUE CHECK

Type for 30 seconds on each line.

Arms quiet.

Feet on floor.

Sharp, quick keystroking.

16	88 cut hay|888 sold cans|88 see mice|888 call homes|8 laugh	12
17	812 stamp cards|368 went in|784 want jobs|851 eat doughnuts	12
18	168 green bushes|814 extra rooms|852 red vans|837 yew trees	12

`01.00` **1-MINUTE OKS**

Take one 1-minute OK timing on each line.

SPEED: 3 errors allowed

ACCURACY: 1 error allowed

19	On June 8 we hired 88 people to work 888 hours on 88 tasks.	12
20	Send 888 packs to 8 clubs for 88 talks on May 8 and June 8.	12

| 1 | 2 | 3 | 4 | 5 | 6 | 7 | 8 | 9 | 10 | 11 | 12 |

POSTTEST

Repeat the Pretest.

WARMUP   Practice the following lines. *Time—2 minutes.*

Fluency	1	Bob Glen may make a tidy profit for eighty bushels of corn.	12
Accuracy	2	Big Vic Knox zealously performs jury duty with quiet class.	24
Numbers	3	Make 8,120 cookies, 375 pies, and 469 cakes for their fair.	36
Symbols	4	dd # dd # dd # jj ^ jj ^ jj ^ ;; [;; [;; [;;] ;;] ;;]	48

PRETEST   Take one 1-minute timing.

5	The adroit pilot from Detroit will rejoin the choir in	12
6	Illinois. She will appoint the national radio choir and the	24
7	junior and senior trios prior to going to Ohio for Antonio.	36

| 1 | 2 | 3 | 4 | 5 | 6 | 7 | 8 | 9 | 10 | 11 | 12 |

PRACTICE   Type lines for speed or accuracy. *Time—3 or 5 minutes.*

Transposition Problems: io

8	lion Ohio riot Audio patio prior union junior lotion period	12
9	Dion trio axiom curio folio Onion radio ratio senior vision	24
10	silo bingo bison Minor piano pilot pivot video widow Wilson	36

oi

11	oil coil coin avoid Boils broil choir doily spoils Illinois	48
12	oink soil void doing going point poise Voice rejoin Detroit	60
13	colic comic Louis movie robin solid toxic boxing Continuous	72

00.12 12-SECOND OKS   Take four 12-second timings on each line.

SPEED: 1 error allowed

ACCURACY: 0 errors allowed

14	action anxious curios devious envious folios furious fusion	
15	adjoin adroit anoint appoint boil boiler boiling boisterous	

| 5 | 10 | 15 | 20 | 25 | 30 | 35 | 40 | 45 | 50 | 55 | 60 |

TECHNIQUE CHECK   Type for 30 seconds on each line.

Eyes on copy.

Eyes don't travel ahead.

Strict attention to copy.

16	optional invoiced accordion hydrofoil dedication noisemaker	12
17	appoints national loitering battalion moisturize elevations	12
18	ambition poisoned captioned ointments federation reservoirs	12

00.30 30-SECOND OKS   Take two 30-second OK timings on each line.

SPEED: 2 errors allowed

ACCURACY: 0 errors allowed

19	My expensive gray hats were covered by fake topaz jonquils.	12
20	Dex hopes to solve jigsaw puzzles more quickly in bifocals.	12
21	Zim peddled unswervingly to buy the antique onyx jackknife.	12

| 1 | 2 | 3 | 4 | 5 | 6 | 7 | 8 | 9 | 10 | 11 | 12 |

POSTTEST   Repeat the Pretest.

WARMUP

Practice the following lines. *Time—2 minutes.*

Fluency	1	The theme for the eighth visit is a big problem for Laurie.	12
Accuracy	2	Bo realized very quickly that jumping was excellent for us.	24
Numbers	3	A man ordered 94 roses, 78 ferns, 126 irises, and 503 mums.	36
Symbols	4	dd # dd # dd # jj ^ jj ^ jj ^ ;; [;; [;; [;;] ;;] ;;]	48

PRETEST

Take one 1-minute timing.

5	Max shopped for 77 days to find 77 items to give to my	12
6	7 fine children for their 7 different birthdays in 7 weeks.	24

| 1 | 2 | 3 | 4 | 5 | 6 | 7 | 8 | 9 | 10 | 11 | 12 |

PRACTICE

Type lines for speed or accuracy. *Time—3 or 5 minutes.*

Key Review: 7

7	jjj juj jjj juj j7j j7j juj jjj j7j j7j j77 j77 j7j 7j7 7j7	12
8	juju juuj ju7j ju7j j77j j77j juju ju7j ju7j j77j j77j j7j7	24
9	7 nap 7 eaves 7 meals 77 homes 77 walks 777 jeers 777 quips	36
10	7 nod 7 elves 7 mists 77 holes 77 weeks 777 jowls 777 query	48
11	jjj juj j7j j77 j77 juuj j77j j77j j7j7 j7j7 7j7j 7j7j 77j7	60
12	The 777 folks drove 777 miles to 77 cities every 77 months.	72

`00.30` 30-SECOND OKS

SPEED: 2 errors allowed

ACCURACY: 0 errors allowed

Take a 30-second OK timing on each line. Repeat.

13	The 76 men lifted 127 trunks and 347 boxes left by 57 boys.	12
14	The 67 women ran 175 days in 273 cities before 47 got sick.	12
15	She bought 712 cows and 347 pigs for 576 farmers on June 7.	12

| 1 | 2 | 3 | 4 | 5 | 6 | 7 | 8 | 9 | 10 | 11 | 12 |

TECHNIQUE CHECK

Smooth stroking, even pace.

Proper finger position and curve.

Space bar—thumb close.

Type for 30 seconds on each line.

16	77 ate meat|7 waited|777 like ham|77 lovely homes|777 pints	12
17	726 cars crashed|174 ate soup|374 sang|725 red tags|7 items	12
18	76 more days|71 happy times|73 baked bread|247 may go|7 run	12

`01.00` 1-MINUTE OKS

SPEED: 3 errors allowed

ACCURACY: 1 error allowed

Take one 1-minute OK timing on each line.

19	A computer ran 777 disks in 77 hours doing 777 jobs for 77.	12
20	You all worked 77 hours on May 7 moving 777 feet of gravel.	12

| 1 | 2 | 3 | 4 | 5 | 6 | 7 | 8 | 9 | 10 | 11 | 12 |

POSTTEST

Repeat the Pretest.

WARMUP   Practice the following lines. *Time—2 minutes.*

Fluency	1	A neighbor may wish to rid the land of eighty dismal signs.	12
Accuracy	2	Holly Pike was fixing my unique adjectives and crazy verbs.	24
Numbers	3	Please ask for 1,356 coats, 7,248 scarves, and 90 new hats.	36
Symbols	4	ff $ ff $ ff $ 11 (11 (11 (;;) ;;) ;;) ;; / ;; / ;; /	48

PRETEST   Take one 1-minute timing.

5	Sara asked Susan about the decrease in necessary sales	12
6	for Texas and Asia. Susan said a resale for fast cash might	24
7	please the harassed cashiers and boost their sad cash flow.	36

| 1 | 2 | 3 | 4 | 5 | 6 | 7 | 8 | 9 | 10 | 11 | 12 |

PRACTICE   Type lines for speed or accuracy. *Time—3 or 5 minutes.*

Transposition Problems: as

	8	ask ash Asia easy fast gash hash areas ideas Please reasons	12
	9	base bask bass cash cast dash Lash erase sofas Texas assets	24
	10	also Bars bays cabs days ears false harsh lapse Marsh raise	36
sa	11	sag sap same sane sash saws essay satin Susan resale Unsaid	48
	12	sad sap sat saw say Mesa Sara salad sales saint saves usage	60
	13	spa Scan seas slab shave small scalps stairs ashtray Asthma	72

00.12 12-SECOND OKS   Take four 12-second timings on each line.

SPEED: 1 error allowed

ACCURACY: 0 errors allowed

14	biased blasts boasts brash brass chased chasm clasp clashed	
15	sabers sables sachets sacked sacred saddens saddest saintly	

     5   10   15   20   25   30   35   40   45   50   55   60

TECHNIQUE CHECK   Type for 30 seconds on each line.

Eyes on copy.

Eyes don't travel ahead.

Strict attention to copy.

16	cashiers nuisance abrasions lifesaver elasticize impassable	12
17	disabled decrease necessary databases passageway ballerinas	12
18	harassed glossary caseloads rehearsal flashlight sabbatical	12

00.30 30-SECOND OKS   Take two 30-second OK timings on each line.

SPEED: 2 errors allowed

ACCURACY: 0 errors allowed

19	The moving Phoenix lawyers quickly briefed frenzied jurors.	12
20	Squire VanDyck was too lazy to pay his men for taxing jobs.	12
21	Verdant July mornings were vibrant except for a quick haze.	12

| 1 | 2 | 3 | 4 | 5 | 6 | 7 | 8 | 9 | 10 | 11 | 12 |

POSTTEST   Repeat the Pretest.

WARMUP

Practice the following lines. *Time—2 minutes.*

Fluency	1	The giant firm may wish to make a goal and then go to work.	12
Accuracy	2	Jim quietly packed crates with seven dozen blue gift boxes.	24
Numbers	3	The 780 girls and 692 boys played 134 hours in 5 nurseries.	36
Symbols	4	ss @ ss @ ss @ jj & jj & jj & ;; = ;; = ;; = ;; + ;; + ;; +	48

PRETEST

Take one 1-minute timing.

5   He caught 666 fish of 6 species in 6 boats using heavy   12

6 line while we caught 66 more fish in 6 hours using 6 poles. 24

| 1 | 2 | 3 | 4 | 5 | 6 | 7 | 8 | 9 | 10 | 11 | 12 |

PRACTICE

Type lines for speed or accuracy. *Time—3 or 5 minutes.*

Key Review: 6

7 fff fff f6f f6f fff f6f f6f f66 f66 fff f6f f6f f66 f66 f6f 12

8 ffff f6f6 ffff f6f6 f66f f66f f6f6 f6f6 f66f f6f6 6f6f 6f6f 24

9 6 sip 6 items 6 aunts 66 ovens 66 tubes 666 palms 666 rates 36

10 6 sat 6 ideas 6 aides 66 oboes 66 tapes 666 plans 666 rafts 48

11 fff f6f f6f f66 f66 f66f f66f f66f f6f6 f6f6 6f6f 6f6f 66f6 60

12 Marvin used 666 cups for 66 guests in 6 days at 666 events. 72

00.30 30-SECOND OKS

SPEED: 2 errors allowed

ACCURACY: 0 errors allowed

Take a 30-second OK timing on each line. Repeat.

13 The 612 visitors bought 546 flags of 136 nations in 6 days. 12

14 The 36 clerks can fix the 641 reports for 562 artists by 6. 12

15 He sent 615 crates to 562 stores in 36 cities and 64 towns. 12

| 1 | 2 | 3 | 4 | 5 | 6 | 7 | 8 | 9 | 10 | 11 | 12 |

TECHNIQUE CHECK

Proper position at machine.

Proper finger position and curve.

Wrists low, not touching.

Type for 30 seconds on each line.

16 66 bid low|66 get fish|66 were lost|666 were ill|666 called 12

17 6 baked pies|65 big sheep|36 enrolled|62 diet|16 race bikes 12

18 62 were wet|216 wrote home|654 will speak|61 can sing|6 sit 12

01.00 1-MINUTE OKS

SPEED: 3 errors allowed

ACCURACY: 1 error allowed

Take one 1-minute OK timing on each line.

19 Amanda scored 66 of 66 points and Randy scored 6 on June 6. 12

20 Jo earned 666 points in 66 races in 6 days and Ed earned 6. 12

| 1 | 2 | 3 | 4 | 5 | 6 | 7 | 8 | 9 | 10 | 11 | 12 |

POSTTEST

Repeat the Pretest.

WARMUP

Practice the following lines. *Time—2 minutes.*

Fluency	1	They may go to the social when the men sign the eighth bid.	12
Accuracy	2	Jack objectively examined prize aquarium fish with Grandma.	24
Numbers	3	We had packed 790 apples, 821 potatoes, and 3,456 tomatoes.	36
Symbols	4	ff % ff % ff % kk * kk * kk * ;; \ ;; \ ;; \ ;; | ;; | ;; |	48

PRETEST

Take one 1-minute timing.

5   Grant carted cartons of pastries from the pantry to my   12

6   cart for this birthday party for Gertrude in Montreal. This   24

7   party will start after the third tour to the district fort.   36

| 1 | 2 | 3 | 4 | 5 | 6 | 7 | 8 | 9 | 10 | 11 | 12 |

PRACTICE

Type lines for speed or accuracy. *Time—3 or 5 minutes.*

Transposition Problems: rt

8   cart Curt dart dirt fort Hart mart part pert port tart yurt   12

9   alert Earth north party births start Martha cartons turtles   24

10   craft draft erupt front Grant Orbit print trout trust wrist   36

tr

11   try entry extra betray Pantry pastry poetry wintry Gertrude   48

12   Actress destroy foxtrot distract district instruct Montreal   60

13   other Otter stair stars steer Terry there third tiers tours   72

00.12 12-SECOND OKS

Take four 12-second timings on each line.

SPEED: 1 error allowed

ACCURACY: 0 errors allowed

14   berths births carted cartel carton forth forte forty fourth

15   pantry pastries contrite contract control contrive contrary

| 5 | 10 | 15 | 20 | 25 | 30 | 35 | 40 | 45 | 50 | 55 | 60 |

TECHNIQUE CHECK

Type for 30 seconds on each line.

Eyes on copy.

16   birthday betrayal advertise keystroke forthright neutralize   12

Eyes don't travel ahead.

17   neutrons departed matriarch cartilage pedestrian heartbeats   12

Strict attention to copy.

18   farthest registry earthworm obstructs introverts restraints   12

00.30 30-SECOND OKS

Take two 30-second OK timings on each line.

SPEED: 2 errors allowed

19   Opaque glass hides exotic birds from view at the junky zoo.   12

ACCURACY: 0 errors allowed

20   Mikey paid his way to join a colorful baroque extravaganza.   12

21   Six jet planes flew quickly over Bend in the azure morning.   12

| 1 | 2 | 3 | 4 | 5 | 6 | 7 | 8 | 9 | 10 | 11 | 12 |

POSTTEST

Repeat the Pretest.

FOR STANDARD KEYBOARDS

WARMUP

Practice the following lines. *Time—2 minutes.*

Fluency	1	The giant firm may wish to make a goal and then go to work.	12
Accuracy	2	Jim quietly packed crates with seven dozen blue gift boxes.	24
Numbers	3	The 780 girls and 692 boys played 134 hours in 5 nurseries.	36
Symbols	4	ss @ ss @ ss @ jj & jj & jj & ;; = ;; = ;; = ;; + ;; + ;; +	48

PRETEST

Take one 1-minute timing.

5 He caught 666 fish of 6 species in 6 boats using heavy   12
6 line while we caught 66 more fish in 6 hours using 6 poles.   24

| 1 | 2 | 3 | 4 | 5 | 6 | 7 | 8 | 9 | 10 | 11 | 12 |

PRACTICE

Type lines for speed or accuracy. *Time—3 or 5 minutes.*

Key Review: 6

7   jjj jjj j6j j6j jjj j6j j6j j66 j66 jjj j6j j6j j66 j66 j6j   12
8   jjjj j6j6 jjjj j6j6 j66j j66j j6j6 j6j6 j66j j6j6 6j6j 6j6j   24
9   6 sip 6 items 6 aunts 66 ovens 66 tubes 666 palms 666 rates   36
10 6 sat 6 ideas 6 aides 66 oboes 66 tapes 666 plans 666 rafts   48
11 jjj j6j j6j j66 j66 j66j j66j j66j j6j6 j6j6 6j6j 6j6j 66j6   60
12 Marvin used 666 cups for 66 guests in 6 days at 666 events.   72

`00.30` 30-SECOND OKS

Take a 30-second OK timing on each line. Repeat.

SPEED: 2 errors allowed

ACCURACY: 0 errors allowed

13 The 612 visitors bought 546 flags of 136 nations in 6 days.   12
14 The 36 clerks can fix the 641 reports for 562 artists by 6.   12
15 He sent 615 crates to 562 stores in 36 cities and 64 towns.   12

| 1 | 2 | 3 | 4 | 5 | 6 | 7 | 8 | 9 | 10 | 11 | 12 |

TECHNIQUE CHECK

Type for 30 seconds on each line.

Proper position at machine.

Proper finger position and curve.

Wrists low, not touching.

16 66 bid low|66 get fish|66 were lost|666 were ill|666 called   12
17 6 baked pies|65 big sheep|36 enrolled|62 diet|16 race bikes   12
18 62 were wet|216 wrote home|654 will speak|61 can sing|6 sit   12

`01.00` 1-MINUTE OKS

Take one 1-minute OK timing on each line.

SPEED: 3 errors allowed

ACCURACY: 1 error allowed

19 Amanda scored 66 of 66 points and Randy scored 6 on June 6.   12
20 Jo earned 666 points in 66 races in 6 days and Ed earned 6.   12

| 1 | 2 | 3 | 4 | 5 | 6 | 7 | 8 | 9 | 10 | 11 | 12 |

POSTTEST

Repeat the Pretest.

WARMUP   Practice the following lines. *Time—2 minutes.*

Fluency	1	Jane Ryan may suspend work by the lake and may blame Doris.	12
Accuracy	2	The jury acquitted Zelma Buck of excessive puzzling wrongs.	24
Numbers	3	My class read 9,082 ads, 765 stories, and 134 old booklets.	36
Symbols	4	kk < kk < kk < 11 > 11 > 11 > ;; { ;; { ;; { ;; } ;; } ;; }	48

PRETEST   Take one 1-minute timing.

5   My niece and her friend received eight pies from Heidi   12

6   for their clients and neighbors. Four dieticians view these   24

7   pies as healthier than fried pies from my other facilities.   36

| 1 | 2 | 3 | 4 | 5 | 6 | 7 | 8 | 9 | 10 | 11 | 12 |

PRACTICE   Type lines for speed or accuracy. *Time—3 or 5 minutes.*

Transposition Problems: ie

8   died diet lied Pier pies tied Brier chief dried views files   12

9   pie brief fried Grief niece plier quiet Yield friend priest   24

10   aisle Diane binder Cinder dinner differ either fiber fidget   36

ei   11   heir rein Veil beige being eight Heidi their veins received   48

12   seize weigh height forfeit Neither Raleigh receipt seizures   60

13   equip Heidi ceiling decline dentist Feeding genuine lentils   72

`00.12` **12-SECOND OKS**   Take four 12-second timings on each line.

SPEED: 1 error allowed

14   adieu afield alien chiefs client crier cries fliers friends

ACCURACY: 0 errors allowed

15   sheik skeins sleigh stein weigh weights weird veils vermeil

| 5 | 10 | 15 | 20 | 25 | 30 | 35 | 40 | 45 | 50 | 55 | 60 |

TECHNIQUE CHECK   Type for 30 seconds on each line.

Eyes on copy.

16   achieves neighbor dietician deceiving facilities foreigners   12

Eyes don't travel ahead.

17   eighties bakeries apartheid galleries weightless efficiency   12

Strict attention to copy.

18   canaries heirloom healthier conceited identities receivable   12

`00.30` **30-SECOND OKS**   Take two 30-second OK timings on each line.

SPEED: 2 errors allowed

19   Max quietly swept my vivid zircon behind a cage of jackals.   12

ACCURACY: 0 errors allowed

20   Quinn saves extra milk for jaguars in the windy public zoo.   12

21   Liz hid the unique black gems in perky wax flowers in Java.   12

| 1 | 2 | 3 | 4 | 5 | 6 | 7 | 8 | 9 | 10 | 11 | 12 |

POSTTEST   Repeat the Pretest.

WARMUP   Practice the following lines. *Time—2 minutes.*

Fluency	1	Dick is busy with the problems of the giant formal socials.	12
Accuracy	2	Zip and Chet will fix the vile rust on my unique black jug.	24
Numbers	3	Class will be held May 5, 6, 7, 8, and 9 for 12,340 pupils.	36
Symbols	4	kk < kk < kk < ll > ll > ll > ;; { ;; { ;; { ;; } ;; } ;; }	48

PRETEST   Take one 1-minute timing.

5	The 55 dads and 55 moms taught 555 boys and 5 girls to	12
6	count to 55 while 5 boys and 555 girls learned how to read.	24

| 1 | 2 | 3 | 4 | 5 | 6 | 7 | 8 | 9 | 10 | 11 | 12 |

PRACTICE   Type lines for speed or accuracy. *Time—3 or 5 minutes.*

Key Review: 5

7	fff fff f5f f5f fff f5f f5f f55 f55 fff f5f f5f f55 f55 5f5	12
8	ffff f5f5 ffff f5f5 f55f f55f f5f5 f5f5 f55f f5f5 5f5f 5f5f	24
9	5 kid 5 gates 5 lamps 55 flags 55 years 555 diets 555 untie	36
10	5 kin 5 goals 5 lions 55 fires 55 yield 555 doors 555 units	48
11	fff f5f f5f f55 f55 f55f f55f f55f f5f5 f5f5 5f5f 5f5f 55f5	60
12	Put 5 stamps on 55 cards for 55 men and 555 women by May 5.	72

00.30 30-SECOND OKS   Take a 30-second OK timing on each line. Repeat.

SPEED: 2 errors allowed

ACCURACY: 0 errors allowed

13	He sent 534 packs of 145 pounds and 15 ounces to 235 towns.	12
14	Sell 541 books and 54 magazines to 145 shops and 523 dorms.	12
15	Give 513 maps to 354 visitors from 245 cities in 15 states.	12

| 1 | 2 | 3 | 4 | 5 | 6 | 7 | 8 | 9 | 10 | 11 | 12 |

TECHNIQUE CHECK   Type for 30 seconds on each line.

Sharp, quick keystroking.

Control hand bounce.

Eyes on copy.

16	55 horse barns|5 big pets|555 blue ties|55 red rocks|5 cats	12
17	54 bones|345 new pups|125 bold men|15 caged rats|52 monkeys	12
18	351 notebooks|235 tablets|451 animals|52 old boats|514 pans	12

01.00 1-MINUTE OKS   Take one 1-minute OK timing on each line.

SPEED: 3 errors allowed

ACCURACY: 1 error allowed

19	He wants 55 cards and 55 pens for 5 students by December 5.	12
20	I need 55 tents and 55 kits for 5 men for 55 days by May 5.	12

| 1 | 2 | 3 | 4 | 5 | 6 | 7 | 8 | 9 | 10 | 11 | 12 |

POSTTEST   Repeat the Pretest.

WARMUP

Practice the following lines. *Time—2 minutes.*

Fluency	1	The profit may go to Rodney if they end the fight for land.	12
Accuracy	2	Banquet voices buzzed with joyful excitement for kind Page.	24
Numbers	3	Cancel 8,354 bids to 2,901 firms in 67 counties before May.	36
Symbols	4	ss @ ss @ ss @ jj & jj & jj & ;; = ;; = ;; = ;; + ;; + ;; +	48

PRETEST

Take one 1-minute timing.

5	The solemn columnists from Denmark condemned an autumn	12
6	consignment for uniforms from government remnants. Steinman	24
7	feels the detainment of the enmeshed remnants was unmarred.	36

| 1 | 2 | 3 | 4 | 5 | 6 | 7 | 8 | 9 | 10 | 11 | 12 |

PRACTICE

Type lines for speed or accuracy. *Time—3 or 5 minutes.*

Transposition Problems: mn	8	Hymns alumni Autumn column condemn solemn calmness gymnasts	12
	9	chimney Dimness remnant calmness insomnia slimness Amnesiac	24
	10	main mean Maine meant moans moons Camping combined commands	36
nm	11	Inmate enmeshed Steinman assignment adjournment consignment	48
	12	Unmade Denmark trainmen governments detainment realignments	60
	13	denim norms anthem inform Norman newsman uniforms Geraniums	72

00.12 12-SECOND OKS

SPEED: 1 error allowed

ACCURACY: 0 errors allowed

Take four 12-second timings on each line.

14	columns columnar condemned columnists indemnify indemnifies	
15	unmet unmerge unmarred unmarked unmapped unmoving unmuzzled	

| 5 | 10 | 15 | 20 | 25 | 30 | 35 | 40 | 45 | 50 | 55 | 60 |

TECHNIQUE CHECK

Eyes on copy.

Eyes don't travel ahead.

Strict attention to copy.

Type for 30 seconds on each line.

16	grimness gunmetal amnesties unmindful insomniacs nonmembers	12
17	cornmeal solemnly rainmaker gymnasium penmanship calumniate	12
18	primness mnemonic unmindful adornment columnists unmailable	12

00.30 30-SECOND OKS

SPEED: 2 errors allowed

ACCURACY: 0 errors allowed

Take two 30-second OK timings on each line.

19	John got very low quiz scores and poor marks on tax briefs.	12
20	Yvonne Belknap fixed with zest a quart jug of mellow cider.	12
21	Crazy Max will quickly juggle nut halves for the baked pie.	12

| 1 | 2 | 3 | 4 | 5 | 6 | 7 | 8 | 9 | 10 | 11 | 12 |

POSTTEST

Repeat the Pretest.

LESSON 100   NUMBER PRACTICE—THE 4 KEY

Practice the following lines. *Time—2 minutes.*

Fluency	1	Nancy Ryan may wish to visit the city with Buckey and Jaye.	12
Accuracy	2	I can pack my boxes with five dozen jugs of liquid varnish.	24
Numbers	3	My 57 boys scored 89 runs in 230 innings in 146 ball games.	36
Symbols	4	ff % ff % ff % kk * kk * kk * ;; \ ;; \ ;; \ ;; | ;; | ;; |	48

PRETEST   Take one 1-minute timing.

5   The September 4 race had 444 men and 444 women running   12

6   44 miles on Highway 4 in 4 early groups and 4 later groups.   24

| 1 | 2 | 3 | 4 | 5 | 6 | 7 | 8 | 9 | 10 | 11 | 12 |

PRACTICE   Type lines for speed or accuracy. *Time—3 or 5 minutes.*

Key Review: 4

7   fff frf fff frf f4f f4f frf fff f4f f4f f44 f44 f4f 4f4 4f4   12

8   frfr frrf fr4f fr4f f44f f44f frfr fr4f fr4f f44f f44f f4f4   24

9   4 bet 4 girls 4 views 44 hands 44 cakes 444 jokes 444 zones   36

10   4 bat 4 guess 4 votes 44 hills 44 cafes 444 jails 444 zeros   48

11   fff frf f4f f44 f44 frrf f44f f44f f4f4 f4f4 4f4f 4f4f 44f4   60

12   Sell 44 bats to 44 boys for 4 games in 4 leagues in 4 days.   72

`00.30` 30-SECOND OKS   Take a 30-second OK timing on each line. Repeat.

SPEED: 2 errors allowed   13   Find 432 clowns to do 241 acts in 143 shows for 241 groups.   12

ACCURACY: 0 errors allowed   14   June 4 or 14 is when 413 men and 242 women run for 4 posts.   12

15   The May 4 guests ate 34 fish served on 24 plates by 14 men.   12

| 1 | 2 | 3 | 4 | 5 | 6 | 7 | 8 | 9 | 10 | 11 | 12 |

TECHNIQUE CHECK   Type for 30 seconds on each line.

Proper finger position and curve.   16   44 gray whales|44 big eggs|44 new jobs|444 hikes|44 carrots   12

Control hand bounce.   17   41 oak tables|34 sunny days|42 city cabs|414 chairs|24 jobs   12

Back erect, lean forward.   18   24 run wild|41 hunt elk|4 fly away|43 seek aid|34 cry aloud   12

`01.00` 1-MINUTE OKS   Take one 1-minute OK timing on each line.

SPEED: 3 errors allowed   19   Buy me 444 tickets for 44 shows for 44 people on January 4.   12

ACCURACY: 1 error allowed   20   We need 44 clerks and 4 stenos to do 444 reports in 4 days.   12

| 1 | 2 | 3 | 4 | 5 | 6 | 7 | 8 | 9 | 10 | 11 | 12 |

POSTTEST   Repeat the Pretest.

WARMUP

Practice the following lines. *Time—2 minutes.*

Fluency	1	If they handle the island firm audit, it may end the fight.	12
Accuracy	2	The judges quickly absolved the crazy man of swiping foxes.	24
Numbers	3	On June 19, 26 of us saw 38 dogs, 47 cats, and 50 chickens.	36
Symbols	4	dd # dd # dd # jj ^ jj ^ jj ^ ;; [;; [;; [;;] ;;] ;;]	48

PRETEST

Take one 1-minute timing.

5	The Norwegian reporters on the weekly news agreed with	12
6	Drew that the very alert hero was dressed in tweed and wore	24
7	a derby. The hero recovered a few jewels from my flowerpot.	36

| 1 | 2 | 3 | 4 | 5 | 6 | 7 | 8 | 9 | 10 | 11 | 12 |

PRACTICE

Type lines for speed or accuracy. *Time—3 or 5 minutes.*

Transposition Problems: er	8	very Hero perk alert clerk derby Query answer banker farmer	12
re	9	read rely wore Korea agree three Pyrex encore mature retire	24
er/re	10	Herb bare pert fired Every siren leery figure either umpire	36
ew	11	ewes dewy sews fewer Lewis chews stews curfew review Andrew	48
we	12	week wear West dwell tweed bower tower blower cobweb Plowed	60
ew/we	13	news wept Yews sweet skews jewel Views snowed mildew trowel	72

00.12 12-SECOND OKS

Take four 12-second timings on each line.

SPEED: 1 error allowed

ACCURACY: 0 errors allowed

14	error erode dream dress serum serve rears ready opera arena
15	newly sewed weary weird crews threw weigh tweet renew sweep

| 5 | 10 | 15 | 20 | 25 | 30 | 35 | 40 | 45 | 50 | 55 | 60 |

TECHNIQUE CHECK

Type for 30 seconds on each line.

Eyes on copy.

Eyes don't travel ahead.

Strict attention to copy.

16	recliner weakness reporters flowerpot researcher midwestern	12
17	driveway recorder viewpoint caretaker eyewitness daydreamer	12
18	remember westward recovered Norwegian breakwater stewardess	12

00.30 30-SECOND OKS

Take two 30-second OK timings on each line.

SPEED: 2 errors allowed

ACCURACY: 0 errors allowed

19	Dave Rex saw zebras at the ranch jump quickly for the gate.	12
20	Grim Bob Kilman was vexed but camped by the fuzzy jonquils.	12
21	One amazing baker was quite excited by the five jelly pies.	12

| 1 | 2 | 3 | 4 | 5 | 6 | 7 | 8 | 9 | 10 | 11 | 12 |

POSTTEST

Repeat the Pretest.

WARMUP

Practice the following lines. *Time—2 minutes.*

Fluency	1	Rob Glen may go to England and Zurich by the eighth of May.	12
Accuracy	2	Josh packed five weighty boxes of frozen quail in my trunk.	24
Numbers	3	We found 7,892 miles of roads in 1,034 counties on 56 maps.	36
Symbols	4	ff $ ff $ ff $ 11 (11 (11 (;;) ;;) ;;) ;; / ;; / ;; /	48

PRETEST

Take one 1-minute timing.

5	The 3 storms wrecked 33 homes in 3 hours while 33 cold	12
6	citizens left 333 cars for 33 storm shelters in 3 counties.	24

| 1 | 2 | 3 | 4 | 5 | 6 | 7 | 8 | 9 | 10 | 11 | 12 |

PRACTICE

Type lines for speed or accuracy. *Time—3 or 5 minutes.*

Key Review: 3

7	ddd ded ddd ded d3d d3d ded ddd d3d d3d d33 d33 d3d 3d3 3d3	12
8	dede deed de3d de3d d33d d33d dede de3d de3d d33d d33d d3d3	24
9	3 owe 3 enter 3 pears 33 weeks 33 names 333 quips 333 mates	36
10	3 out 3 exits 3 pelts 33 watch 33 notes 333 quays 333 mines	48
11	ddd ded d3d d33 d33 deed d33d d33d d3d3 d3d3 3d3d 3d3d 33d3	60
12	The 333 people swam in 33 races in 33 days using 333 pools.	72

`00.30` **30-SECOND OKS**

Take a 30-second OK timing on each line. Repeat.

SPEED: 2 errors allowed

ACCURACY: 0 errors allowed

13	The 32 nurses served 31 patients in 23 days in 3 hospitals.	12
14	Watch 13 big firms sell 321 items to 132 groups in 3 hours.	12
15	Rent 322 rooms to 13 tenants and 31 rooms to the 3 schools.	12

| 1 | 2 | 3 | 4 | 5 | 6 | 7 | 8 | 9 | 10 | 11 | 12 |

TECHNIQUE CHECK

Type for 30 seconds on each line.

Eyes on copy.

Proper position at machine.

Proper finger position and curve.

16	3 new groups|33 fir trees|333 grew figs|33 ride bikes|3 jog	12
17	13 run races|32 new students|31 new chairs|123 grow berries	12
18	31 new bags|312 wet mats|231 egg cups|23 more ideas|32 fish	12

`01.00` **1-MINUTE OKS**

Take one 1-minute OK timing on each line.

SPEED: 3 errors allowed

ACCURACY: 1 error allowed

19	Put 333 boxes of paper in 3 rooms by 33 desks for 33 women.	12
20	Sail 33 hours in 3 days in 3 boats for 3 bosses of 3 firms.	12

| 1 | 2 | 3 | 4 | 5 | 6 | 7 | 8 | 9 | 10 | 11 | 12 |

POSTTEST

Repeat the Pretest.

WARMUP   Practice the following lines. *Time—2 minutes.*

Fluency	1	Clair and Bob paid Helen for the land she owns by the quay.	12
Accuracy	2	Mary Kimmel joined us to explore big white caves of quartz.	24
Numbers	3	The 90 men and 87 boys ran 14 miles, swam 26, and biked 35.	36
Symbols	4	ff $ ff $ ff $ 11 (11 (11 (;;) ;;) ;;) ;; / ;; / ;; /	48

PRETEST   Take one 1-minute timing.

      5   The cartoonist reported that story about some bellhops   12

      6   who threw spoiled tomatoes at four actors in the opera. The   24

      7   hotel noted the story and deported the bellhops to my town.   36

     | 1 | 2 | 3 | 4 | 5 | 6 | 7 | 8 | 9 | 10 | 11 | 12 |

PRACTICE   Type lines for speed or accuracy. *Time—3 or 5 minutes.*

Transposition Problems: op	8	opal open cope Opera lopes mopes ropes canopy Europe gallop	
po	9	poem pout upon epoch sport depot Vapor deport Impose report	12
op/po	10	hope pony Tops spoil poppy Kapok stoop oppose troops tipoff	24
ot	11	both dots Iota booth froth Quota riots otters hotels allots	36
to	12	toad town toys Atoms stone stove actor tutors grotto Tomato	48
ot/to	13	moth toot Note store photo story tooth vetoes bottom Cotton	60

     72

⏱ 00.12   12-SECOND OKS   Take four 12-second timings on each line.

SPEED: 1 error allowed   14   opals optic tempo hippo copes adopt polio pours elope spots

ACCURACY: 0 errors allowed   15   other total token topic voter rotor stove stows broth autos

     | 5   10   15   20   25   30   35   40   45   50   55   60 |

TECHNIQUE CHECK   Type for 30 seconds on each line.

Eyes on copy.   16   opposing opponent antelopes evaporate apostrophe deposition

Eyes don't travel ahead.   17   bellhops flagpole developer allotment cartoonist clothespin   12

Strict attention to copy.   18   elevator barefoot defectors emotional totalities footlights   12

     12

⏱ 00.30   30-SECOND OKS   Take two 30-second OK timings on each line. Repeat.

SPEED: 2 errors allowed   19   Vera May Clark will seize and box her quota of grape juice.   12

ACCURACY: 0 errors allowed   20   Crazy mechanics walked to fix big jeeps for the vice squad.   12

     21   Wilma Burton has quoted zany poems and five exciting jokes.   12

     | 1 | 2 | 3 | 4 | 5 | 6 | 7 | 8 | 9 | 10 | 11 | 12 | 12

POSTTEST   Repeat the Pretest.

LESSON 98   NUMBER PRACTICE—THE 2 KEY

WARMUP   Practice the following lines. *Time—2 minutes.*

Fluency	1	Their busy neighbor got six or eight mementos for the city.	12
Accuracy	2	Jack Daw quietly explains the behavior of gazelles in camp.	24
Numbers	3	Kelli ordered for 3,075 firms, 981 schools, and 246 groups.	36
Symbols	4	dd # dd # dd # jj ^ jj ^ jj ^ ;; [;; [;; [;;] ;;] ;;]	48

PRETEST   Take one 1-minute timing.

5	On May 2 we sent 222 pets to 22 agencies to distribute	12
6	to 222 folks in 222 homes in 2 towns in 2 days and 2 hours.	24

| 1 | 2 | 3 | 4 | 5 | 6 | 7 | 8 | 9 | 10 | 11 | 12 |

PRACTICE   Type lines for speed or accuracy. *Time—3 or 5 minutes.*

Key Review: 2

7	sss sws sss sws s2s s2s sws sss s2s s2s s22 s22 s2s 2s2 2s2	12
8	swsw swws sw2s sw2s s22s s22s swsw sw2s sw2s s22s s22s s2s2	24
9	2 sew 2 yards 2 acres 22 units 22 trees 222 irons 222 ropes	36
10	2 see 2 yawns 2 admit 22 unite 22 tires 222 idols 222 rides	48
11	sss sws s2s s22 s22 swws s22s s22s s2s2 s2s2 2s2s 2s2s 22s2	60
12	May 2 is 2 days and 22 hours after 2 boys and 22 girls ran.	72

⏱ 00.30 30-SECOND OKS   Take a 30-second OK timing on each line. Repeat.

SPEED: 2 errors allowed

ACCURACY: 0 errors allowed

13	The 212 people left when their 21 cabins burned on June 22.	12
14	Watch 112 bike 122 miles after swimming 2 miles in 2 hours.	12
15	The 12 children played 21 games and ate 22 meals in 2 days.	12

| 1 | 2 | 3 | 4 | 5 | 6 | 7 | 8 | 9 | 10 | 11 | 12 |

TECHNIQUE CHECK   Type for 30 seconds on each line.

Wrists low, not touching.

Smooth stroking, even pace.

Space bar—thumb close.

16	2 white rats|22 wool hats|222 invitations|22 roses|22 nails	12
17	21 old cars|12 orders|21 pecan tarts|212 fried clams|2 pies	12
18	22 more men|212 fur capes|211 good ideas|2 new shifts|2 ran	12

⏱ 01.00 1-MINUTE OKS   Take one 1-minute OK timing on each line.

SPEED: 3 errors allowed

ACCURACY: 1 error allowed

19	The 22 farms grew 22 fruits and 22 vegetables on 222 acres.	12
20	Fix 22 steaks in 2 minutes and fix 222 snacks for 22 girls.	12

| 1 | 2 | 3 | 4 | 5 | 6 | 7 | 8 | 9 | 10 | 11 | 12 |

POSTTEST   Repeat the Pretest.

WARMUP

Practice the following lines. *Time—2 minutes.*

Fluency	1	The eight chaps may go right to the rocks with Sue and Jay.	12
Accuracy	2	Kirby played mighty fine sax with the Victory Jazz Quartet.	24
Numbers	3	I got 27 apples, 58 plums, 39 kiwis, 46 pears, and 10 bags.	36
Symbols	4	ff % ff % ff % kk * kk * kk * ;; \ ;; \ ;; \ ;; | ;; | ;; |	48

PRETEST

Take one 1-minute timing.

5	His swell old colleague from Sweden was sworn into the	12
6	golf and polo clubs. The folks swiftly swayed him to answer	24
7	the bold questions about local lobbyists and the newscasts.	36

| 1 | 2 | 3 | 4 | 5 | 6 | 7 | 8 | 9 | 10 | 11 | 12 |

PRACTICE

Type lines for speed or accuracy. *Time—3 or 5 minutes.*

Transposition Problems: lo	8	load lock lone loans local alone blows Colony Igloos velour	12
ol	9	Oleo bold golf color folks polka yolks behold Arnold patrol	24
lo/ol	10	hole solo Polo elope tolls gloom Volts fellow symbol gallon	36
sw	11	swam Swan sway swank sweat swift swarm swampy answer Oswego	48
ws	12	bows hews Jaws draws Flaws glows snows allows bylaws elbows	60
sw/ws	13	swap Laws swum views swirl thaws sworn widows Sweden oxbows	72

00.12 12-SECOND OKS

Take four 12-second timings on each line.

SPEED: 1 error allowed	14	lobby loamy older extol cloak float atoll scold glory extol
ACCURACY: 0 errors allowed	15	swell swirl blows brews sword sworn slows stews swift crews

| 5 | 10 | 15 | 20 | 25 | 30 | 35 | 40 | 45 | 50 | 55 | 60 |

TECHNIQUE CHECK

Type for 30 seconds on each line.

Eyes on copy.	16	lobbyist gasworks melodious passwords loganberry swallowing	12
Eyes don't travel ahead.	17	lawsuits absolute bungalows colleague fellowship enrollment	12
Strict attention to copy.	18	closeups menswear flagpoles newscasts allotments sweatshirt	12

00.30 30-SECOND OKS

Take two 30-second OK timings on each line. Repeat.

SPEED: 2 errors allowed	19	Quin plucked a zither with vigor as six men ate beef jerky.	12
ACCURACY: 0 errors allowed	20	Phil may view and judge sixty lizards or fifty black quail.	12
	21	Bankruptcy forces Zelda to give her exotic quince jam away.	12

| 1 | 2 | 3 | 4 | 5 | 6 | 7 | 8 | 9 | 10 | 11 | 12 |

POSTTEST

Repeat the Pretest.

LESSON 97   NUMBER PRACTICE—THE 1 KEY

WARMUP

Practice the following lines. *Time—2 minutes.*

Fluency	1	He may wish to fix the ancient oak chair and the ivory box.	12
Accuracy	2	Quaint little pixies jumped over forty big rocks with zeal.	24
Numbers	3	All 387 workers may receive $1,260 today and $945 tomorrow.	36
Symbols	4	ss @ ss @ ss @ jj & jj & jj & ;; = ;; = ;; = ;; + ;; + ;; +	48

PRETEST

Do not use lowercase letter "l" for the number 1.

Take one 1-minute timing.

5   Jane wants 111 ideas on her desk from 11 staff members   12

6 when the June 11 group of 111 meet for 11 hours 11 minutes.   24

| 1 | 2 | 3 | 4 | 5 | 6 | 7 | 8 | 9 | 10 | 11 | 12 |

PRACTICE

Key Review: 1

Type lines for speed or accuracy. *Time—3 or 5 minutes.*

7 aaa aqa aaa aqa a1a a1a aqa aaa a1a a1a a11 a11 a1a 1a1 1a1   12

8 aqaq aqqa aq1a aq1a a11a a11a aqaq aq1a aq1a a11a a11a a1a11   24

9 1 hog 1 gable 1 jewel 11 faces 11 kings 111 dials 111 lease   36

10 1 hem 1 giant 1 judge 11 files 11 knees 111 ducks 111 learn   48

11 aaa aqa a1a a11 a11 aqqa a11a a11a a1a1 a1a1 1a1a 1a1a 11a1   60

12 Send 1 man to 11 shops to see 111 cars for 11 sales routes.   72

⏱ 00.30 30-SECOND OKS

SPEED: 2 errors allowed

ACCURACY: 0 errors allowed

Take a 30-second OK timing on each line. Repeat.

13 Ship 111 packages in 11 days for 111 meetings in 1 country.   12

14 Write 11 letters and 1 memo for 11 staff writers by May 11.   12

15 Wrap 111 fine gifts for 11 parties in 11 days in 11 cities.   12

| 1 | 2 | 3 | 4 | 5 | 6 | 7 | 8 | 9 | 10 | 11 | 12 |

TECHNIQUE CHECK

Feet on floor.

Sharp, quick keystroking.

Control hand bounce.

Type for 30 seconds on each line.

16 11 new toys|1 palm tree|111 good meals|11 fun trips|11 cats   12

17 1 red sock|11 fine cups|111 old pans|11 cloth hats|11 races   12

18 111 fuzzy sheep|11 hours|1 new idea|11 warm cookies|11 days   12

⏱ 01.00 1-MINUTE OKS

SPEED: 3 errors allowed

ACCURACY: 1 error allowed

Take one 1-minute OK timing on each line.

19 Ed sent 111 cards in 11 days to 11 friends in 11 countries.   12

20 Kate swam 11 miles in 11 hours and 11 minutes for 111 days.   12

| 1 | 2 | 3 | 4 | 5 | 6 | 7 | 8 | 9 | 10 | 11 | 12 |

POSTTEST

Repeat the Pretest.

WARMUP

Practice the following lines. *Time—2 minutes.*

Fluency	1	Doris is busy with the firm but may go to Lake City for us.	12
Accuracy	2	Kimberly recognized the export volume for unique wine jars.	24
Numbers	3	Get 43 saws, 59 clips, 68 pliers, and 10 drills for 72 men.	36
Symbols	4	kk < kk < kk < 11 > 11 > 11 > ;; { ;; { ;; { ;; } ;; } ;; }	48

PRETEST

Take one 1-minute timing.

5	Derek and Hugo haggled about hiring eight dressmakers.	12
6	They ought not to dicker about hiring because having enough	24
7	skilled handworkers and fabric lengths kindles high growth.	36

| 1 | 2 | 3 | 4 | 5 | 6 | 7 | 8 | 9 | 10 | 11 | 12 |

PRACTICE

Type lines for speed or accuracy. *Time—3 or 5 minutes.*

Transposition Problems: d-k	8	duke dank deck Derek disks ducky drank Darken dicker docker	12
k-d	9	kids Kind skid kedge knead Kodak kudzu kidney kidded kidnap	24
d-k/k-d	10	Dusk kudo dark kneed dinky kinds ducky kindle donkey Kinder	36
g-h	11	Gash gosh gush aught laugh eight ghost growth Length sleigh	48
h-g	12	hogs Huge hugs hangs hinge hedge Shrug haggle highly having	60
g-h/h-g	13	high Hugo sigh thing light thong ought hunger Enough hiring	72

00.12 12-SECOND OKS

Take four 12-second timings on each line.

SPEED: 1 error allowed

ACCURACY: 0 errors allowed

14	drake drink biked hiked ducks dunks baked faked desks asked
15	sighs sight hogan huger right tight hoagy thigh tough shags

| 5 | 10 | 15 | 20 | 25 | 30 | 35 | 40 | 45 | 50 | 55 | 60 |

TECHNIQUE CHECK

Type for 30 seconds on each line.

Eyes on copy.

Eyes don't travel ahead.

Strict attention to copy.

16	darkness regrowth daybreaks eightieth deadlocked farsighted	12
17	behaving keyboard bothering kidnapper purchasing handworker	12
18	diskette goldfish kickstand sagebrush dressmaker outshining	12

00.30 30-SECOND OKS

Take two 30-second OK timings on each line. Repeat.

SPEED: 2 errors allowed

ACCURACY: 0 errors allowed

19	Liz Carver may quit doing tax forms with Becky Poe in June.	12
20	Mac Park had five extra jobs mining white or yellow quartz.	12
21	Skip gave Dexter the quickly melting frozen strawberry jam.	12

| 1 | 2 | 3 | 4 | 5 | 6 | 7 | 8 | 9 | 10 | 11 | 12 |

POSTTEST

Repeat the Pretest.

NUMBER PRACTICE LESSONS

CONTENT

The ten Number Practice lessons in this section provide you with separate lessons for each of the numeric digits.

OBJECTIVE

To increase stroking speed and accuracy in typing numbers.

TECHNIQUE TIP

Adjust chair height so the back of the chair supports your lower back.

WARMUP	Practice the following lines. *Time—2 minutes.*	
Fluency	1 Chris did go to town with vigor to do the usual civic duty.	12
Accuracy	2 Nine excited journalists flew high over Mozambique Parkway.	24
Numbers	3 On May 10, 39 girls and 48 boys need 56 sets of 27 tickets.	36
Symbols	4 ss @ ss @ ss @ jj & jj & jj & ;; = ;; = ;; = ;; + ;; + ;; +	48

PRETEST   Take one 1-minute timing.

5   Clever Calvin carved beautiful figures of chipmunk and   12

6   beaver for the youngsters of the Yukon while Buddy supplied   24

7   yummy yogurt for the brave youth by the cavern in the cove.   36

| 1 | 2 | 3 | 4 | 5 | 6 | 7 | 8 | 9 | 10 | 11 | 12 |

PRACTICE   Type lines for speed or accuracy. *Time—3 or 5 minutes.*

Transposition Problems: b, v	8 verb vibe bevy brave vibex above Bevel adverb Viable braver	12
c, v	9 cave Cove vice voice civil Vouch vocal active cavity novice	24
b, v / c, v	10 vacant canvas Behave verbal avocado receive Observe verbena	36
i, u / u, i	11 unit quit Lieu incur guide virus minus tulips Studio liquid	48
u, y / y, u	12 buoy duly your yummy hurry Yukon yucca Uneasy jaunty yogurt	60
u, i / u, y	13 Turkey injury hungry unique younger impulse Playful cruises	72

[00.12] 12-SECOND OKS   Take four 12-second timings on each line.

SPEED: 1 error allowed   14   curve havoc bravo vibes crave evict breve verbs cover vinca

ACCURACY: 0 errors allowed   15   cubic input youth buddy unify mixup bayou buggy lucid yours

| 5 | 10 | 15 | 20 | 25 | 30 | 35 | 40 | 45 | 50 | 55 | 60 |

TECHNIQUE CHECK   Type for 30 seconds on each line.

Eyes on copy.   16   behavior altitude adverbial beautiful believable acquiesced   12

Eyes don't travel ahead.   17   unicycle vehicles unusually revocable youngsters observance   12

Strict attention to copy.   18   beverage chipmunk boulevard delicious invincible youthfully   12

[00.30] 30-SECOND OKS   Take two 30-second OK timings on each line. Repeat.

SPEED: 2 errors allowed   19   Tracy Bond mixed seven quarts of zesty jam with green kelp.   12

ACCURACY: 0 errors allowed   20   Jock was relaxing quietly in his plum vest and fine blazer.   12

21   Ralph Jackson always visits dozens of exquisite big motels.   12

| 1 | 2 | 3 | 4 | 5 | 6 | 7 | 8 | 9 | 10 | 11 | 12 |

POSTTEST   Repeat the Pretest.

NUMBER PRACTICE ENTRY AND EXIT TIMINGS

Practice the following lines. *Time—2 minutes.*

Fluency	1	field world amend vigor cycle whale right shelf their title	12
Accuracy	2	joker quote ivory waltz excel fight blame corps novel muted	24
Numbers	3	and 1 and 2 and 3 and 4 and 5 and 6 and 7 and 8 and 9 and 0	36
Symbols	4	ff $ ff $ ff $ ll (ll (ll (;;) ;;) ;;) kk * kk * kk *	48

`01.00` **TIMING A**

Take one 1-minute timing on lines 5–9. Type each line once.
Repeat if time allows.

Numbers in Phrases

5	6 run 8 went home 92 play ball 304 ate lunch 571 see whales	12
6	8 did 6 busy days 49 will sail 573 can speak 201 are purple	24
7	4 ask 7 cars left 39 were lost 628 big towns 105 cut papers	36
8	9 bid 4 like corn 36 work well 185 wed today 720 got better	48
9	6 cry 8 were here 72 push back 403 run races 591 bid higher	60

| 1 | 2 | 3 | 4 | 5 | 6 | 7 | 8 | 9 | 10 | 11 | 12 |

`01.00` **TIMING B**

Take one 1-minute timing on lines 10–14. Type each line once.
Repeat if time allows.

Numbers in Sentences

10	Get 548 tickets for 139 guests for 60 parties on 27 yachts.	12
11	The 27 men lifted 890 trucks and 146 boxes left by 35 boys.	24
12	She put 352 boxes and 790 sacks on 415 tables for 68 hours.	36
13	They sent 854 packages of 93 pounds 12 ounces to 706 towns.	48
14	The 30 clerks can fix the 784 reports for 569 people by 12.	60

| 1 | 2 | 3 | 4 | 5 | 6 | 7 | 8 | 9 | 10 | 11 | 12 |

`01.00` **TIMING C**

Take one 1-minute timing on lines 15–19. Type as a paragraph.
Repeat if time allows.

Numbers in Paragraph

15	The harbor seals number around 289,478. Flipper weighs	12
16	about 260 pounds. This seal will dive 600 feet and hold its	24
17	breath 25 to 29 minutes. Each grown seal needs to eat about	36
18	4 to 11 percent of its body weight daily and lives 17 to 33	48
19	years. The female will produce 15 pups during her lifetime.	60

| 1 | 2 | 3 | 4 | 5 | 6 | 7 | 8 | 9 | 10 | 11 | 12 |

Frequently Misspelled Words Practice

Lessons 67–71

CONTENT
Commonly misspelled words are the focus of the five lessons in this section.

OBJECTIVE
To improve stroking speed and accuracy by typing the most frequently misspelled English words.

TECHNIQUE TIP

Avoid touching the keyboard with your wrists.

Number Practice

Lessons 97–106

NUMBER PRACTICE ENTRY TIMINGS

CONTENT

This section provides three timings for measuring skill in typing numbers in phrases, in sentences, and in a paragraph.

OBJECTIVE

To determine initial speed and accuracy in typing numbers.

NUMBER PRACTICE EXIT TIMINGS

OBJECTIVE

To measure speed and accuracy in typing numbers after completing the practice lessons.

After completing the Number Practice Exit Timings, compare your scores on these timings with the scores you achieved on the Number Practice Entry Timings, and note your skill gain!

LESSON 67 FREQUENTLY MISSPELLED WORDS

WARMUP		Practice the following lines. *Time—2 minutes.*	
Fluency	1	risks goals foams laugh they flap rich own and rub to by do	12
Accuracy	2	dive quit bake jogs ways zinc fish milk pays text fill grew	24
Numbers	3	may 1 may 2 may 3 may 4 may 5 may 6 may 7 may 8 may 9 may 0	36
Symbols	4	dd # dd # dd # jj ^ jj ^ jj ^ ;; [;; [;; [;;] ;;] ;;]	48

PRETEST Take one 1-minute timing.

5	The Berkeley attorney benefited from the business. She	12
6	basically had my consignment from the Caribbean and offered	24
7	bargains to raise capital for an architect near bankruptcy.	36

| 1 | 2 | 3 | 4 | 5 | 6 | 7 | 8 | 9 | 10 | 11 | 12 |

PRACTICE 1 Type lines for speed or accuracy. *Time—3 or 5 minutes.*

8	Aging answer absence adjacent amortize Accompany attendance	12
9	aisle Accrue acquire analysis argument architect Apparently	24
10	buses bureau Bargain brochure bulletin Beginning bookkeeper	36
11	biased bazaar believe Boundary becoming business Bankruptcy	48
12	Chief column concede calendar Canceled committee comparison	60
13	candor Census collate capital campaign Conscious convenient	72

00.30 30-SECOND OKS Take a 30-second OK timing on each line. Repeat.

SPEED: 2 errors allowed

ACCURACY: 0 errors allowed

14	convenient buses|collate our brochure|canceled the bulletin	12
15	business bankruptcy|campaign committee|beginning comparison	12
16	offered capital|beginning attorney|basically they benefited	12

| 1 | 2 | 3 | 4 | 5 | 6 | 7 | 8 | 9 | 10 | 11 | 12 |

PRACTICE 2 Type for 30 seconds on each line.

17	article attorney benefited criticism continuous accommodate	12
18	address Berkeley arbitrary Caribbean arithmetic consignment	12
19	basically changeable achievement cancellation chronological	12

01.00 1-MINUTE OKS Take one 1-minute OK timing on each line.

SPEED: 3 errors allowed

ACCURACY: 1 error allowed

20	An aging bookkeeper bargains with architects in the bazaar.	12
21	The changeable consignment was canceled by my bureau chief.	12

| 1 | 2 | 3 | 4 | 5 | 6 | 7 | 8 | 9 | 10 | 11 | 12 |

POSTTEST Repeat the Pretest.

WARMUP Practice the following lines. *Time—2 minutes.*

Fluency	1	Blair Durham may rush in the auto to sign the chapel audit.	12
Accuracy	2	Kirby plays expert jazz guitar with fervor on my cold quay.	24
Numbers	3	She sews 9,325 sleeves, 1,204 skirts, and 687 coat pockets.	36
Symbols	4	kk < kk < kk < ll > ll > ll > ;; { ;; { ;; { ;; } ;; } ;; }	48

PRETEST Take one 1-minute timing.

5	The interview--the basis of a job search--requires the	12
6	applicant to be organized (well rehearsed). Why is this the	24
7	case? Who profits? Both the applicant and the employer will	36
8	profit--from time saved and a better employee-to-job match.	48

| 1 | 2 | 3 | 4 | 5 | 6 | 7 | 8 | 9 | 10 | 11 | 12 |

PRACTICE Type lines for speed or accuracy. *Time—3 or 5 minutes.*

Dash	9	;-- ;-- now--run now--run ;-- ;-- yes--now yes--now ;-- ;--	12
	10	;-- swim--here iron--later tag--items maybe--yes skip--jump	24
Parentheses	11	l(l ;); (sell) (seek) (arrive) (wish) (this) (that) (hopes)	36
	12	l(l ;); (go) (watch) (chair) (bag) (rent) (serves) (covers)	48
Question Mark	13	;?; ;?; me? now? away? both? later? maybe? salad? tomorrow?	60
	14	;?; ;?; no? yes? when? case? where? never? chair? whenever?	72

`00.12` 12-SECOND OKS Take four 12-second OK timings on each line.

SPEED: 1 error allowed

ACCURACY: 0 errors allowed

15	Did she need it--the one we found yesterday--to do the job?	
16	Will he send Sam (the doctor) to get them for Max (my dog)?	

| 5 | 10 | 15 | 20 | 25 | 30 | 35 | 40 | 45 | 50 | 55 | 60 |

TECHNIQUE CHECK Type for 30 seconds on each line.

Efficient use of shift keys.

Arms quiet.

Sharp, quick keystroking.

17	Can we go? Send it--now. Is she (Sara) ready? Call Vi--now.	12
18	Please--wait. Yes--ask him. Will he (George) find her? Why?	12
19	Do you help? Can you (or Patsy) find it? Can you--will you?	12

`00.30` 30-SECOND OKS Take a 30-second OK timing on each line. Repeat.

SPEED: 2 errors allowed

ACCURACY: 0 errors allowed

20	Will you please send me (or Earl) to buy--or rent--the car?	12
21	Can George (Long) find the path to home--and school--alone?	12
22	Can Brian run the machine--the lathe--today (and tomorrow)?	12

| 1 | 2 | 3 | 4 | 5 | 6 | 7 | 8 | 9 | 10 | 11 | 12 |

POSTTEST Repeat the Pretest.

LESSON 68 FREQUENTLY MISSPELLED WORDS

WARMUP — Practice the following lines. *Time—2 minutes.*

Fluency	1	downs usual cubic title maid wish risk jam sue woe he us so	12
Accuracy	2	vial mine fake rips quip tubs good chat jaws yarn axes raze	24
Numbers	3	own 1 own 2 own 3 own 4 own 5 own 6 own 7 own 8 own 9 own 0	36
Symbols	4	ff $ ff $ ff $ 11 (11 (11 (;;) ;;) ;;) ;; / ;; / ;; /	48

PRETEST — Take one 1-minute timing.

```
 5      Their guardian was disappointed that the extraordinary     12
 6  entrepreneur was in debt. The discrepancy in this extension    24
 7  definitely dissatisfied the embarrassed facility directors.    36
```
| 1 | 2 | 3 | 4 | 5 | 6 | 7 | 8 | 9 | 10 | 11 | 12 |

PRACTICE 1 — Type lines for speed or accuracy. *Time—3 or 5 minutes.*

```
 8  Debt devise develop deficit definite Disappoint discrepancy    12
 9  describe Dependent disappear defendant dissatisfied Dessert    24
10  effect eighth Either entity Effective existence explanation    36
11  excel exceed expense Envelope extension excellent Embarrass    48
12  forty Forth fiscal fulfill freight foreign fragile February    60
13  gauge general Grammar gesture Grateful guarantee government    72
```

[00.30] 30-SECOND OKS — Take a 30-second OK timing on each line. Repeat.

SPEED: 2 errors allowed
ACCURACY: 0 errors allowed

```
14  develop effective grammar|foreign government|fiscal expense    12
15  fragile existence|excellent defendants|definite discrepancy    12
16  disappointed director|exceed the debt|dissatisfied guardian    12
```
| 1 | 2 | 3 | 4 | 5 | 6 | 7 | 8 | 9 | 10 | 11 | 12 |

PRACTICE 2 — Type for 30 seconds on each line.

```
17  deductible further defense eligible field guardian grievous    12
18  entitled entrepreneur extraordinary financial employee gray    12
19  delinquent extension function facility definitely directors    12
```

[01.00] 1-MINUTE OKS — Take one 1-minute OK timing on each line.

SPEED: 3 errors allowed
ACCURACY: 1 error allowed

```
20  The entrepreneur made extraordinary guarantees in February.    12
21  The general described my extension of the defense facility.    12
```
| 1 | 2 | 3 | 4 | 5 | 6 | 7 | 8 | 9 | 10 | 11 | 12 |

POSTTEST — Repeat the Pretest.

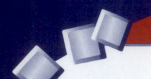

WARMUP

Practice the following lines. *Time—2 minutes.*

Fluency	1	Dick works for the town, but he may wish to work for Burke.	12
Accuracy	2	Lazy Quinn and big Jake wore extra vests to the golf camps.	24
Numbers	3	There are 7,890 cars, 2,314 trucks, and 56 bikes in my lot.	36
Symbols	4	ff % ff % ff % kk * kk * kk * ;; \ ;; \ ;; \ ;; | ;; | ;; |	48

PRETEST

Take one 1-minute timing.

```
 5        "Wait: Matt can run; Kirby can jog; Paula can ride the     12
 6   bicycle," said Steve. "No," said Matt, "We have to fix this     24
 7   bike." "If I can't repair it," said Paula, "I'll take it to     36
 8   Bella's shop: it's the only shop open for Saturday's race."     48
```

| 1 | 2 | 3 | 4 | 5 | 6 | 7 | 8 | 9 | 10 | 11 | 12 |

PRACTICE

Type lines for speed or accuracy. *Time—3 or 5 minutes.*

Semi-colon	9	;;; ;;; tans; tans; soil; soil; soil; loads; loads; ;;; ;;;	12
Colon	10	;:; ;:; said: said: paid: paid: paid: asked: asked: ;:; ;:;	24
Apostrophe	11	;'; ;'; can't can't won't won't won't aren't aren't ;'; ;';	36
Quotation Marks	12	;"; ;"; "jog" "jog" "ail" "ail" "ail" "home" "home" ;"; ;";	48
	13	turn; mind; over; send; mail; lists: learns: deals: search:	60
	14	isn't can't won't don't we're "at" "do" "to" "go" "us" "it"	72

00.12 12-SECOND OKS

Take four 12-second OK timings on each line.

SPEED: 1 error allowed

ACCURACY: 0 errors allowed

```
15   Wait: Mark can work; he can plan; the boss may sign a card.
16   "Kaye went home," I said, and she won't or can't come back.
```

| 5 | 10 | 15 | 20 | 25 | 30 | 35 | 40 | 45 | 50 | 55 | 60 |

TECHNIQUE CHECK

Type for 30 seconds on each line.

Smooth stroking, even pace.

Control hand bounce.

Wrists low, not touching.

```
17   Dear Mike: Dear Edie: Gentlemen: Notice: see; ask; fly; go;    12
18   "she won't go" "we're going on" "they won't" "today's menu"    12
19   for her; to him: "run" see us; "isn't here" we go; I won't:    12
```

00.30 30-SECOND OKS

Take a 30-second OK timing on each line. Repeat.

SPEED: 2 errors allowed

ACCURACY: 0 errors allowed

```
20   "No," Joy said, "this shop's hats aren't what we must buy."    12
21   The boy's and girl's words rang out: "Let's run after six."    12
22   "She isn't going; she must work," said Roy to the new boss.    12
```

| 1 | 2 | 3 | 4 | 5 | 6 | 7 | 8 | 9 | 10 | 11 | 12 |

POSTTEST

Repeat the Pretest.

LESSON 69 FREQUENTLY MISSPELLED WORDS

WARMUP   Practice the following lines. *Time—2 minutes.*

Fluency | 1 | fuels worms tutor whale down mend owls may aid six if it or | 12
Accuracy | 2 | quay jinx link back food home vase page zero area wage time | 24
Numbers | 3 | sub 1 sub 2 sub 3 sub 4 sub 5 sub 6 sub 7 sub 8 sub 9 sub 0 | 36
Symbols | 4 | ff % ff % ff % kk * kk * kk * ;; \ ;; \ ;; \ ;; | ;; | ;; | | 48

PRETEST   Take one 1-minute timing.

5   The likable niece of my neighbor negotiated an interim   12
6   judgment against a health industry. The issues of hazardous   24
7   materials is a concern of labor and the insurance industry.   36

| 1 | 2 | 3 | 4 | 5 | 6 | 7 | 8 | 9 | 10 | 11 | 12 |

PRACTICE 1   Type lines for speed or accuracy. *Time—3 or 5 minutes.*

8   Harass height hygiene humorous hindrance Hazardous interest   12
9   initial industry Included itinerary Insurance indispensable   24
10   interim Internal important immediate initiative Interfering   36
11   judgment lose lease Likable liability Laboratory lieutenant   48
12   Library minimum misspell Mortgage maintenance miscellaneous   60
13   motor Material ninety nuclear nuisance Necessary noticeable   72

`00.30` **30-SECOND OKS**   Take a 30-second OK timing on each line. Repeat.

SPEED: 2 errors allowed
ACCURACY: 0 errors allowed

14   mortgage insurance|miscellaneous material|important library   12
15   nuclear laboratory|necessary maintenance|hazardous industry   12
16   interim itinerary|negotiated labor concerns|humorous nieces   12

| 1 | 2 | 3 | 4 | 5 | 6 | 7 | 8 | 9 | 10 | 11 | 12 |

PRACTICE 2   Type for 30 seconds on each line.

17   heir labor lying nickel license integrate mediocre maneuver   12
18   niece ninth mileage movable negotiate legitimate nonchalant   12
19   issue health limited neighbor lightning miniature indicated   12

`01.00` **1-MINUTE OKS**   Take one 1-minute OK timing on each line.

SPEED: 3 errors allowed
ACCURACY: 1 error allowed

20   The interfering neighbor will lose his lease in a judgment.   12
21   Health issues indicated necessary hygiene is indispensable.   12

| 1 | 2 | 3 | 4 | 5 | 6 | 7 | 8 | 9 | 10 | 11 | 12 |

POSTTEST   Repeat the Pretest.

WARMUP Practice the following lines. *Time—2 minutes.*

Fluency	1	Helen Glen paid for half of the ducks and half the turkeys.	12
Accuracy	2	Hefty Stuart gave Pam quaint zircon and black onyx jewelry.	24
Numbers	3	Dana needs 149 plates, 680 cups, 235 bowls, and 7 platters.	36
Symbols	4	ff $ ff $ ff $ 11 (11 (11 (;;) ;;) ;;) ;; / ;; / ;; /	48

PRETEST Take one 1-minute timing.

5   A world-class yachtsman is currently planning a be-all   12
6   and end-all voyage. The around-the-world adventure to those   24
7   tropical blue-green seas and faraway cities of exotic lands   36
8   required a staff of able-bodied and self-motivated sailors.   48

| 1 | 2 | 3 | 4 | 5 | 6 | 7 | 8 | 9 | 10 | 11 | 12 |

PRACTICE Type lines for speed or accuracy. *Time—3 or 5 minutes.*

Hyphen
9   ;;; ;-; ;;; ;-; -;- -;- ;;; ;-; ;;; ;-; -;- -;- ;;; ;-; -;-   12
10   ;-; -;- up- to- be- ;-; -;- go- in- as- ;-; -;- at- it- no-   24
11   ivy- hop- high- warm- well- claim- annual- bottom- nonstop-   36
12   sad- old- poor- four- buff- right- profit- strong- strange-   48
13   well-read world-class blue-green month-to-month no-nonsense   60
14   able-bodied first-class son-in-law world-weary high-powered   72

`00.12` 12-SECOND OKS Take four 12-second OK timings on each line.

SPEED: 1 error allowed
15   A high-powered car ran a world-class race on one-way roads.

ACCURACY: 0 errors allowed
16   Her father-in-law is a good-natured man and a self-starter.

| 5 | 10 | 15 | 20 | 25 | 30 | 35 | 40 | 45 | 50 | 55 | 60 |

TECHNIQUE CHECK Type for 30 seconds on each line.

Space bar—thumb close.
17   first-class tickets|old-time fairs|senior-citizen discounts   12

Arms quiet.
18   two-quart jars|blue-green rugs|three-way tie|soon-forgotten   12

Feet on floor.
19   high-powered boats|one-on-one meeting|ever-changing weather   12

`00.30` 30-SECOND OKS Take a 30-second OK timing on each line. Repeat.

SPEED: 2 errors allowed
20   We took twenty-two high-priced cars to a first-class hotel.   12

ACCURACY: 0 errors allowed
21   My brother-in-law had low-level talks about duty-free laws.   12

22   A well-read man did much-needed work for my well-known inn.   12

| 1 | 2 | 3 | 4 | 5 | 6 | 7 | 8 | 9 | 10 | 11 | 12 |

POSTTEST Repeat the Pretest.

LESSON 70 FREQUENTLY MISSPELLED WORDS

WARMUP

Practice the following lines. *Time—2 minutes.*

Fluency	1	turns panel their forms with sick sock for icy key me of to	12
Accuracy	2	calm very quiz wake hoax page bead junk star fate give cafe	24
Numbers	3	sit 1 sit 2 sit 3 sit 4 sit 5 sit 6 sit 7 sit 8 sit 9 sit 0	36
Symbols	4	kk < kk < kk < ll > ll > ll > ;; { ;; { ;; { ;; } ;; } ;; }	48

PRETEST

Take one 1-minute timing.

```
 5      The question of the practice of plagiarism occurred to    12
 6   five psychology professors from Pittsburgh. Our opinion was  24
 7   that their personnel pamphlet was an exact replica of ours.  36
```
| 1 | 2 | 3 | 4 | 5 | 6 | 7 | 8 | 9 | 10 | 11 | 12 |

PRACTICE 1

Type lines for speed or accuracy. *Time—3 or 5 minutes.*

```
 8   opinion Offered omitted offense Occasion omission obedience  12
 9   Pastime present premium Proceed privilege probably proposal  24
10   parallel possible Personnel pamphlets plagiarism Pittsburgh  36
11   property Provided prestige Prominent psychology politically  48
12   prior possess Quantity questionnaire Rhythm receive receipt  60
13   Rescind reference recognize recommend restaurant Remittance  72
```

`00.30` **30-SECOND OKS**

SPEED: 2 errors allowed

ACCURACY: 0 errors allowed

Take a 30-second OK timing on each line. Repeat.

```
14   restaurant personnel|possible omissions|prior questionnaire  12
15   rescind proposals|politically prominent|provided privileges  12
16   question that receipt|required practice|possessed a replica  12
```
| 1 | 2 | 3 | 4 | 5 | 6 | 7 | 8 | 9 | 10 | 11 | 12 |

PRACTICE 2

Type for 30 seconds on each line.

```
17   practice question position prejudice ridiculous opportunity  12
18   replica required occurred professor precedence requirements  12
19   optimism relevant physician procedure promissory resistance  12
```

`01.00` **1-MINUTE OKS**

SPEED: 3 errors allowed

ACCURACY: 1 error allowed

Take one 1-minute OK timing on each line.

```
20   The Pittsburgh professor of psychology offered her opinion.  12
21   An opportunity for the plagiarism of pamphlets is possible.  12
```
| 1 | 2 | 3 | 4 | 5 | 6 | 7 | 8 | 9 | 10 | 11 | 12 |

POSTTEST

Repeat the Pretest.

Practice the following lines. *Time—2 minutes.*

Fluency	1	Blanche may go to work for the auditor to pay for the boat.	12
Accuracy	2	Both Kathy and Glenn viewed the six frozen quince jam pies.	24
Numbers	3	Mail cards to 1,297 men, 480 women, and 356 boys in Oregon.	36
Symbols	4	dd # dd # dd # jj ^ jj ^ jj ^ ;; [;; [;; [;;] ;;] ;;]	48

PRETEST Take one 1-minute timing.

5   Rt. Rev. A. J. Cole served in the U.S. Army for twenty   12
6   years in the U.S.A. before transferring to our hospitals in   24
7   St. Thomas, U.S. Virgin Islands. She retired to the city of   36
8   St. Louis to earn a Ph.D. A. J. Cole graduated with honors.   48

| 1 | 2 | 3 | 4 | 5 | 6 | 7 | 8 | 9 | 10 | 11 | 12 |

PRACTICE Type lines for speed or accuracy. *Time—3 or 5 minutes.*

Period	9	lll l.l lll l.l .l. .l. l.l lll l.l ... l.l .l. .l. l.l ..l	12
	10	l.l jr. jr. l.l sr. sr. l.l co. co. l.l f.o.b. l.l c.o.d.	24
	11	do. it. try. cup. dish. pack. dull. film. town. logo. drip.	36
	12	is. me. few. bar. hula. bulb. dead. ride. cuff. flag. roar.	48
	13	go. be. fun. hop. mash. back. fall. trim. down. zero. soap.	60
	14	no. us. sad. jab. area. slab. sled. view. leaf. deer. miss.	72

00.12 12-SECOND OKS Take four 12-second OK timings on each line.

SPEED: 1 error allowed
ACCURACY: 0 errors allowed

15   Wait. You must go now. The car is waiting. Get your luggage.
16   Send it c.o.d. Dr. Green needs to go. Use the a.m. delivery.

| 5 | 10 | 15 | 20 | 25 | 30 | 35 | 40 | 45 | 50 | 55 | 60 |

TECHNIQUE CHECK Type for 30 seconds on each line.

Eyes on copy.
Proper position at machine.
Sharp, quick keystroking.

17   Please run fast. Sign up now. Find a book. See me. You may.   12
18   Do sit down. He may fly soon. Order c.o.d. Go away. See it.   12
19   Use a p.m. flight. Seek his help. Run for office. Hire her.   12

00.30 30-SECOND OKS Take a 30-second OK timing on each line. Repeat.

SPEED: 2 errors allowed
ACCURACY: 0 errors allowed

20   Dr. Daly and Dr. Finch would require them to ship it c.o.d.   12
21   B.J. earned a B.A. from Stanford and plans to get an M.B.A.   12
22   Go to St. Paul or St. Jude at 3 p.m. to see Mrs. B. J. Lee.   12

| 1 | 2 | 3 | 4 | 5 | 6 | 7 | 8 | 9 | 10 | 11 | 12 |

POSTTEST Repeat the Pretest.

LESSON 71 FREQUENTLY MISSPELLED WORDS

WARMUP
Practice the following lines. *Time—2 minutes.*

Fluency	1	autos lapel cycle visit then rush turn dye sit ham go is by	12
Accuracy	2	curb stay move goes quid zone taxi vest walk high five jump	24
Numbers	3	jam 1 jam 2 jam 3 jam 4 jam 5 jam 6 jam 7 jam 8 jam 9 jam 0	36
Symbols	4	ss @ ss @ ss @ jj & jj & jj & ;; = ;; = ;; = ;; + ;; + ;; +	48

PRETEST
Take one 1-minute timing.

5   On Tuesday or Wednesday my secretary will schedule our   12
6   unforgettable surprise brunch of vegetable sandwiches. This   24
7   lunch will occur in the vicinity of my satellite warehouse.   36

| 1 | 2 | 3 | 4 | 5 | 6 | 7 | 8 | 9 | 10 | 11 | 12 |

PRACTICE 1
Type lines for speed or accuracy. *Time—3 or 5 minutes.*

8   seize sizable Sandwich schedule separate surprise Sincerely   12
9   Suing similar summary Special strength secretary sustenance   24
10   truly Their theory tariff totaled Tuesday tragedy threshold   36
11   Toward through Usage unique utilize unanimous unforgettable   48
12   volume Vacuum victim vicinity vengeance Versatile vegetable   60
13   wield weird Which wholly warranty Wednesday warehouse yield   72

`00.30` 30-SECOND OKS

SPEED: 2 errors allowed
ACCURACY: 0 errors allowed

Take a 30-second OK timing on each line. Repeat.

14   vegetable sandwich|victims of vengeance|my special warranty   12
15   separate tragedy|utilize my big vacuum|unforgettable theory   12
16   through a unique satellite|by the vicinity|similar schedule   12

| 1 | 2 | 3 | 4 | 5 | 6 | 7 | 8 | 9 | 10 | 11 | 12 |

PRACTICE 2
Type for 30 seconds on each line.

17   scissors usually whether tentative transferred simultaneous   12
18   waiver succeed sponsor withhold strength subpoena therefore   12
19   salable tendency seniority satellite thoroughly transparent   12

`01.00` 1-MINUTE OKS

SPEED: 3 errors allowed
ACCURACY: 1 error allowed

Take one 1-minute OK timing on each line.

20   The sponsors transferred that satellite to their warehouse.   12
21   The Tuesday schedule will surprise the versatile secretary.   12

| 1 | 2 | 3 | 4 | 5 | 6 | 7 | 8 | 9 | 10 | 11 | 12 |

POSTTEST
Repeat the Pretest.

WARMUP   Practice the following lines. *Time—2 minutes.*

Fluency	1	They may pay for the signs and risk a fight with Doris May.	12
Accuracy	2	Jacky saw foxgloves quietly waving in the breeze by a dump.	24
Numbers	3	Send 985 orders with 213 pencils, 450 pens, and 67 tablets.	36
Symbols	4	ss @ ss @ ss @ jj & jj & jj & ;; = ;; = ;; = ;; + ;; + ;; +	48

PRETEST   Take one 1-minute timing.

5   When buying a new computer, you should read, talk, and   12

6   think about available features. Price, of course, should be   24

7   considered, but you must also ponder speed, memory, modems,   36

8   monitors, and printers. True, there are many, many options.   48

| 1 | 2 | 3 | 4 | 5 | 6 | 7 | 8 | 9 | 10 | 11 | 12 |

PRACTICE   Type lines for speed or accuracy. *Time—3 or 5 minutes.*

Comma   9   kkk k,k kkk k,k ,k, ,k, k,k kkk k,k ,,, k,k ,k, ,k, k,k ,,k   12

10   k,k of, of, k,k us, us, k,k to, to, k,k do, do, k,k so, so,   24

11   flip, drum, barn, pony, bank, chin, slim, hobo, fish, will,   36

12   aqua, band, chow, pert, pets, roar, bang, reef, free, crib,   48

13   drop, swim, town, jury, walk, swan, trim, polo, dish, sell,   60

14   papa, food, flew, suit, pets, four, frog, beef, come, crab,   72

[00.12] 12-SECOND OKS   Take four 12-second OK timings on each line.

SPEED: 1 error allowed   15   Buy wax, brooms, pans, and soap to clean, scrub, or polish.

ACCURACY: 0 errors allowed   16   We walk, run, and talk while seeing the zoo, city, and sea.

| 5 | 10 | 15 | 20 | 25 | 30 | 35 | 40 | 45 | 50 | 55 | 60 |

TECHNIQUE CHECK   Type for 30 seconds on each line.

Proper finger position and curve.   17   feed birds, have fun, wash hair, take this, see the wolves,   12

Control hand bounce.   18   pack a bag, go on, send away, find a job, hire her, go out,   12

Wrists low, not touching.   19   to work, go swim, play a tune, serve four, buy food, a bug,   12

[00.30] 30-SECOND OKS   Take a 30-second OK timing on each line. Repeat.

SPEED: 2 errors allowed   20   She will, of course, mail the letters, packages, and bills.   12

ACCURACY: 0 errors allowed   21   In the evening, my aunts, uncles, and cousins visit a park.   12

22   We seek help, however, from all men, women, girls, or boys.   12

| 1 | 2 | 3 | 4 | 5 | 6 | 7 | 8 | 9 | 10 | 11 | 12 |

POSTTEST   Repeat the Pretest.

Alternate-Hand Words Practice

Lessons 72–76

CONTENT

Each of the five lessons in this section builds speed through practice on words that require the alternate use of the right and left hands.

OBJECTIVE

To improve stroking speed and accuracy and to maintain the stroking rate achieved during 12-second timings or 30-second timings.

TECHNIQUE TIP

Keep the backs of your hands at the same angle as the keyboard.

Punctuation Practice

Lessons 92–96

CONTENT

Intensive practice on all punctuation keys is provided in the five lessons in this section.

OBJECTIVE

To improve stroking speed and accuracy on the punctuation keys.

TECHNIQUE TIP

Be sure to take a break and change position, walk around, or stretch when your muscles are tired.

LESSON 72   ALTERNATE-HAND WORDS

WARMUP	Practice the following lines. *Time—2 minutes.*	
Fluency	1 nap apt sit bye rid spa dog fix sod due via cod fog eye yam	12
Accuracy	2 nun zip jaw his fur dig bay qua vex mix kit ilk gab elf cod	24
Numbers	3 aid 1 aid 2 aid 3 aid 4 aid 5 aid 6 aid 7 aid 8 aid 9 aid 0	36
Symbols	4 dd # dd # dd # jj ^ jj ^ jj ^ ;; [;; [;; [;;] ;;] ;;]	48

PRETEST

Take one 1-minute timing.

5   My mama may visit the haughty tutor from England. Mama   12
6 owns a chair and urn of rigid enamels. She also owns a clay   24
7 owl. This tutor and Mama work with burlap and cork mementos   36
8 for the visitor from the Orient. Their works focus on owls.   48

| 1 | 2 | 3 | 4 | 5 | 6 | 7 | 8 | 9 | 10 | 11 | 12 |

PRACTICE 1

Type lines for speed or accuracy. *Time—3 or 5 minutes.*

9 clan Born sigh heir urns Pane duel sick jams span idle laid   12
10 land flay form turn When wish they Mama fork owls foam snow   24
11 Vigor their slept right bucks Works focus visit soaps signs   36
12 burns Risks title shame chair tutor forms Autos shelf curls   48
13 she dial rigid tight Orient peptic Enamels visitor mementos   60

`00.12` 12-SECOND TIMINGS

Total words typed × 5 = wpm

Take three 12-second timings on each line.

14 The tutor with the tight curls may wish for the right fork.
15 A haughty visitor slept and Mama laid burlap on this shelf.
16 Andy may wish to duel for the idle land and the clan signs.

| 5 | 10 | 15 | 20 | 25 | 30 | 35 | 40 | 45 | 50 | 55 | 60 |

PRACTICE 2

Type for 30 seconds on each line.

17 key burlap dismay theory haughty socials tutorial amendment   12
18 mama owls|they slept|idle works|their visitor|burns a chair   12
19 Ken Andy Duane Sydney Dudley Bowman England Guthrie Langley   12

`00.30` 30-SECOND TIMINGS

Total words typed × 2 = wpm

Take two 30-second timings on each line.

20 The tutor with the tight curls may wish for the right fork.   12
21 A haughty visitor slept and Mama laid burlap on this shelf.   12
22 Andy may wish to duel for the idle land and the clan signs.   12

| 1 | 2 | 3 | 4 | 5 | 6 | 7 | 8 | 9 | 10 | 11 | 12 |

POSTTEST

Repeat the Pretest.

LESSON 91   LEFT-HAND WORDS

WARMUP		Practice the following lines. *Time—2 minutes.*	
Fluency	1	Vivian may blame both the city and the girls for the signs.	12
Accuracy	2	John Bille was vexed after jacking up his shaky quiz marks.	24
Numbers	3	Send 90 coats, 81 shirts, 27 hats, 36 skirts, and 45 vests.	36
Symbols	4	kk < kk < kk < ll > ll > ll > ;; { ;; { ;; { ;; } ;; } ;; }	48

PRETEST

Take one 1-minute timing.

5   You saw him crate up a pumpkin at my garage in west Joplin.   12

| 1 | 2 | 3 | 4 | 5 | 6 | 7 | 8 | 9 | 10 | 11 | 12 |

PRACTICE 1

Type lines for speed or accuracy. *Time—3 minutes.*

Left-Hand Practice

6   Age saw tear were rear west crate cedar Waste craft extract   12
7   fee Dab gear fear Vase text bears aware graze dread garbage   24
8   cat Ear gaze ware sear care geese areas asset Texas weavers   36
9   bat fat tact Czar star grab draft vexes sweet edged Webster   48
10   Rex age sear raft east debt seat avers beard Garage grasses   60

PRACTICE 2

Type lines for speed or accuracy. *Time—2 minutes.*

Right-Hand Practice

11   you ink polo pump Jill holy union junky Milly plump minimum   12
12   him pip Polk jump Lump pony milky Lilly puppy plunk pillion   24
13   Kim Hun punk lull pull upon loon unpin nylon Joplin pumpkin   36

PRACTICE 3

Type for 30 seconds on each line.

Left Hand: All Fingers

14   targets breed grave adage xebec data care edge deed dad rag   12
15   rafters tweed zebra creed swabs west raft weds raze sew bat   12
16   freezes fever abate vexes egret gaze vase brag fret Eve wax   12

⟦00.30⟧ 30-SECOND OKS

Take a 30-second OK timing on each line. Repeat.

SPEED: 2 errors allowed

ACCURACY: 0 errors allowed

17   dad ink area pump weed John waste pinky grass inulin adverb   12
18   sew pip deed pulp axes pool after Nikki stews pompon accede   12
19   ear Kim aged loin saws inky wedge puppy barge hookup bearer   12

| 1 | 2 | 3 | 4 | 5 | 6 | 7 | 8 | 9 | 10 | 11 | 12 |

POSTTEST

Repeat the Pretest.

WARMUP

Practice the following lines. *Time—2 minutes.*

Fluency	1	tie did wit and cot man rob foe oak map fit wow toe fox owl	12
Accuracy	2	cad wax bed zap fur keg rot pen end joy hum lay qua sip vat	24
Numbers	3	eye 1 eye 2 eye 3 eye 4 eye 5 eye 6 eye 7 eye 8 eye 9 eye 0	36
Symbols	4	ff $ ff $ ff $ 11 (11 (11 (;;) ;;) ;;) ;; / ;; / ;; /	48

PRETEST

Take one 1-minute timing.

5	Blair may go with my neighbor to the docks to do field	12
6	work. They may wish to fight the busy city auditor about my	24
7	penalty for their work. This auditor may blame them for the	36
8	rocks that were thrown at those antique autos on the docks.	48

| 1 | 2 | 3 | 4 | 5 | 6 | 7 | 8 | 9 | 10 | 11 | 12 |

PRACTICE 1

Type lines for speed or accuracy. *Time—3 or 5 minutes.*

9	dock vial Gown hens Kept glen lame hair coal flap duty sign	12
10	pair Body oaks clan down city busy tick pens auto pays Jane	24
11	slang rocks sighs forks angle ducks bowls Vials corks Handy	36
12	chaps blame girls vivid civic clans Prowl sight lapel Tusks	48
13	did work field fight profit Panels visuals Auditor neighbor	60

[00.12] 12-SECOND TIMINGS

Total words typed × 5 = wpm

Take three 12-second timings on each line.

14	The pair of girls kept their keys for the authentic panels.
15	The busy chap with the bowls cut my hair down by the docks.
16	The busy field auditor ducks rocks thrown by that neighbor.

| 5 | 10 | 15 | 20 | 25 | 30 | 35 | 40 | 45 | 50 | 55 | 60 |

PRACTICE 2

Type for 30 seconds on each line.

17	cob laughs enamel thrown penalty antique problems authentic	12
18	lame ducks|vivid panels|civic work|busy auditor|handy bowls	12
19	Leo Guam Blair Auburn Peoria Zurich Borland Dubuque Rickels	12

[00.30] 30-SECOND TIMINGS

Total words typed × 2 = wpm

Take two 30-second timings on each line.

20	The pair of girls kept their keys for the authentic panels.	12
21	The busy chap with the bowls cut my hair down by the docks.	12
22	The busy field auditor ducks rocks thrown by that neighbor.	12

| 1 | 2 | 3 | 4 | 5 | 6 | 7 | 8 | 9 | 10 | 11 | 12 |

POSTTEST

Repeat the Pretest.

WARMUP Practice the following lines. *Time—2 minutes.*

Fluency	1	A big, rich clan may wish to fish for the old, giant whale.	12
Accuracy	2	The goofy squad jumped over a box and seized the balky cow.	24
Numbers	3	Type 178 letters, 36 memos, 250 reports, and 49 tables now.	36
Symbols	4	ff % ff % ff % kk * kk * kk * ;; \ ;; \ ;; \ ;;	;;	;;		48

PRETEST Take one 1-minute timing.

5   Weave my tattered pink sweater on a loom at my secret mill.   12

| 1 | 2 | 3 | 4 | 5 | 6 | 7 | 8 | 9 | 10 | 11 | 12 |

PRACTICE 1 Type lines for speed or accuracy. *Time—3 minutes.*

Left-Hand Practice

6   dad red Zest west vast waft weave breed tears trace Sweater   12
7   ear vat fate fast brag tart taste Verse beast baste Extract   24
8   Tag bad were garb ever rear crass defer vests bread Stewart   36
9   sat bat seat Sara eggs brew stage draft fever Steve barters   48
10 Rex eat wart fact test verb eager secret tattered Aggravate   60

PRACTICE 2 Type lines for speed or accuracy. *Time—2 minutes.*

Right-Hand Practice

11 mum Ill mill loom pink Lyon nippy plump minim Junin mullion   12
12 ilk pun pomp milk hook Yolk lymph kinky onion jumpy Phillip   24
13 lop nun hull loom honk Ohio nylon hooky imply Kippy minikin   36

PRACTICE 3 Type for 30 seconds on each line.

Left Hand:
First and Fourth Fingers

14 Barbara staff award greet refer saga gate area raft bag fat   12
15 garters versa zebra graft agate data verb fret Bart tab bat   12
16 bazaars beret abate craze Grace brag aver faze afar wax zag   12

⟦00.30⟧ 30-SECOND OKS Take a 30-second OK timing on each line. Repeat.

SPEED: 2 errors allowed

ACCURACY: 0 errors allowed

17 see mum wade hoop saga milk award lymph evade minion secede   12
18 add oil dear only stew join dread yummy creed kimono defeat   12
19 sax hum weds link adds pulp adder union gazed pippin crazed   12

| 1 | 2 | 3 | 4 | 5 | 6 | 7 | 8 | 9 | 10 | 11 | 12 |

POSTTEST Repeat the Pretest.

WARMUP

Practice the following lines. *Time—2 minutes.*

Fluency	1	bit sir hay icy bus dig big urn dye got lay dug pen sue pal	12
Accuracy	2	fit kip ado own que let hot bud jig yet zoo vet cam sir axe	24
Numbers	3	key 1 key 2 key 3 key 4 key 5 key 6 key 7 key 8 key 9 key 0	36
Symbols	4	ff % ff % ff % kk * kk * kk * ;; \ ;; \ ;; \ ;;	;;	;;		48

PRETEST

Take one 1-minute timing.

5   The big town may rush eighty bushels of corn and lambs   12

6   to the docks. The rich firm may amend its goals to purchase   24

7   turkeys. That town may also augment the quantity of turkeys   36

8   and corn. This work may shape the social goals of the firm.   48

| 1 | 2 | 3 | 4 | 5 | 6 | 7 | 8 | 9 | 10 | 11 | 12 |

PRACTICE 1

Type lines for speed or accuracy. *Time—3 or 5 minutes.*

9   Ruby wick Make lens risk snap hems mend lamb held pale rich   12

10   lend bowl worn pals rush owns melt Torn Oboe pant corn envy   24

11   World towns docks duels throw firms tusks flaps gland Soaks   36

12   slays toxic socks shape Panel amend gowns spend Goals cycle   48

13   bid air blend burial Lapels formal Audible suspend downtown   60

`00.12` 12-SECOND TIMINGS

Total words typed × 5 = wpm

Take three 12-second timings on each line.

14   The rich towns own the eighty docks and they may mend them.

15   The big town may amend or suspend the formal toxic air bid.

16   Blanche may shape the worn lapels and hem the formal gowns.

| 5 | 10 | 15 | 20 | 25 | 30 | 35 | 40 | 45 | 50 | 55 | 60 |

PRACTICE 2

Type for 30 seconds on each line.

17   dog burlap turkey eighty bushels augment quantity flamencos   12

18   rich towns|worn socks|torn hems|world docks|the formal gown   12

19   Tod Dick Heidi Durham Rodney Laurie Claudia Dickens Blanche   12

`00.30` 30-SECOND TIMINGS

Total words typed × 2 = wpm

Take two 30-second timings on each line.

20   The rich towns own the eighty docks and they may mend them.   12

21   The big town may amend or suspend the formal toxic air bid.   12

22   Blanche may shape the worn lapels and hem the formal gowns.   12

| 1 | 2 | 3 | 4 | 5 | 6 | 7 | 8 | 9 | 10 | 11 | 12 |

POSTTEST

Repeat the Pretest.

WARMUP   Practice the following lines. *Time—2 minutes.*

Fluency	1	Helena and Clair wish for both of the ancient ivory panels.	12
Accuracy	2	Pam has fixed the prized quilt with very strong black jute.	24
Numbers	3	Anita bought 45 books, 761 pencils, and 309 pens on May 28.	36
Symbols	4	ff $ ff $ ff $ 11 (11 (11 (;;) ;;) ;;) ;; / ;; / ;; /	48

PRETEST   Take one 1-minute timing.

5   Brave Phillip fed him a lollipop as you fed my sweet puppy.   12

| 1 | 2 | 3 | 4 | 5 | 6 | 7 | 8 | 9 | 10 | 11 | 12 |

PRACTICE 1   Type lines for speed or accuracy. *Time—3 minutes.*

Left-Hand Practice

6	gag Wet edge rare sage bear Brave tweed defer weeds targets	12
7	cab rag date test stew Awed greed graze serve brags Caterer	24
8	ate Get data deaf seat Vest verse sweet treat stage retrace	36
9	fed cat Brad wade tare garb evade farce verge Grace adverse	48
10	Wes tea crew best beat acre radar staff Edgar Starr streets	60

PRACTICE 2   Type lines for speed or accuracy. *Time—2 minutes.*

Right-Hand Practice

11	him kin pill kiln July jump puppy pulpy pupil mummy Milikin	12
12	oil hip nook oily mink only Holly onion Yukon lumpy plumply	24
13	Jim Lou kilo loin only look hook imply pinky knoll lollipop	36

PRACTICE 3   Type for 30 seconds on each line.

Left Hand:
Third and Fourth Fingers

14	grasses award brass waste sweat aware sews razz Bees was sax	12
15	bazaars craze swear abase taxes swats area adze West wax saw	12
16	swagger asset dazed abaca zebra avast czar swab axes zag Aza	12

`00.30` 30-SECOND OKS   Take a 30-second OK timing on each line. Repeat.

SPEED: 2 errors allowed

ACCURACY: 0 errors allowed

17	zag you vest hymn feed pomp waxes unpin straw pippin grazes	12
18	get kin edge poll dart mink deter Milly abate Philip street	12
19	wax pup faze kink sets pump aware pupil greed unholy fewest	12

| 1 | 2 | 3 | 4 | 5 | 6 | 7 | 8 | 9 | 10 | 11 | 12 |

POSTTEST   Repeat the Pretest.

WARMUP

Practice the following lines. *Time—2 minutes.*

Fluency	1	aid jam for die key yen pan men irk row own cow may cut hem	12
Accuracy	2	put lot her zag sop fix mud quo ban wet gum coy job via kid	24
Numbers	3	got 1 got 2 got 3 got 4 got 5 got 6 got 7 got 8 got 9 got 0	36
Symbols	4	kk < kk < kk < 11 > 11 > 11 > ;; { ;; { ;; { ;; } ;; } ;; }	48

PRETEST

Take one 1-minute timing.

5   Henry may bicycle downtown to the lake. He may halt by   12
6   the bush and fish. Panama may roam down the lane to buy the   24
7   fish for the neurotic widow. The maid may fix a big dish of   36
8   fish and ham and hand it to the widow to eat by the chapel.   48

| 1 | 2 | 3 | 4 | 5 | 6 | 7 | 8 | 9 | 10 | 11 | 12 |

PRACTICE 1

Type lines for speed or accuracy. *Time—3 or 5 minutes.*

9   lake maps Buck dual such male chap Maid tidy gush name firm   12
10   bush Irks fish hams halt lane soap Fowl sock hand them dish   24
11   rotor dials robot Widow roams Henry ivory hairy bland flays   36
12   usual Aisle fuels title coals theme Laugh spans turns cubic   48
13   big Element formals downtown Neurotic endowment entitlement   60

`00.12` 12-SECOND TIMINGS

Total words typed × 5 = wpm

Take three 12-second timings on each line.

14   The tidy maid may fix hams and fowl and fish for the widow.
15   Neurotic Leland may roam down to the big city lake to fish.
16   The chaps may go downtown to fix the handle of the bicycle.

| 5 | 10 | 15 | 20 | 25 | 30 | 35 | 40 | 45 | 50 | 55 | 60 |

PRACTICE 2

Type for 30 seconds on each line.

17   corps chapel bushel handle bicycle torment apricot neuritis   12
18   bicycle corps|apricot socks|soap dish|lake fish|firm bushel   12
19   Bob Glen Cyrus Panama Vivian Leland Orlando Janeiro Langley   12

`00.30` 30-SECOND TIMINGS

Total words typed × 2 = wpm

Take two 30-second timings on each line.

20   The tidy maid may fix hams and fowl and fish for the widow.   12
21   Neurotic Leland may roam down to the big city lake to fish.   12
22   The chaps may go downtown to fix the handle of the bicycle.   12

| 1 | 2 | 3 | 4 | 5 | 6 | 7 | 8 | 9 | 10 | 11 | 12 |

POSTTEST

Repeat the Pretest.

WARMUP

Practice the following lines. *Time—2 minutes.*

Fluency	1	The busy auditor may work to amend the downtown city title.	12
Accuracy	2	Exhausted vandals grasp jittery zebras from warm quicksand.	24
Numbers	3	Buy 29 pears, 41 carrots, 36 yams, 58 apples, and 70 beans.	36
Symbols	4	dd # dd # dd # jj ^ jj ^ jj ^ ;; [;; [;; [;;] ;;] ;;]	48

PRETEST

Take one 1-minute timing.

5   Joy gave my dad my sweetest yummy dessert in a Kokomo cafe.   12

| 1 | 2 | 3 | 4 | 5 | 6 | 7 | 8 | 9 | 10 | 11 | 12 |

PRACTICE 1

Type lines for speed or accuracy. *Time—3 minutes.*

Left-Hand Practice

6   sat cab seat Gave draw erst beret crate erase taxes Dessert   12
7   bee Rag cafe dare eggs Tess farce fewer cease tests created   24
8   set Dad ease acts race brew greet treat stage taste Adverbs   36
9   Ted was gate Fred crab grew evade baste refer brave reserve   48
10   vet wee veer case fret Ward avert grave added Greta regrets   60

PRACTICE 2

Type lines for speed or accuracy. *Time—2 minutes.*

Right-Hand Practice

11   joy him moon John upon pool yummy lolly phony Polly pumpkin   12
12   pup mom poll hill moll Milo unpin Jimmy pulpy humph opinion   24
13   pop Lil poi loll hymn honk null poppy hilly Kokomo sweetest   36

PRACTICE 3

Type for 30 seconds on each line.

Left Hand:
Second and Third Fingers

14   arcades sweet brass asset evade deed edge axed deer dad sew   12
15   cascade vexes adder geese cease stew sets seed west add was   12
16   ragweed deter edged weeds xebec deed aces weds cede bed wax   12

⏱ 00.30 30-SECOND OKS

Take a 30-second OK timing on each line. Repeat.

SPEED: 2 errors allowed

ACCURACY: 0 errors allowed

17   axe you saws hump seed jump verge nippy fever limply career   12
18   fee joy data kiln czar lull swear milky cedar poplin secret   12
19   wed ilk barb pool fare pony sexes poppy refer hominy strata   12

| 1 | 2 | 3 | 4 | 5 | 6 | 7 | 8 | 9 | 10 | 11 | 12 |

POSTTEST

Repeat the Pretest.

WARMUP

Practice the following lines. *Time—2 minutes.*

Fluency	1	six the air pep fir box end bow bob but sob rib woe pay tow	12
Accuracy	2	hem jar eve bat mix sit zip led met que kit fox now gym cub	24
Numbers	3	own 1 own 2 own 3 own 4 own 5 own 6 own 7 own 8 own 9 own 0	36
Symbols	4	ss @ ss @ ss @ jj & jj & jj & ;; = ;; = ;; = ;; + ;; + ;; +	48

PRETEST

Take one 1-minute timing.

5   The giant auto firm paid for half of the fuel to bring   12
6   my authentic bugle corps to the island. Their chairman also   24
7   paid for half. She may audit the profits for the social. We   36
8   may give the profits to the town to fix the big burnt sign.   48

| 1 | 2 | 3 | 4 | 5 | 6 | 7 | 8 | 9 | 10 | 11 | 12 |

PRACTICE 1

Type lines for speed or accuracy. *Time—3 or 5 minutes.*

9   Ruby then duck burn pelt roam goal Paid soak tusk slam town   12
10   laps also curl cork furl girl slap half fuel with Both Isle   24
11   audit endow Burnt giant wicks snaps bugle Proxy corns prism   36
12   rifle borne signs autos Virus usury Japan eight whale elbow   48
13   May vow rock signal island social surname Ancient authentic   60

`00.12` 12-SECOND TIMINGS

Total words typed × 5 = wpm

Take three 12-second timings on each line.

14   The ancient and authentic bugle corps may pay for my rifle.
15   Clement paid the social chairmen for the eight whale signs.
16   Lakeman is the surname of the pale girl with the half curl.

| 5 | 10 | 15 | 20 | 25 | 30 | 35 | 40 | 45 | 50 | 55 | 60 |

PRACTICE 2

Type for 30 seconds on each line.

17   and dismal enrich profit visible fusible chairman cornfield   12
18   auto signals|also visible|burnt cornfield|the dismal profit   12
19   Sue Kent Provo Burien Helena Nalepa Lakeman Maybury Clement   12

`00.30` 30-SECOND TIMINGS

Total words typed × 2 = wpm

Take two 30-second timings on each line.

20   The ancient and authentic bugle corps may pay for my rifle.   12
21   Clement paid the social chairmen for the eight whale signs.   12
22   Lakeman is the surname of the pale girl with the half curl.   12

| 1 | 2 | 3 | 4 | 5 | 6 | 7 | 8 | 9 | 10 | 11 | 12 |

POSTTEST

Repeat the Pretest.

WARMUP   Practice the following lines. *Time—2 minutes.*

Fluency	1	The panels wish to aid the town and fix the signs and maps.	12
Accuracy	2	Sixteen black squid gazed upon my seven swarming jellyfish.	24
Numbers	3	She gave 468 papers to 279 people in 150 houses on April 3.	36
Symbols	4	ss @ ss @ ss @ jj & jj & jj & ;; = ;; = ;; = ;; + ;; + ;; +	48

PRETEST   Take one 1-minute timing.

5   My carefree nonunion caterers join a jolly debate in Texas.   12

| 1 | 2 | 3 | 4 | 5 | 6 | 7 | 8 | 9 | 10 | 11 | 12 |

PRACTICE 1   Type lines for speed or accuracy. *Time—3 minutes.*

Left-Hand Practice

6	red ate date fear Bart cast Cedar adage defer react average	12
7	was far seat Acts rare drag graft waste beard Texas cabbage	24
8	fat Bad read aged Drab debt great asset tears aware careers	36
9	Eve cab dear area feet ever zebra weave serve Bette affects	48
10	sea Abe scab gave safe Steve fewer debate caterers carefree	60

PRACTICE 2   Type lines for speed or accuracy. *Time—2 minutes.*

Right-Hand Practice

11	pin Jon join limp kill puny jolly Holly polio Hoppy million	12
12	inn Lyn lily link pull Kimi loony yummy pinky mummy mullion	24
13	mop ohm hulk Lynn mull hoop mump junky ninny Molly nonunion	36

PRACTICE 3   Type for 30 seconds on each line.

Left Hand:
First and Second Fingers

14	careers treat great geese dread brat deer edge verb tar fee	12
15	beavers craft wedge cedar tract beet brag tree reed tab err	12
16	adverbs verge cadet dazed avert read tart garb fret cad wee	12

[00.30] 30-SECOND OKS   Take a 30-second OK timing on each line. Repeat.

SPEED: 2 errors allowed

ACCURACY: 0 errors allowed

17	bar pop verb kilo afar Mimi zebra plump taste mukluk tarter	12
18	wax ill deed noun fret puny tract junky grate Kokomo secede	12
19	egg mop swab Lynn card pink egret onion dazed pipkin barber	12

| 1 | 2 | 3 | 4 | 5 | 6 | 7 | 8 | 9 | 10 | 11 | 12 |

POSTTEST   Repeat the Pretest.

Double-Letter Words Practice

Lessons 77–81

CONTENT

The five lessons in this section provide practice in typing all the double-letter combinations in English words. These lessons will help overcome the common problem of misstroking the second letter in double-letter combinations.

OBJECTIVE

To improve stroking speed and accuracy in typing words containing double letters.

TECHNIQUE TIP

Position the monitor so that the top of the screen is just below eye level.

WARMUP		Practice the following lines. *Time—2 minutes.*	
Fluency	1	The girls kept the title to the lake and the ancient autos.	12
Accuracy	2	A jovial workman quickly fixes the big red azalea planters.	24
Numbers	3	Get the 368 memos to 472 companies in 50 states in 19 days.	36
Symbols	4	kk < kk < kk < ll > ll > ll > ;; { ;; { ;; { ;; } ;; } ;; }	48

PRETEST   Take one 1-minute timing.

5   You saw him crate up a pumpkin at my garage in west Joplin.   12

| 1 | 2 | 3 | 4 | 5 | 6 | 7 | 8 | 9 | 10 | 11 | 12 |

PRACTICE 1   Type lines for speed or accuracy. *Time—3 minutes.*

Right-Hand Practice

6   you lip milk hull only link Puppy unpin imply Holly pumpkin   12
7   mop him Moon pool null hunk pupil phony mummy Yukon homonym   24
8   pun ink pink honk look pulp Polly onion kinky lumpy Opinion   36
9   ill hip mink noun oily plum Molly jolly nylon Johny million   48
10   pin pop only hump milk puny Milly lumpy plunk Joplin kimono   60

PRACTICE 2   Type lines for speed or accuracy. *Time—2 minutes.*

Left-Hand Practice

11   Dew bet aged edge west gate Aware crate draft grass decades   12
12   dad eve Bate gaze weed Fast water after grade cater badgers   24
13   are saw Cage face tear test Wart terse bears garage gadgets   36

PRACTICE 3   Type for 30 seconds on each line.

Right Hand: All Fingers

14   minimum imply jolly hilly Yukon look July hoop moon pin ink   12
15   Phillip jumpy union pinky mummy mill oily noun limp Lil pop   12
16   minikin hoppy unpin yummy knoll null pump Lyon only you Jon   12

00.30 30-SECOND OKS   Take a 30-second OK timing on each line. Repeat.

SPEED: 2 errors allowed

ACCURACY: 0 errors allowed

17   oil axe Niki dead mink swab poppy fewer plunk crazed unhook   12
18   nil wed link webs hill deed pulpy dread puppy Dexter pipkin   12
19   pop zag pill debt pink raze knoll graze phony adverb Philip   12

| 1 | 2 | 3 | 4 | 5 | 6 | 7 | 8 | 9 | 10 | 11 | 12 |

POSTTEST   Repeat the Pretest.

WARMUP

Practice the following lines. *Time—2 minutes.*

Fluency	1	She may aid the social with half the ham and half the corn.	12
Accuracy	2	Kay judged the extra power of a unique salve on bad eczema.	24
Numbers	3	Jan sold 280 oils, 169 paints, 357 charcoals, and 4 frames.	36
Symbols	4	dd # dd # dd # jj ^ jj ^ jj ^ ;; [;; [;; [;;] ;;] ;;]	48

PRETEST

Take one 1-minute timing.

5   Successful Abby met an eccentric peddler at the midday   12

6 bazaar in Morocco. She added piccolos to her accounts. Abby   24

7 then accepted the reddest saddles for her sobbing toddlers.   36

   | 1 | 2 | 3 | 4 | 5 | 6 | 7 | 8 | 9 | 10 | 11 | 12 |

PRACTICE

Type lines for speed or accuracy. *Time—3 or 5 minutes.*

8 aardvark Bazaar abbey babble bobbin bubbles Cabbage dribble   12

9 Ebbs gabby hobby jabbed lobby accent hiccup Occurs piccolos   24

10 mecca raccoon soccer succumb tobacco Vaccine Yucca zucchini   36

11 Addled buddy cheddar daddy eddy fiddle gladden huddle Kiddy   48

12 Odd adds ladder middle paddle reddest saddle toddler Wedded   60

13 baa cabby chubby Fibbed accept access account Midday shoddy   72

⏱00.12 12-SECOND OKS

SPEED: 1 error allowed

ACCURACY: 0 errors allowed

Take four 12-second OK timings on each line.

14 My toddler dribbles on Daddy while my chubby kiddy hiccups.

15 A gabby cabby fibbed about accepting cabbage at the bazaar.

   5   10   15   20   25   30   35   40   45   50   55   60

TECHNIQUE CHECK

Sharp, quick keystroking.

Feet on floor.

Efficient use of shift keys.

Type for 30 seconds on each line.

16 extra acre|lava area|grab bag|club band|epic case|need data   12

17 sobbing Debby|successful addition|saddest eccentric peddler   12

18 Aaron Isaac Abby Bobby Libby Robby Morocco Todd Teddy Addie   12

⏱00.30 30-SECOND OKS

SPEED: 2 errors allowed

ACCURACY: 0 errors allowed

Take a 30-second OK timing on each line. Repeat.

19 Isaac babbled when Aaron played fiddle in the middle lobby.   12

20 My shoddy raccoon accepts the reddest cabbage and zucchini.   12

21 My buddy Todd gave a piccolo and saddle to Abby in Morocco.   12

   | 1 | 2 | 3 | 4 | 5 | 6 | 7 | 8 | 9 | 10 | 11 | 12 |

POSTTEST

Repeat the Pretest.

WARMUP

Practice the following lines. *Time—2 minutes.*

Fluency	1	They lend the disks to the visitor and then go to the city.	12
Accuracy	2	Vi Joss rode quickly by with a fixed gaze on the pale moon.	24
Numbers	3	Send 68 boys and 70 girls to 125 towns in 39 days on May 4.	36
Symbols	4	ff % ff % ff % kk * kk * kk * ;; \ ;; \ ;; \ ;; | ;; | ;; |	48

PRETEST

Take one 1-minute timing.

5 Weave my tattered pink sweater on a loom at my secret mill.   12

    | 1 | 2 | 3 | 4 | 5 | 6 | 7 | 8 | 9 | 10 | 11 | 12 |

PRACTICE 1

Type lines for speed or accuracy. *Time—3 minutes.*

Right-Hand Practice

	6	him nun pink poll jump Lynn Yukon lumpy onion plump homonym	12
	7	Joy pop mump loom mill only loony nippy pupil Holly million	24
	8	imp You mull yolk mink pool unpin nylon Polly jumpy opinion	36
	9	lip mop Look hook lump polo hilly Jimmy phony nylon minimum	48
	10	inn oil Lily link noon upon jump polio knoll Junin monopoly	60

PRACTICE 2

Type lines for speed or accuracy. *Time—2 minutes.*

Left-Hand Practice

	11	fed war Date sees seed Crew weave tweet great trace secrets	12
	12	tab web Zest scab Bead care verse rafts brace saber sweater	24
	13	bad Fee sew Area wage east rave scarf fever secret tattered	36

PRACTICE 3

Type for 30 seconds on each line.

Right Hand:
First and Fourth Fingers

	14	minimum Polly union jumpy yummy John junk pulp hump joy you	12
	15	homonym unpin Yukon phony nylon July hymn noun Lynn mom pup	12
	16	minikin nippy union pupil plump Juno pomp pump jump pop ohm	12

⎡00.30⎤ 30-SECOND OKS

Take a 30-second OK timing on each line. Repeat.

SPEED: 2 errors allowed

ACCURACY: 0 errors allowed

	17	ill sew tart look Mimi brat nylon greed pinky better pippin	12
	18	ink tag kilo verb polo grab ninny sexes mummy Caesar minion	12
	19	pun Ada pulp area lion data milky zebra jumpy career hominy	12

    | 1 | 2 | 3 | 4 | 5 | 6 | 7 | 8 | 9 | 10 | 11 | 12 |

POSTTEST

Repeat the Pretest.

WARMUP

Practice the following lines. *Time—2 minutes.*

Fluency	1	They made a giant profit and now they wish to visit Sydney.	12
Accuracy	2	Peg just moved back home and made extra fuzzy white quilts.	24
Numbers	3	My 359 oak, 246 pine, and 78 fir trees were cut on June 10.	36
Symbols	4	ff $ ff $ ff $ 11 (11 (11 (;;) ;;) ;;) ;; / ;; / ;; /	48

PRETEST

Take one 1-minute timing.

5	The teens were taxiing to go skiing with toboggans and	12
6	duffels. The foggy day made them wish for green Hawaii. Lee	24
7	offered muffins and waffles and suggested my cliffside inn.	36

| 1 | 2 | 3 | 4 | 5 | 6 | 7 | 8 | 9 | 10 | 11 | 12 |

PRACTICE

Type lines for speed or accuracy. *Time—3 or 5 minutes.*

8	Agree bee beef career deeds eels flee free green heed Jeers	12
9	Knee lee meet need speed affect Buffalo cliff duffel effect	24
10	fluff giraffe huffy layoff Muffin off Cuffs puffins waffles	36
11	baggage Buggy digging foggy giggle Jogger muggy piggy saggy	48
12	shaggy suggests Tagging toboggan Wiggles bathhouse fishhook	60
13	tee teen Raffle sheriff dagger eggs Withhold taxiing skiing	72

00.12 12-SECOND OKS

SPEED: 1 error allowed

ACCURACY: 0 errors allowed

Take four 12-second OK timings on each line.

14	Reed suggests the jogger eat muffins and eggs for the meet.	
15	The sheriff and teen were tagging the baggage and toboggan.	

| 5 | 10 | 15 | 20 | 25 | 30 | 35 | 40 | 45 | 50 | 55 | 60 |

TECHNIQUE CHECK

Proper position at machine.

Space bar—thumb close.

Efficient use of shift keys.

Type for 30 seconds on each line.

16	bite each|golf free|hang gift|rush help|brief form|ski inns	12
17	three offices|offers coffee|soggy luggage|logger hitchhikes	12
18	Reed Leed Aileen Greece Clifford Aggie Peggy Hawaii Pompeii	12

00.30 30-SECOND OKS

SPEED: 2 errors allowed

ACCURACY: 0 errors allowed

Take a 30-second OK timing on each line. Repeat.

19	A logger needs to hitchhike to the office to flee the bees.	12
20	Aileen Leed agreed to offer coffee and three soggy waffles.	12
21	Shaggy buffalo differ from speedy giraffes and wiggly eels.	12

| 1 | 2 | 3 | 4 | 5 | 6 | 7 | 8 | 9 | 10 | 11 | 12 |

POSTTEST

Repeat the Pretest.

WARMUP   Practice the following lines. *Time—2 minutes.*

Fluency	1	The chairman may wish to pay the men for their eight signs.	12
Accuracy	2	My squad asked James to give a box of prized white candles.	24
Numbers	3	Buy 49 to 50 cups for $16.73 for the August 28 opening day.	36
Symbols	4	ff $ ff $ ff $ ll (ll (ll (;;) ;;) ;;) ;; / ;; / ;; /	48

PRETEST   Take one 1-minute timing.

5   Brave Phillip fed him a lollipop as you fed my sweet puppy.   12

| 1 | 2 | 3 | 4 | 5 | 6 | 7 | 8 | 9 | 10 | 11 | 12 |

PRACTICE 1   Type lines for speed or accuracy. *Time—3 minutes.*

Right-Hand Practice

6	You him kink hoop holy yolk hilly pupil knoll Jimmy minimum	12
7	oil hum Milk kill loop nook loony puppy jolly Polly homonym	24
8	hop lip monk upon noun lily Yukon lymph union plump Phillip	36
9	kin pun Lion noun mill pill phony Nylon ninny poppy pumpkin	48
10	mom ink mommy milky nippy Kokomo monopoly Honolulu lollipop	60

PRACTICE 2   Type lines for speed or accuracy. *Time—2 minutes.*

Left-Hand Practice

11	fed era case beds rage debt Brave fewer badge tease Average	12
12	Tar add west vase brew sear sweet agree wafer Weave sweater	24
13	age set garb were wear acts Cease eager award Dazed garbage	36

PRACTICE 3   Type for 30 seconds on each line.

Right Hand:
Third and Fourth Fingers

14	million plump hilly pupil jolly lull plum only loom pup oil	12
15	mullion knoll Molly poppy Holly look pool poll polo ill pop	12
16	pumpkin holly Polly knoll loony loop pomp loon lull lop Lon	12

⌈00.30⌋ 30-SECOND OKS   Take a 30-second OK timing on each line. Repeat.

SPEED: 2 errors allowed

ACCURACY: 0 errors allowed

17	kin bag pool edge yolk gaze kinky creed Nikki decade poplin	12
18	nun fat hymn adze noun dear Jimmy beard nippy assets pompon	12
19	ilk Wes kink weed pomp razz lippy adder unpin bazaar unholy	12

| 1 | 2 | 3 | 4 | 5 | 6 | 7 | 8 | 9 | 10 | 11 | 12 |

POSTTEST   Repeat the Pretest.

WARMUP

Practice the following lines. *Time—2 minutes.*

Fluency	1	The rich widow blames the firm for the fight with the town.	12
Accuracy	2	Big Squire Whittman played a very exotic kazoo for a julep.	24
Numbers	3	Mail a payment of $14,579 by May 20 to receive a $368 gift.	36
Symbols	4	ff % ff % ff % kk * kk * kk * ;; \ ;; \ ;; \ ;; | ;; | ;; |	48

PRETEST

Take one 1-minute timing.

5	My bookkeeper planned to sell books and knickknacks in	12
6	the hallway of the summer school annex. She enrolled all of	24
7	the swimming teammates who train in an immense indoor pool.	36

| 1 | 2 | 3 | 4 | 5 | 6 | 7 | 8 | 9 | 10 | 11 | 12 |

PRACTICE

Type lines for speed or accuracy. *Time—3 or 5 minutes.*

8	Bookkeeper jackknife stockkeeper knickknack trekked Yakking	12
9	all Alley calls dwell enrolls fell gallon hallway Ill jelly	24
10	Comma drummer grammar hummed immense Mummy summer teammates	36
11	Annex bunny cannon funny granny Kennel manner penny zinnias	48
12	book Choose door floor football good hood Indoor looks wood	60
13	trekker Bell ill commit ammonia dinner Planned school pools	72

00.12 12-SECOND OKS

SPEED: 1 error allowed

ACCURACY: 0 errors allowed

Take four 12-second OK timings on each line.

14	Our funny teammates fell ill from too much summer football.	
15	My bookkeeper planned to enroll in school and choose books.	

| 5 | 10 | 15 | 20 | 25 | 30 | 35 | 40 | 45 | 50 | 55 | 60 |

TECHNIQUE CHECK

Proper finger position and curve.

Eyes on copy.

Efficient use of shift keys.

Type for 30 seconds on each line.

16	back kick|cool lake|full load|warm milk|sign note|veto once	12
17	illegal dilemma|annual winner|summoned swimmers|poodle food	12
18	Jill Ellen Tammy Jimmy Ann Johnny Kenneth Minny Booth Woody	12

00.30 30-SECOND OKS

SPEED: 2 errors allowed

ACCURACY: 0 errors allowed

Take a 30-second OK timing on each line. Repeat.

19	All swimmers summoned to the pool trekked by Granny and me.	12
20	The good drummer hummed in the hallway of an immense annex.	12
21	Jimmy and Kenneth choose to work on the indoor wood floors.	12

| 1 | 2 | 3 | 4 | 5 | 6 | 7 | 8 | 9 | 10 | 11 | 12 |

POSTTEST

Repeat the Pretest.

LESSON 83 RIGHT-HAND WORDS

LESSON 83 | RIGHT-HAND WORDS

WARMUP

Practice the following lines. *Time—2 minutes.*

Fluency	1	Dixie and Blanche do not envy Duane the shape of the chair.	12
Accuracy	2	Kimmy saw novel plaques of azure jade at a Chicago exhibit.	24
Numbers	3	We need 286 stenos, 175 clerks, and 94 auditors by June 30.	36
Symbols	4	dd # dd # dd # jj ^ jj ^ jj ^ ;; [;; [;; [;;] ;;] ;;]	48

PRETEST

Take one 1-minute timing.

5 Joy gave my dad my sweetest yummy dessert in a Kokomo cafe. 12

| 1 | 2 | 3 | 4 | 5 | 6 | 7 | 8 | 9 | 10 | 11 | 12 |

PRACTICE 1

Right-Hand Practice

Type lines for speed or accuracy. *Time—3 minutes.*

6 ply lip jump join only lily Yummy nylon onion uphill Unhook 12
7 oil mon Jill lion pink monk poppy imply pupil Kimono phylum 24
8 ill Ink junk kiln limp poll Hilly phony lymph pompom minion 36
9 joy you pump upon Ohio hook nippy milky yummy Kokomo pippin 48
10 mop pop Polk pill plum hymn unpin jumpy plunk uphill Johnny 60

PRACTICE 2

Left-Hand Practice

Type lines for speed or accuracy. *Time—2 minutes.*

11 cab Rat gave deer case fear Geese dread feast waves taffeta 12
12 web dad Cafe cave west ward crate evade Verse wrest decrees 24
13 bag vex Tea vest gear cart beat seat wedge Dessert sweetest 36

PRACTICE 3

Right Hand:
Second and Third Fingers

Type for 30 seconds on each line.

14 million jolly knoll Molly holly milk link loom kiln ink oil 12
15 mullion milky Polly knoll jolly lull poll mink loll ill kin 12
16 minikin pinky loony holly knoll look polo kink pink lop Lon 12

00.30 30-SECOND OKS

SPEED: 2 errors allowed

ACCURACY: 0 errors allowed

Take a 30-second OK timing on each line. Repeat.

17 pup get join raze pump Brad hilly extra imply excess mukluk 12
18 ohm vet hump deed join west lymph asset Kimmy beggar kimono 12
19 you see poll eggs puny Fred jolly award jumpy savage hominy 12

| 1 | 2 | 3 | 4 | 5 | 6 | 7 | 8 | 9 | 10 | 11 | 12 |

POSTTEST

Repeat the Pretest.

WARMUP Practice the following lines. *Time—2 minutes.*

Fluency	1	Bob and Al may go to visit Zurich with their rich neighbor.	12
Accuracy	2	Vick quickly fixed the big worn zipper on my gray jodhpurs.	24
Numbers	3	The scores on the French test were 100, 93, 82, 74, and 65.	36
Symbols	4	kk < kk < kk < 11 > 11 > 11 > ;; { ;; { ;; { ;; } ;; } ;; }	48

PRETEST Take one 1-minute timing.

5 The boss had the need to irrigate to avoid the useless   12
6 loss of barrels and barrels of berries and carrots. She was   24
7 obsessed with worry and wanted to avoid an excessive error.   36

| 1 | 2 | 3 | 4 | 5 | 6 | 7 | 8 | 9 | 10 | 11 | 12 |

PRACTICE Type lines for speed or accuracy. *Time—3 or 5 minutes.*

8 Appear copper equipped happen Oppose puppet ripped shoppers   12
9 Puppies topping upper Zippy barrels berries carrots earring   24
10 hurry Jarred marry occurred purr Quarry sorry warrant worry   36
11 assets Boss chess dismiss essay floss glass hiss Issue loss   48
12 Mass obsess pass recess remiss scissors Toss useless vessel   60
13 appetite apply appoint carry Error Irrigate message classes   72

00.12 12-SECOND OKS Take four 12-second OK timings on each line.

SPEED: 1 error allowed

ACCURACY: 0 errors allowed

14 My remiss boss was sorry about the loss of a copper quarry.
15 An obsessed shopper passed barrels of carrots and earrings.

| 5 | 10 | 15 | 20 | 25 | 30 | 35 | 40 | 45 | 50 | 55 | 60 |

TECHNIQUE CHECK Type for 30 seconds on each line.

Smooth stroking, even pace.

Wrists low, not touching.

Efficient use of shift keys.

16 help pack|trap pets|your rate|wear red|hums songs|buys silk   12
17 support appeals|borrow currency|ageless actress|furry puppy   12
18 Poppy Harry Jerry Terry Morrow Missouri Ross Melissa Vassar   12

00.30 30-SECOND OKS Take a 30-second OK timing on each line. Repeat.

SPEED: 2 errors allowed

ACCURACY: 0 errors allowed

19 Terry Morrow wrote an essay on the upper classes of Vassar.   12
20 Harry and Melissa dismissed the ageless actress in a hurry.   12
21 The furry puppy ripped and tossed the puppet until useless.   12

| 1 | 2 | 3 | 4 | 5 | 6 | 7 | 8 | 9 | 10 | 11 | 12 |

POSTTEST Repeat the Pretest.

WARMUP   Practice the following lines. *Time—2 minutes.*

Fluency	1	I may go right to the field to end the fight for the title.	12
Accuracy	2	Bey hopes five dozen oranges will make six quarts of juice.	24
Numbers	3	I sing 14 songs 7 times to 65 groups on May 28, 29, and 30.	36
Symbols	4	ss @ ss @ ss @ jj & jj & jj & ;; = ;; = ;; = ;; + ;; + ;; +	48

PRETEST   Take one 1-minute timing.

5   My carefree nonunion caterers join a jolly debate in Texas.   12

| 1 | 2 | 3 | 4 | 5 | 6 | 7 | 8 | 9 | 10 | 11 | 12 |

PRACTICE 1   Type lines for speed or accuracy. *Time—3 minutes.*

Right-Hand Practice

6	him Ply pony pool hymn polo phony imply Yummy pupil opinion	12
7	Imp you only Hull join poll pulpy hilly nylon unpin million	24
8	hum pin oily hulk kink pink pinky Molly ninny Yukon minimum	36
9	hip non upon plum mink Jill Holly union poppy onion pumpkin	48
10	ohm inn limp nook kiln hulk Loop lion pupil Unholy monopoly	60

PRACTICE 2   Type lines for speed or accuracy. *Time—2 minutes.*

Left-Hand Practice

11	Ace vat acre dead weed reef eases breed Carve brass scatter	12
12	fat see bade race dead fret barge Dazed trade Texas extract	24
13	Was arc deed vast crab Texts baste debate caterers carefree	36

PRACTICE 3   Type for 30 seconds on each line.

Right Hand:
First and Second Fingers

14	homonym nylon jumpy union Jimmy pink noun milk hymn joy him	12
15	minimum mummy lymph Yukon phony July mink holy link kin ink	12
16	minikin Johny ninny jumpy yummy kink hump kiln link inn mum	12

`00.30` 30-SECOND OKS   Take a 30-second OK timing on each line. Repeat.

SPEED: 2 errors allowed

ACCURACY: 0 errors allowed

17	mop ace milk verb nook brag plump refer Molly target pompom	12
18	kin wed hook saws poll ease lumpy react plump Baxter hookup	12
19	inn sax loll raft oily drab loony abate pupil treats Joplin	12

| 1 | 2 | 3 | 4 | 5 | 6 | 7 | 8 | 9 | 10 | 11 | 12 |

POSTTEST   Repeat the Pretest.

LESSON 81   DOUBLE-LETTER WORDS

WARMUP

Practice the following lines. *Time—2 minutes.*

Fluency	1	Eighty of my men did handle their big social ritual in May.	12
Accuracy	2	Jacob Fritz or Kevin will pass the required geometry exams.	24
Numbers	3	Maryanne has 136 gallon, 245 quart, and 79 or 80 pint jars.	36
Symbols	4	ss @ ss @ ss @ jj & jj & jj & ;; = ;; = ;; = ;; + ;; + ;; +	48

PRETEST

Take one 1-minute timing.

5   The dazzling attorney wore a pretty cotton muumuu to a   12

6   snazzy pizza parlor. She ate a pizza dinner as my jazz band   24

7   dazzled attendees above the clatter of hollowware platters.   36

| 1 | 2 | 3 | 4 | 5 | 6 | 7 | 8 | 9 | 10 | 11 | 12 |

PRACTICE

Type lines for speed or accuracy. *Time—3 or 5 minutes.*

8   attacks attorney Batters better cattle clatter gritty Mitts   12

9   mottos Otters petty platter Quitting settled unbutton witty   24

10   Vacuums muumuu continuum revving Powwow glowworm hollowware   36

11   blizzards Buzzers dazzle drizzle fizz Embezzle dizzy fizzle   48

12   frizzle fuzz Gizzards grizzly Jazz muzzle nozzle pizza razz   60

13   attend battery cotton Vacuuming revved sizzle Puzzle snazzy   72

`00.12` 12-SECOND OKS

SPEED: 1 error allowed

ACCURACY: 0 errors allowed

Take four 12-second OK timings on each line.

14   A dazzling attorney in the snazzy cotton muumuu liked jazz.

15   The batter vacuumed the gritty mitt and ate sizzling pizza.

| 5 | 10 | 15 | 20 | 25 | 30 | 35 | 40 | 45 | 50 | 55 | 60 |

TECHNIQUE CHECK

Control hand bounce.

Arms quiet.

Efficient use of shift keys.

Type for 30 seconds on each line.

16   hot tip|last time|you used|bureau unit|slow walk|grew wheat   12

17   boycott attempt|pretty kitty|quizzed embezzler|little jetty   12

18   Abbott Calcutta Emmett Patty Pittsburgh Seattle Yvette Buzz   12

`00.30` 30-SECOND OKS

SPEED: 2 errors allowed

ACCURACY: 0 errors allowed

Take a 30-second OK timing on each line. Repeat.

19   The pretty kitty is puzzled by the drizzle from the nozzle.   12

20   A muzzled grizzly attempted an attack on my settled cattle.   12

21   Emmett Abbott from Calcutta embezzled the better batteries.   12

| 1 | 2 | 3 | 4 | 5 | 6 | 7 | 8 | 9 | 10 | 11 | 12 |

POSTTEST

Repeat the Pretest.

DIAGNOSTIC TIMINGS

WARMUP		Practice the following lines. *Time—2 minutes.*	
Fluency	1	a b c d e f g h i j k l m n o p q r s t u v w x y z xyz xyz	12
Accuracy	2	cam vet zoo yet jig bud axe sir qua own kin pit fit hot let	24
Numbers	3	Walk 14 or 15 blocks in 36 minutes to see the 8 navy ships.	36
Symbols	4	ss @ ss @ ff $ ff $ jj & jj & kk * kk * aa ! aa ! ll > 11 >	48

TIMING A

Take one 1-minute timing on lines 5–9. Type each line once. Repeat if time allows.

Left-Hand Words

5	was far bad sat bee dad tea gag wet tag eat red saw ear age	12
6	date cast rare draw brew test awed vest garb were vase care	24
7	read debt gave eggs fret beat sage tart verb star raft ever	36
8	defer serve taxes avert sweet evade bread eager crate asset	48
9	aware graft brave erase farce tweed draft tears waste dread	60

| 1 | 2 | 3 | 4 | 5 | 6 | 7 | 8 | 9 | 10 | 11 | 12 |

TIMING B

Right-Hand Words

Take one 1-minute timing on lines 10–14. Type each line once. Repeat if time allows.

10	pin hip you oil ink pop him lip mom joy mop inn mum ill pun	12
11	milk pool only mill lily noun pink kiln join hulk yolk link	24
12	plum honk noon loom upon monk junk lion mink nook polo hoop	36
13	pupil poppy imply onion hilly union lumpy polio holly jumpy	48
14	lymph knoll nylon phony unpin pulpy plunk jolly plump yummy	60

| 1 | 2 | 3 | 4 | 5 | 6 | 7 | 8 | 9 | 10 | 11 | 12 |

Right-Hand and Left-Hand Words Lessons

CONTENT

The lessons in this section are designed to reduce or eliminate the stroking imbalance between your hands.

OBJECTIVE

To increase the stroking speed and accuracy of the weaker hand until it equals that of the stronger hand.

CONTENT

A surprising number of English words are typed entirely with the fingers of one hand, and most people typing over 30 words per minute have a stroking speed imbalance between their hands. The diagnostic timings and the ten lessons in this section are designed to detect and reduce or eliminate this stroking imbalance.

OBJECTIVE

To determine the stroking imbalance between right and left hands and to identify the lessons that should be completed.

TECHNIQUE TIP

Rest your eyes occasionally by looking away from the screen.

The following tables show which lessons will help you reduce or eliminate the stroking imbalance that may occur if you have a weak right hand or a weak left hand. After you complete the Diagnostic Timing on page 98, look at the tables shown below to determine the appropriate lesson assignments that will help you.

If your scores on the Diagnostic Timing indicate you have a weak right hand, type the following lesson assignments as indicated by your speed and error differences on the timing.

The symbol ≥ means equal to or greater than.

The symbol < means less than.

Speed Difference	Error Difference ≥ 5	Error Difference < 5
	Lesson Assignments:	Lesson Assignments:
5 or fewer words	82, 83, 84, 85, 91	82, 83, 84, 90, 91
6 to 8 words	82, 83, 84, 85, 86	82, 83, 84, 85, 91
9 or more words	82, 83, 84, 85, 86	82, 83, 84, 85, 86

If your scores on the Diagnostic Timing indicate you have a weak left hand, type the following lesson assignments as indicated by your speed and error differences on the timing.

Speed Difference	Error Difference ≥ 5	Error Difference < 5
	Lesson Assignments:	Lesson Assignments:
5 or fewer words	87, 88, 89, 90, 86	87, 88, 89, 85, 86
6 to 8 words	87, 88, 89, 90, 91	87, 88, 89, 90, 86
9 or more words	87, 88, 89, 90, 91	87, 88, 89, 90, 91